RHEINGOLD

THE GERMAN WINE RENAISSANCE

BY

OWEN BIRD

Published 2005 by arima publishing

www.arimapublishing.com

ISBN 1-84549-079-7

Printed and bound in the United Kingdom

Typeset in Garamond 12/16

arima publishing
ASK House, Northgate Avenue
Bury St Edmunds, Suffolk IP32 6BB
t: (+44) 01284 700321

www.arimapublishing.com

To Elmar Schwarz with much affection and thanks.

Contents

Acknowledgements

With any work, no matter how flawed, there are people that need to be thanked for encouraging the budding author. All good yarns should have a beginning, middle, and end. English wine writer Tom Stevenson inadvertently provided the catalyst, Tim Pearce provided encouragement as only great mate can when there seemed no end in sight, and Tom Benns said he would proof read it all but not, apparently, until he receives his free published hardback copy.

None of this would have been possible without the introduction to real German wine by Elmar Schwarz one bleak January day in the Rheingau. The German word for weather is, most appropriately, *wetter*.

It is to the many producers, winemakers, representative bodies, and their staff whom I am indebted. Discussions with such fine and dedicated people led over time to the formation of the ideas contained herein. I never imagined our many personal communications would transform into a book based largely on my highly opinionated comments. To those who have given freely of their time I am most grateful and sincerely hope that even if they do not agree with what I have written it will at least provoke debate, preferably over a good glass of Riesling.

The VDP, Verband Deutsche Prädikatsweingüter, deserve a special mention especially the assistance from Hilke Nagel and Eva Raps who both put up with my worse than atrocious German grammar, understood what I was trying to accomplish perhaps better than I did, thought it would be useful, prodded me to fly in for tastings, and streamlined winemaker contacts. Vielen Danke. I hope that in some way this work is a small step in communicating what the VDP and leading German producers are trying to accomplish.

Thanks also go to Rob Hay of Chard Farm in New Zealand, who made many nights of freezing de-acidification and filtration pass *very very* slowly by informing me that, "minus 14 isn't cold mate, now when I was working in Germany...", and so began various armchair travels with him through German regions and their wines. When you are on the other side of the world, sighting a wine label is a wonderful way to reminisce over regions, towns, and people. Good company always makes good wine better.

Sincere thanks to Dr. Rolf Klein of Meininger Verlag, who was the first German I met who could get his head around the idea of a Tasmanian, ex-barrister, flying winemaker, sometimes touching down in *das Vaterland*, being passionate about German wines, and who dreamed about making wine in his country, before the world caught on to what true wine *cognoscenti* have known for years.

Thanks to arima publishers, Richard Franklin, and his team. English wine writer Rosemary George MW wished me all the best and in her ever direct style jokingly informed me that this was no way to write a book. First, better to come up with a concept, convince a publisher it was a good idea, blow the retainer, miss all the deadlines, and hide from the editor! Hilary Lumsden, who did not publish the book, but was instrumental in giving me help as to how to get it published.

To Pierpaolo Petrassi MW, his thirst for knowledge in areas other than his existing substantial expertise kept me burning the midnight oil in what I could increasingly see was not just of interest to me. Natalia Posadas-Dickson and "El Escocés Volando", Norrel Robertson MW formed what I would like to think as a formidable winemaking team of which it was a privilege to be a member of during the writing of this book.

Lastly, to the Deutsche Wine Institute, with whose help this book would never have been written.

Any errors of fact and judgement remain mine and have likely arisen from trying to pull together rough notes I made on the back of airline boarding passes.

Owen Bird
Weinheim, Germany
September 2005

Foreword

Der Schatz der Deutschen

Der mythische Nibelungenhort, das Rheingold, als Metapher für Wein?
Wer einen Goldklumpen in der Hand hält – siehe das Märchen vom Hans
im Glück – , ist sich nicht immer bewusst, welchen Schatz er da besitzt.
Gut, wenn dann jemand kommt und einem die Augen öffnet. Owen Bird,
international erfahrener Weinmacher, hat sich dies vorgenommen. Seine
Aussage: Eure Rieslinge sind grandios und gehören zur Weltspitze, aber
ihr Deutschen vergesst vor lauter Bescheidenheit und komplizierter
Bedenkenträgerei, mit diesem Pfund zu wuchern. Nur so ist zu erklären,
dass den deutschen Spitzenwinzern erst in jüngster Zeit internationale
Aufmerksamkeit zuteil geworden ist. Gelingt es ihnen, an die einstige
Bedeutung der deutschen Rieslinge in der Welt anzuschließen? Owen
Bird ist sich sicher. Nur sollten einige Hemmnisse speziell des
Weingesetzes vorher beseitigt werden. Mit dem objektiven Blick des
Außenseiters analysiert Bird nicht nur die Qualitäten und das Terroir der
deutschen Spitzenlagen in den einzelnen Anbaugebieten, sondern seziert
auch die deutsche Winzerschaft im Licht der Marktinteressen. Und die,
bemerkt Owen Bird, haben auf einem der größten Weinmärkte der Welt
leider immer noch mehr die Masse als die Klasse im Blick. Die
Perspektive des neutralen Beobachters macht dieses Buch besonders
lesens- und bedenkenswert, denn hier werden die Dinge klar beim
Namen genannt. Es ist das leidenschaftliche Plädoyer eines Liebhabers
deutscher Weine – ein wahrer Schatz, um den uns die Welt beneiden
könnte.

Dr. Rolf Klein
Chefredakteur Weinwelt

The Treasure of the Germans

The mystic „*Nibelungenhort*", of Rhinegold as a metapher for wine?
Who holds a gold nugget in their hand – like in the fairytale of „Hans im Luck" – is not always conscious of true treasure they really possess. Fortunate, then when someone comes along and opens their eyes. Owen Bird, internationally experienced winemaker, has done this. His statement, „your Rieslings are great and belong to the worldclass elite of wines, but you Germans forget to make a profit from this and remain with modesty and honest hesitation". That is the only explanation for why only lately the top German winemakers have sought international attention. Will they be able to reclaim the former importance and reputation of German Riesling in the world? Owen Bird is sure of it. Before it can take place he feels some changes, especially regarding the German wine law, should take place. With the objective view of an outsider Bird analyses not only the qualities and the terroir of the German elite vineyards in the single „*Anbaugebiete*", but discusses the German winemaking in the light of market interests. And these, states Owen Bird, in one of the biggest wine markets in the world they still have in mind more mass than class. The perspective of a neutral observer makes this book particularly worth reading and considering, because he „calls a spade a spade". It is the passionate plea of a lover of german wine – a true treasure, the world could envy us for.

Dr. Rolf Klein
Chefredakteur Weinwelt

Introduction

Another meddling foreigner writing a book about German wine! Will I get away with the excuse of the natives not being able to see the forest for the trees, or should that be the wines for the vines? No. The reason behind it, if truth be-known, is that Germans will not take you seriously unless you have written a book. Bang goes that theory.

The reasons for writing this book are very simple. Riesling, being the most noble of white wines is very easy to get excited about. Winemakers tend to be passionate people, and the more great Riesling I tasted the more I was upset that the German industry had fallen so low in terms of world wine opinion. This book is an attempt to communicate that passion and hopefully redress the balance in whatever small way.

It had always been a dream of mine to work with Riesling and I had always felt there could only be one place in which the truly great could be made. The more I taste the more I remain of that opinion. Who will give me back my misspent youth drinking anything other than great German Riesling?

Germans do a lot of things very well. Take their automobile industry. It was not long ago names such as Rolls Royce, Bentley, Jaguar, Triumph, MG, and Rover were the marquees of desire. Do the English still make cars or are they limited to providing team management for Formula One missiles propelled by German engines? Anything of automotive value the English were still doing was bought up by Germans in a *post-Thatcherzeit Fire Sale* and turned into something the world wanted.

Arguably German cars are at the pinnacle of performance and quality as are their Rieslings. Why then do they have people lining up for the former and seemingly few takers for the latter? German car sales demonstrate there is no real post-WWII xenophobic attitude to their products. Wine experts place Riesling as the most noble of white wines and German Riesling as the pinnacle of its varietal expression. Meanwhile consumers have bought elsewhere. I will attempt to explain this gap between wine expert and wine consumer opinion in the chapters that follow.

Is Riesling "World Famous in Germany" merely because it is too difficult to understand? I do not believe so. Consumers seem to understand New World Riesling. What is more, the American market, with all its fast-food kitsch seems to be leading the Renaissance for German Riesling. During the so called "varietal revolution" whereby New World producers seemingly made things easy for the consumer, Riesling stood alone as a classic variety which had always been declared as such. There was no need to get under the bonnet to understand that Burgundy was Pinot Noir and that behind Sancerre was Sauvignon Blanc. Those who write about the "varietal revolution" conveniently forget this fact. The German industry woes had and have a deeper source.

I should clarify from the outset the terms Old and New World in terms of winemaking. For the purposes of this book, the Old World refers to the classic European wine producing countries and the New World refers to Australia, New Zealand, South America and the United States of America despite the fact that we could likely term the USA old New World nowadays.

Hugh Johnson states, "...while the greatest German wines have never diminished in stature, their reputation sank in the past thirty years. During that time, new wine law/label terminology made it difficult for anyone but a true connoisseur to easily seek out these great wines, and the precise meanings of renowned site-names lost much of their significance."[1]

Labelling has often been blamed as if simply sorting it out would reverse the sales avalanche. Realistically, poor labelling has merely made some wines "un-user friendly" and/or unattractive. The use of gothic script gives an old fashioned and potentially a frightening appearance. More to the point, the German problem in labelling is with too much unspecific information being passed off as specific. That is, the use of regional, town, and catch-all vineyard territory names is abused in order to give the consumer some illusion that the £2.99 wine in their hands has some noble estate parentage. Mutton dressed up as lamb. The source for this legalised "fraud" can be traced to the fountain of shoddy "sticking plaster" wine regulations placed over a veritable sales haemorrhage by German legislators.

Consumers moved away from buying German wine for a combination of reasons which deserve consideration including the rise of "sweet and cheap", the New World "revolution", poor marketing, lack of understanding consumer taste changes, and a swing towards red wine consumption. In short, the industry has only itself to blame for the present state of affairs and only the industry that can reverse this situation.

Are German wines merely victims of fashion or is this something more permanent? Fashion is fickle but, as anyone who ever bought a Hawaiian shirt knows, some boomerangs just don't come back. My

---

[1] VDP Handbook, Grosses Gewächs No.1, Berlin 2002.

premise is that quality German wines have the potential to again rule the ranks of white wine respect through the application of what would appear to be commonsense principles of presenting a quality product to the public.

The trend for red wine consumption, despite making matters difficult at present, can be positive for German Riesling when consumers return to white wine. Red wine consumption means consumers are looking for more complexity, structure, and flavour in their wines. This is a great opportunity for German Riesling and bad news for bulk Italian lightweights such as Orvieto[2] and Frascati. Consumers will look to whites with a high expression of fruit and ones easily matched to a diverse modern kitchen. Why drink taste the same Chardonnay[3] when there are diverse fruit driven Rieslings with a pedigree available at highly competitive, if not comparatively low prices?

There are a plethora of red grape varieties vying for contention as producing the most noble of red wines. In terms of white wine nobility there is no doubt that Riesling remains pre-eminent. Despite the disregard that German wine has been dragged into, no-one has managed to elevate the proletarian workhorse variety of Chardonnay to the throne Riesling so richly deserves, despite it being the grape in noble Burgundian wines such as Puligny-Montrachet and Corton-Charlemagne. Much of the thanks for this ironically are due to influential English wine journalists such as Hugh Johnson and Jancis Robinson MW publicly asserting their passion for Riesling.[4]

The challenge for German winemakers is how to correctly anticipate

---

[2] The following is an extract from English musician Brian Eno's diary entry for 26th of August 1995, "Pissed into an empty wine bottle so I could continue watching *Monty Python*, and suddenly thought, I've never tasted my own piss, so I drank a little…just like Orvieto Classico." Probably more of a general consumer impression rather than one of an acknowledged expert but a winemaker friend having replicated the experiment, (sans *Monty Python*), verifies Eno's opinion. Name withheld to protect the guilty.

[3] As a flying winemaker having made considerable volumes of commercial "international" style Chardonnay the challenge has often been to try to set such wines apart by virtue of accenting just enough terroir whilst remaining acceptable to their target consumers who are generally looking for fruit impact.

[4] I state ironically as the German wine industry has produced few native champions of Riesling during this period of their wine history whereas names such as Johnson, Robinson MW, Brook, and Pigott were champions of the traditional German expression of Riesling. A shameful result for such "defenders of the faith" was when Pigott located a historic map basically defining the cru status of German vineyards. The response from the DWI was to withdraw his funds and to take to Hugh Johnson with a stick. The DWI continues with a similar approach to the present day.

customer tastes and to serve these without abandoning the positive aspects of their tradition. In fact, tradition can be harnessed to work in a positive way for producers. A better understanding of market price points, (a combination of marketing, quality, and flavours for a price), what their target markets should actually be, and how to go about promoting within those markets is essential learning material for German producers.

This is not a text on the history of the German wine industry or a baseless ranking of wine producers; such works exist by other authors. I have written as I speak, which for some might be too direct or tend to the irreverent. You can take the man out of Australia but you cannot take the Australian out of the man! I hope whatever the written style, or lack of it, that my serious message is communicated.

The first part of the book examines the background to the German wine industry development to the point of crisis and its comical regulation. Basically it is a section on how the industry arrived to its present state.

The second part of the book deals with Riesling and the potential renaissance for German producers. Riesling is integral to this revival. This part is presented as an encapsulation of the changes that have taken place internally and externally to the German wine industry in the last 30 years. Important considerations are the altered playing field forced upon Old World producers with the rise of New World winemaking. German producers are aware of the decline in their popularity but frequently unaware of the reasons. If you do not understand the cause it is very difficult to define a strategic solution. Further consideration is given to the advent of "flying winemaking" and its effect on the global wine market. I cite the New World's current direction and beseech German producers not to miss this trend.

When varietal labelling "revolutionised" wine marketing the producers of German Riesling stood by and did not mention that this was exactly what they had been doing for years. German producers, or at least their representative bodies, seemed shy. The New World has now "discovered" terroir, despite many winemakers being reluctant to admit so publicly. New World winemakers previously dismissed terroir as a concept designed by the French to justify high prices for wines. Extensive vine plantings in the New World have meant that in search of markets they have flooded, or will shortly do so, the world with taste the same wines and now need a way to differentiate their production. As a result, we will see a rise in single vineyard and small regional denominations from the

New World in an attempt to have a peg upon which to hang their marketing.

Germany is awash with regional distinctions and should not now run to release clumped together wines without a declared connection to the land and climate from which they originate in the thought that they are taking on the New World at their own game. The winemaking history and geography of Germany's wine regions lend itself to an effective discussion on terroir and provides a perfect case study of its affect on wine. To date, German producers have not been successful in defining regional distinctions to the majority of wine buyers. The same cannot be said for producers in France, Italy, or Spain. People will look for a Bordeaux, Burgundy, Chianti, Barolo, or Rjoca with the idea that this nonclamenture defines a wine style. The vast majority of consumers do not think of the designations of Rheingau, Pfalz, or Mosel-Saar-Ruwer in the same way. Rather Riesling is Riesling.

Does this mean educating buyers and the wine public in regional distinctions? I think not. Consumers and those with greater interest will delve deeper. Part of the success of "Brand Australia's" success is that journalists and consumers really are not fussed which particular district from which the wine originates. The easily written steps for Germany's return must be based first on the re-elevation of Riesling in the consumer's mind to that of the greatest white wine. Second, developing the *Grosses Gewächs, Erste Lage, Erstes Gewächs,* and *Edelsüsser* Spitzenwein classification system as a guarantee to the consumer that such categorised wine should be regarded at the pinnacle of German wines is essential. Thirdly, these elite wines will then provide the "lessons" as to winemaking styles, aspects of regionalism, and ultimately individual terroir characteristics. The regional distinctions will happen by default and with concentration on what should be the least complicated way of presenting the greatness of many German wines.

The efforts in making such regional distinctions apparent will be very difficult. In a world constantly compacted into needing to get its message across in shorter and short (sic) time, it will be nigh on impossible to train the majority of wine consumers as to the differences between regions and even particular vineyards. Riesling, like Pinot Noir, seems to adapt with its own particular style to its own microclimate. Add in vintage-to-vintage variations and the fact that the winemaking on any estate will change over time means there is a lot to explain. As a result, it is necessary for German producers to abandon their fear of elitism and show off their best producers, vineyards, and wines as something of which to be especially proud. In order to do this, one needs to focus on providing convincing, concise, and accurate information on terroir. This has been learnt over generations and it is important to demonstrate this in site-specific wines, which set themselves apart from any others in the world.

The steps German producers should take in order to regain the respect of the wine drinker are then considered. My discussion is based upon two tenants originating from my former legal and economic disciplines. The elite German producers have suffered from "guilt by association" with the poor quality "sweet and cheap" wines. Such an undeserving loss of reputation must have been heartbreaking to quality producers as making good wine is not something that one can do without passion, energy, or emotion. Elite producers must rise above this negative association and present a clear message to consumers regarding the quality of their wine.

The renaissance arrives via the "trickledown effect". Producers have to embrace the work of the best in their industry and recognise the image of German wine will be led by the elite and most importantly rest on the greatness of Riesling. In times past this was an anathema, with the concept being to lead with the worst, a strategy that has done more damage than good. For some reason Germans wanted to avoid an association of being arrogant about their elite, or avoid the creation of an elite. Our society is structured as such. No armies won the Cold War; that was taken care of by the likes of Mercedes-Benz and Ferrari, as one will quickly see travelling through any of the former Eastern Bloc countries.

It is high time for German producers to make more of a fuss about the best in their branch without petty jealousy. Every other wine nation does so, whereas Germany seemingly does not want to place a few producers on a pedestal lest it suggest an arrogance of character. English wine writer Tom Stevenson points out, "…every wine writer agrees that German wines are underrated, and the only course of action is to rebuild their reputation on the back of the Riesling grape variety."[5] This revival of reputation flows from the concentration on elite Riesling. Concentrating on the best of the best will bring a reversal of fortune to the much maligned German wine industry.

It is essential for the future well being of the German industry to capitalise upon its strengths and educate the market. This is easier said than done. In order to ensure the industry survives and potentially flourishes the work will need to be done in order to draw attention to top quality German Riesling and, therefore, wine. Producers will need to

---

[5] Page 259, Tom Stevenson The New Sotheby's Wine Encyclopaedia, DK, 1999.

bring in a new generation of German wine drinkers, both at home and abroad. At present, Australian and New Zealand producers are mimicking German winemaking and adapting their traditional packaging. This might surprise German producers who are trying in many cases to "hide" their wine in untraditional packaging. The New World track record indicates they are very good at kidnapping wine styles and markets. In many ways, one now looks to Australia as the "home" of Syrah[6] and New Zealand as the focal point for Sauvignon Blanc rather than their French origins.

German producers cannot be complacent. New World winemakers will, if given half a chance, kidnap what the "man on the Clapham omnibus"[7] has as his idea of Riesling. That is, if German producers do not assert their styles, terroirs, and differences they will run the risk of New World producers training the market as to what Riesling should taste like. One already sees journalists in the United Kingdom making differences between Clare Valley and Eden Valley Rieslings on a far greater scale than they do for trying to explain the differences between Mosel and Rheingau styles. One German producer[8] is on record that if there is a "Riesling Renaissance" that it will come from Australian producers rather than German. I sincerely hope that this is not the case. German producers and their representative bodies must rapidly realise this threat in order to correctly react.

The third part of the book deals with an examination of the steps to renaissance through the efforts made by both the Deutsche Wein Institute (DWI) and the Verband Deutsche Prädikatsweingüter (VDP). The DWI is banking on releasing wines under the moniker of "Classic" and "Selection" whereas the VDP have taken the more difficult and long overdue approach of classifying German terroir. My argument, as will be seen, suggests the VDP system is the best path to follow but this does not mean that the DWI effort cannot exist or that it is without its uses. Some members of the VDP also use the DWI system of "Classic" and "Selection", which suggests at a practical level producers might use them in combination. It is clear that the President of the VDP is of the view that the way back, particularly for the elite estates of German wine, is to place the greatest possible emphasis on terroir. He describes this as the

---

[6] Referred to as Shiraz in Australia.

[7] The standard reasonable member of the public as so defined in McQuire v Western Morning News Co. (1903) 2 K.B. 100 at 109.

[8] Ernst Loosen, personal communication, lending his considerable weight to this argument especially given the energy and work Herr Loosen has placed into redressing the image and fortunes of German wine.

soil, microclimate, vine, clone, winemaking/vineyard handwork, and intuition.[9]

The fourth and final part to the book deals with an individual analysis of the classification system ratified by VDP members. This consists of a breakdown in the various Grosses Gewächs with a description of the sites and some of the wines that result. Where appropriate this description includes notes from the actual winemaker. The VDP have not limited the use of the classification model to only their members and nor have I. In theory it is applicable to all producers and I hope that some producers growing grape within the various *Gewächs* will also adopt the classification even if they chose to remain outside the VDP. It would give credibility to the system.

The German wine industry is an underdog in the world of wine. This has a lot to do with relying for many years in fighting on international markets with "sweet and cheap" products. Many of its players are dedicated and creative people who deserve to gain greater recognition for the world-class products they produce. Times have passed where it was good enough to watch market share slip away. Top German producers must be proactive in developing "Brand Germany" and this brand must focus on the best of what Germany has to fight with. The Blue Nuns and Liebfrauen should not be on the battlefield.

---

[9] Personal communication.

Part One

Background

Once Upon a Wine

For all intensive purposes religious orders were responsible for the commercial cultivation of the Riesling grape in Germany. Naturally, Riesling as a grape variety existed prior to the intervention of religious orders but the determination that Riesling was the ideal grape for the German terroir is found in the studious application monks gave to its clonal selection. In his classic work, <u>Story of Wine</u>, Hugh Johnson establishes the Cistercian Order of Burgundian origins got the ball rolling in the Rheingau. The order was more than likely the first "multinational" corporation and had fingers in basically every agricultural pie. Anti-Globalisation protestors would have had a field day up against this lot being able to mount protests from forestry to fishing.

Wine was one of their business divisions and early attempts at replicating the success of Burgundy are recorded from about 1136. These industrious monks were soon a major force along the Rhine with a headquarters at Kloster Eberbach on land granted by the Archbishop of Mainz. Kloster Eberbach is under *denkmalschutz*, or historic protection, and is well worth a visit today, particularly to witness the skill with which the historic nature of the building is maintained whilst allowing within a modern winemaking operation.

One of the first lessons of winemaking in Germany was discovered here, but he who does not study the past is bound to repeat its failures. The monks soon found that despite their best efforts they did not produce a red wine capable of competing with those made by their Burgundian brethren. The present day market demand for red wines means many German producers are expecting such a level of global warming that they persist with attempts to produce Syrah, despite the fact that southern France is flooded with the stuff at bargain basement prices.

Trial and error eventually determined that Riesling was the variety ideally suited to the steep slopes and particular growing season. If there was ever a case for terroir needing to be made, this historical demonstration provides exactly that. Riesling thrived. Despite the debate surrounding who found it, where, and when, the fact of the matter remains this Order set the standards of quality for the time. The region became synonymous with Riesling, the first documentary evidence of the variety found in 1435. The earnings from wine production, despite vines covering a minor percentage of the estate, accounted for a major proportion of Kloster income. Naturally, this made it an attractive business and one with a product relatively easily compared by consumers.

Not only did other religious orders expand to compete but private wineries entered the market.

The Rhein River provided an expansion highway for the wine industry. Such a fast method of transport facilitated trade. Ports sprang up along its course. Naturally, our perennial favourite the taxman was not far behind and, as with most trade, he had screwed it to the point of submission by the time the so-called Thirty Years' War broke out. A series of bad seasons, rape, pillage, and all the blokes off smashing up other blokes' estates meant that the industry hit rock bottom. Vineyards, cellars, transport kegs, and boats were all *kaput*.

Fortunately for the industry, and particularly Riesling, the church again took up the reins through massive replanting of vineyards. Given the ravages of war, flat fertile land was turned over to the planting of food crops where boom times had seen expansive plantings of vines. This meant vines were pushed back up the slopes where the land was harder to work and less productive; ideal conditions for grapevines. It is the very fact that the vine must struggle and the soil difficult to sustain any other type of crop that often makes the grapes from those vineyards so special.

The Church was instrumental in this replanting. They artfully negotiated tax exemptions which gave them an immediate competitive advantage but at the same time did allow for studious progression of vineyard development. Taxes by their very nature are a distortion of the market but we can see that during these times they also provided a guarantee of quality. By taxing highly at source the wines became more expensive. The overseas markets were happy to buy wines that were expensive as long as they were of excellent quality. A wine of poor quality but with a high tax basis meant that it would find little custom. The better wines were thus exported. Leaping forward into the 20th and 21st Centuries we can see that the reverse resulted. High taxes imposed at market mean the cheapest wines are exported.

Riesling is a particularly hardy variety and as will be detailed later, its natural acid structure allows its wines to keep. It was able to withstand the vagaries of the climate better than other varieties and thus was a natural crop of choice for the monks given winemaking knowledge of the day. This success was soon replicated by other religious orders insisting they also needed Riesling vines. This meant Riesling found a home and its own individual expression in different regions such as Deidesheim (Pfalz) under the patronage of the Bishop of Speyer and with the Benedictines in the Mosel-Saar-Ruwer. We can parallel such a swift "copy cat" system of planting with what we have witnessed in the New World.[10]

Winemaking methods were also riding a steep learning curve. Allowing a longer ripening period provided more precious lush wines. Precious wines were set aside for placement in a cabinet like cellar.[11] There has been considerable debate over the derivation of this term but it is clear that *kellermeisters* were keeping the best vineyard production for such wines. Leaving harvest until October must have meant harvesting grapes affected with *botrytis cinerea* or noble rot but then it would have just been termed rot. Hugh Johnson states, "The Rheingau poses a similar question to Sauternes: was there a real reluctance to use rotten grapes to make sweet wine, or was it just something nobody liked to admit?"[12] The multinational monks must have had their own public relations "spin doctors". Johnson again, "In Germany history is made characteristically tidy. 1775 was the first official *Spätlese* or late-gathered, vintage."[13]

This all took place on the 50th Parallel at Schloss Johannisberg in the Rheingau. Basically it came about due to a communications cock up. The estate owner had to give the order to harvest but as he was without a cellphone, the messenger boy took nearly two weeks, (the return ride no doubt with some roadside pub and wenching delays included), to bring the blessing from the holidaying owner. (Winemakers might rightly wonder how much has actually changed in 230 years).

As a result, all the other estates were "home and hosed", well finished with harvest but Schloss Johannisberg was left with fields of rotten grapes. The resulting wines from these late harvested grapes were so extraordinary that *Spätlese*, or late harvesting, was set into law, the government reacting with a speed to put most to shame nowadays. As the 19th Century kicked off, there was a great leap forward in the quality of

---

[10] Start up regions in the New World had little to go by when planting other than a suspicion that the climate was similar to somewhere in the Old World. One can still read pioneering growers statements that they were reminded of parts of Europe they had travelled through or immigrants grew what their families grew at home. Later we would see statements such as, "northern Tasmania has a climate better than Bordeaux", but through trial and error it was found that terroir has more to do with lines on a map or rainfall statistics. Despite all the analysis, what grew well in an area often was the result of trial and error; witness Sauvignon Blanc in Marlbourgh, New Zealand and Shiraz in various regions of Australia. Once a grower proved a region suited to a variety others soon followed. This often worked on a regional basis and did not work on a national scale much like the Franconians finding their region was better suited to Silvaner rather than Riesling

[11] Ending up as the category Kabinett.

[12] p291, Hugh Johnson, <u>Story of Wine</u>, Mitchell Beazley, London (1994).

[13] ibid

Riesling and the door was open to the noblest of wines from *Auslese,* *Beerenauslese,* and *Trockenbeerenauslese.*

Tariffs and taxes were the foundation of the next crucial stage of German wine history. The Prussians pulled it all together via the skilful use of taxation rather than their famed military science. Given the speed of transportation and the breadth of the territory involved, (roughly present day Germany and part of Poland), it was basically the periods equivalent of the European Union. Austria was absent from these plans, but what's new? This Customs Union, *Zollverein,* produced a tax equalisation, meaning that the better wines could be moved around within this *Zollverein* without fiscal penalty. Customers were thus able to select wines grown from where they were produced at their best.

Economic unification was naturally hastened by the coming of the railroad. Easier travel brought a basic form of wine tourism and allowed wines to be shipped to destinations over the horizon. By the mid 19th Century German wine was the favoured white at the royal courts of Europe. The best producers of the Rheingau were effectively aristocratic "first growths" and the wines sold for the highest of prices. Taxation charges reflected this and we can imagine that from natural selection better wines received better prices. As the providence of the wines was easily ascertained duties could be assessed on a vineyards potential earnings. Through taxation records an effective rating of the terroirs was made.[14]

During this period at the pinnacle of wine world respect the top estates concentrated on producing a flagship wines which were more than likely to be Riesling. Recorded "mouthwitness" testimony indicates that these wines were dry and they were fermented more fully rather than having the fermentation stopped in order to maintain residual sweetness. As a result, they were drier and higher in alcohol. They were cuvees of great structure, body, high alcohol, and high acid allowing them to retain their freshness even as they aged.[15] They were designed for long term cellaring and the aromas they generated after long periods of correct aging were integral to their style.

---

[14] English wine writer Stuart Pigott rejuvenated this system and his excellent efforts will be discussed later.

[15] A cuvee is a considered blend of wines from different vineyards where the resultant wine is theoretically an improvement over the individual components. A winemaker might try to utilise overt characteristics of say fruit with another wine with better acid structure in order to create a blended wine with fruit and acid. This is the essence of great winemaking and blending.

Wineries lost focus on the flagship that had made their name when they started to try to provide a wine in every quality structure[16] from every little named vineyard plot and variety. Not only did this completely confuse the customers, (and more than likely the winemaker), but it meant that the producers had moved away from doing what had given them success and made their name in the first place. Trying to be all things to all people by filling all the categories was and is not a successful strategy. Many German wineries have still not learnt this basic lesson and continue to attempt an annual production release of over fifty wines.

Both World Wars were obviously devastating for the industry and the Third Reich's centrally planned command economy bringing all aspects to the business under political direction was not ever going to be a recipe for quality. This takes no account of the loss of wise traditional wine merchants through persecution. Under National Socialism the Reich's control of agriculture extended to wine and the same management team that gave birth to the *Volkswagen* also thought that a *Volksgetränk* was a ripper idea. It was totally unsuccessful but post war a similar product took export markets by storm, no prizes for guessing what it was called.

The period since the Second World War has been, like for so many industries in Germany, one of major growth and upheaval.[17] Export growth outstripped wine production. Demand was met with planting on fields with no history of vine cultivation or the ability to make anything of quality. Rather they were suited to tractors and easy to harvest. This was the first turn of the viscous circle of poor wine, powerful co-ops, and the dragging down of the best. As we have seen, in the 18th Century the increased demand for food had pushed vines up onto the less fertile slopes, so producing the stresses great vines require. Now vines were spreading out onto the flatter lands in the quest for mass production. Suffice to say these changes made the material available for bulk sweet wine production, especially when combined with technical winemaking advances.

The export demand for "sweet and cheap" wines meant new vineyards were planted. Commercial winemaking requires commercial vineyard planting where co-operatives can farm easily. The tractor axel dictated row widths and trellising arrangements. Gone was the desire to limit the vines growing space[18] and corresponding ability to concentrate flavours.

---

[16] QbA (*Qualitätswein bestimmter Anbaugebiete*) level wines to *Trockenbeerenauslese*.

[17] Referred to as the *Wirtschaftswunder* or "economic miracle" in Germany.

[18] Both root zone and leaf canopy light interception are important to bring in balance for quality grape production. In general terms, a vine with too much root access to water

In order to gain volumes, as quantity was what was demanded not quality, the growers planted high-yielding grape varieties on highly fertile soil.

Many of the high yielding grape varieties were developed at the research institute Geisenheim. Their research pushed vine crosses that ensured early ripening before the weather turned foul and gave high crop levels. Fruit flavours were not an important consideration. A similar event occurred around this time in the Italian industry with varieties such as Lambrusco and Pagadebit. Pagadebit translates like it sounds, "pay the debts" and is a high yielding variety designed for that purpose, when people were paying for volume. These things come full circle and nowadays no one can be found who wants to buy a litre of the stuff much the same can be said for Germany's national grape embarrassment Müller-Thurgau.

The need to produce economies of scale with these plantings meant mechanical harvesting of grapes. Mechanically harvesting[19] can produce wines of good quality but I am yet to see a world-class wine resulting from this method of harvest. The idea was to merely bring it in and ferment the stuff. Generally no chapitalisation[20] took place so low alcohols were the norm due to the fact that the producers of such wine were unwilling to spend the money on sugar. The winemaking part really only came into play after fermentation when the wines were basically centrifuged and prepared for bottling using all the high tech gear. The wines are "fixed" and cleaned up using technical methods that will be discussed later.

At around this time, there was also a push to downplay the importance of named single vineyard sites (*Einzellagen*). We will see that laws were changed which reduced the number of single vineyard sites but inexplicably expanded the areas they covered. The elite were shouted

---

and soil nutrients will channel its energy into vine growth. Larger space in which to spread the foliage means bigger plants and potentially more grape bunches. The more bunches the less concentration of vine resources and thus more dilute flavours. Close spacing of vines means roots have a small area in which to work and foliage is limited so resulting in a greater concentration on pushing energy into the grape bunch.

[19] Mechanical harvesting works basically by a self-propelled machine straddling the vine row and beating the fruit zone with soft rods in order to knock the grapes from the bunch. This is then collected either in on-board holding tanks or spat into trailers. Naturally, the must arrives at the winery with a high level of MOG (Material Other than Grape) such as leaves, fencing nails, snails, irrigation sprinkler heads, and from time-to-time snakes. All good protein.

[20] The process of adding sugar to the grape must in order to achieve a higher level of alcohol named after the Frenchman Chapital who developed it.

down as an old boys club at wanting to preserve their special names because they saw themselves as the "Grand Cru" estates. Disappointingly for the industry, this meant an erosion of the elite names and a dilution of many that remained. The results for the industry were exceptionally painful.

The "need" for egalitarianism might well look different if you were from outside of the elite. Certainly, a case can be mounted that one can make good wine and in some cases great wine without having a named site. No matter how long one has been out of New World winemaking there is always a sense of this sort of equalitarian attitude within you. It is a mistake to compare generations of experience resulting in named single vineyards with the rapid discovery of good sites in the New World. At the same time, when markets hit rock bottom it did not matter if you had a great old vineyard name or a general estate.

Despite poor sales of German wine we can see in general the "recognised" vineyard sites are still producing the best wines. This begs the question of those egalitarians, if there was nothing economically to be gained from selling wines from these "recognised" sites as all wineries were effectively receiving the same price per bottle as the other, then why when such sites become available for sale are they always more expensive than the others? These sites change hands at higher prices because of the quality of production they can give, not the economic return at any particular moment.

A great winemaker can produce good wines from lesser sites. A good winemaker can do the same with wine from a great site. One only needs to look at the wines of Basserman-Jordan prior to Ullrich Mell taking over the winemaking to be convinced that a great winemaker can work wonders on great material. The loss of Frank John from Reichsrat von Buhl has seen the reverse take place. These two men were disciples of German winemaking doyen Herr Gunter Schwarz who was able to turn great wines from the vineyards at Müller Catoir despite their lack of cru status.[21]

This modern period also saw German wine legislation step into line with the European Economic Community and rather than enshrine quality the resultant legislation provided an incentive to produce rubbish.

---

[21] I have only ever met briefly with two of these three winemakers and so my statements are based on an impartial assessment of their wines rather than any personal bias and I have taken the example using two of the Pfalz "B's" (Basserman and von Buhl) and a third winery in the region.

Liebfraumilch rapidly became the public face of German wine.[22] Germans were happy to drink their best wine at home and export the rubbish. It did not really matter what was leaving the country as local wine customers were happy to deal directly with quality producers.

---

[22] The ambassadors for German wine were the milk from a nice lady, (literal translation of Liebfraumilch) and a Blue Nun, the name I find most amusing given that in German slang to be drunk is to be *blau* (blue).

Hell's Own Vineyard

If religious orders were responsible for the foundation of the German wine industry then the nuns and the Church of Our Lady in Worms can be said to have produced its virtual destruction. If you were not aware, German wine has an image problem worse Michael Jackson. Like "Wacco Jacko", some people love it, some people hate it, but all agree that they really don't understand it. And that's just the Germans!

Stop anyone in the street and ask them what they know about German wine and the universal response will be to look at you strangely and sometimes respond with "Liebfraumilch". What most company chairmen would give to have such power of name or brand recognition? Nothing else in the wine industry goes close. Even so, Liebfraumilch is proof that not all publicity is good publicity.

One would expect Germany to be awash with the stuff. Ninety-nine percent of it is exported.[23] That imbibed in Germany is generally done so by the dwindling numbers of American military staff. Germans know the reputation of it but not often what it actually tastes like. The Liebfraumilch export cascade is single-handedly responsible for the image problem with German wine today. This wine created the "sweet and cheap" image with which, despite all the valiant efforts of quality producers, Germany remains associated.

This wine is case positive in how a bad apple can ruin a bunch, and more to the point that the Germans drink their best wines at home and export their rubbish whereas other major wine producing countries do the opposite. This is only to the detriment of the industry as a whole.

In theory there is an actual vineyard from where this originates. I state in theory as the actual vineyard has little to do with the wine apart from the donation of its name. One can see "Hell's Own Vineyard" in Worms as they travel on the Ryanair bus to Frankfurt Hahn airport, (readers can infer no expense has been squandered in the research for this book). Frankfurt Hahn is decked with banners informing you that you are entering the gateway to Blue Nun Country. This in itself should be enough to make you want to get straight back on the plane. Talk about putting your worst tourism foot forward.

The Deutsche Wine Institute (DWI), as part of their commitment to promoting members production, give a glowing description of Liebfraumilch as; "Liebfraumilch [is a] mild QbA wine from the

---

23 The DWI would not release the sales statistics/exports of Liebfraumilch to me.

Rheingau, Nahe, Rheinhessen, or Pfalz with at least 70% of Riesling, Müller-Thurgau, Silvaner, or Kerner. A varietal designation on the label is not permitted."

And why would one need to?[24]

The Rheinhessen is a beautiful region, not alone for its vineyards. It really does not deserve the following plug from the DWI, "this region boasts the world's largest acreage planted with the ancient variety Silvaner and is the birthplace of Liebfraumilch, the soft, mellow white wine originally made from grapes grown in vineyards surrounding the Liebfrauenkirche or Church of Our Lady in Worms."[25] There is a certain factual correctness to this statement. The wine is soft; the soft underbelly of the entire German wine industry.

In recent years Liebfraumilch has improved in quality. This is not saying much really but given that the DWI channels considerable effort into finding ways to make the stuff better it is a core achievement. This low quality wine that has caused such devastation for the German wine industry has its composition enshrined in legislation. This is nothing more than a convincing demonstration of comical wine legislation and the misplaced focus by the custodians of its regulation. The DWI should have "bitten the bullet" on this many years ago but instead they have continued to perpetuate the problem.

Taking the legislation apart we can see that the wine is a complete nothingness in terms of identity. The permissible varieties are white, and can be grown in just about every German wine region. The logic behind this cannot be explained especially when we consider that Germans have been so particular in their classification of thousands of small vineyard sites. There is nothing in the wine legislation about what can or cannot be done on the great individual vineyards. At the same time there is a complete section of legislation to regulate a wine style, (Liebfraumilch) covering a plethora of varieties and regions that have no individual style whatsoever. Individual treatment for the most unspecific of wines. If it walks like a duck and quacks like a duck it must be Liebfraumilch.

This generic wine is more suitable to be seen as a brand. It accounts for around a third of total wine exports and ninety-nine percent of the German wine image. Originally there was an individual wine produced from a small vineyard surrounding the Liebfrauenkirch in Worms. This is where the image of German wine is buried. The Church of Our Lady

---

[24] Source, DWI Internet site.
[25] Ibid

vineyard likely does not produce anything special but likely has always given an inoffensive potentially enjoyable wine. This small patch of vineyard belongs to the Liebfrauenstift-Kirchenstuek, which comprises part of the overall *Grosslage* of Liebfrauenmorgen. This in itself is uninteresting except for the fact to demonstrate it actually exists as a plot of land with vines growing on it, despite it bearing no relation to the wine sold as Liebfraumilch today.[26] As we will see, German wine laws have permitted and encouraged such absurd results which have no parallel in any other industry.

In 1910, the Worms Chamber of Commerce classified the wine but more as a name of fantasy and no restrictions were really applied to the use of this "trademark". As a result it was a catch all, "slap a Liebfraumilch label on it and ship it overseas cheap" designation. So much so that generally over one third of all the wines blended to make a Liebfraumilch were produced in regions other than the regions bordering the Rhein. It is ironic that in an industry known around the world for overkill in describing wine origin had as the birth of its malaise a wine designed as a brand fifty years before this was *de rigueur* and with a wine made far away from its expressed vineyard location.

The wine laws of 1971, which will be discussed shortly, should have put a stop to this debacle. Vested interests were to perpetuate the problem. Powerful co-ops and large bottlers had made considerable money from buying bulk wine, blending it, filtering it to nothingness, and selling it as Liebfraumilch. Their growers had survived and in some cases thrived but the basis to their business was the ability to supply quantity rather than quality. These growers were inexorably linked to the large co-ops and bottlers so needing Liebfraumilch to continue if they were to as well. Politicians in charge of making laws were unlikely to hear pleas of small quality producers but rather the large players. He who "pays the piper calls the tune", and requests from the small elite were not going to be heard. Despite all attempts you cannot legislate Liebfraumilch into quality. Legislation was bent and built around a product that should have been hidden away.

As a result the laws were framed to so as enshrine Liebfraumilch. Despite some tidying up around the edges so that Rhein regions, (Rheinhessen, Rheingau, Rheinpfalz, and Nahe), could produce the wine

---

[26] If anything positive can be found in this is that at least it exists, rather than a multitude of the "famous" Australian wines named after a spurious connection to things such as local hills, creeks, flats, mountains, sacred koala resting places, and valleys when they are actually made of component wines trucked in from around a nation the size of Europe.

it could still be composed from wines produced in any or all of the regions. It is merely mutton dressed up as lamb. Further amendments have only served to make the production more regional based which now must be listed on the label but this is far too little too late and of no interest to the intended consumer.

Considering matters from a winemaking perspective Liebfraumilch should be stripped of its place in German wine law and reclassified as a table wine (*Deutsche Tafelwein*). This would then allow it to be a blend of grapes more suitable to the intended style of the wine, its quality level, and target market. The wine, if you ever drink it, can be at best clean, non-specific, and other times just bloody dreadful. This all has to do with the base components and given that anyone can really produce it, it is a lottery.

At the end of the day you generally pay for what you get. It works as a brand and as a result, it does not require a specific classification. *Tafelwein* would be a suitable category for the wine. The wine is targeted at an audience that is not looking for complexity.[27] They want consistent fresh fruity notes, a grape taste, with a good lashing of sugar, zippy acid, and importantly it has to be alcoholic.

This sort of wine can be better delivered using some aromatic varieties that grow well in Germany but are not permitted in the Liebfraumilch blend legally. In fact, some producers who have used the sensible winemaking practice of adding some süss reserve[28] made from such aromatic varieties have found that their wines do not pass the sensorial examination required of German wines[29] as they are considered untypical! Hard really to say what is untypical of a wine that has no chance of being typical given its array of potential grape and regional mix. It does not matter what the legislation says, you could require it to be filtered through a pair of old underpants, the customer recognises the brand and this product has, historically, been so constructed that it does not matter what is it's composition.

Liebfraumilch is going to remain and as such we must accept that fact.

---

[27] Through bitter experience, despite consumers of such wines not looking for complexity they are often the hardest to please and straight onto the winery if they detect the smallest departure from previous bottlings, even if such departures are improvements. Consumers of less commercial wines tend to appreciate factors of vintage variation.

[28] *Süssreserve* is discussed in detail later in this book.

[29] This is the granting of an APN, or *Amtliche Prüfungsnummer*, is discussed in an Appendix One.

It would be better not to have the restrictive confines of enforced legislation and allow winemakers to at least produce a wine better suited to the tastes of such consumers. In such a case, it could work towards having a reputation similar to Asti Spumante where an unabashed sweet aromatic bubbly serves a market and is at least of a uniform standard. Sweet "leg opener" it might be, but at least consistent in quality and built with the appropriate base material correct for the style.

English wine writer Patrick Mathews quotes leading producer Ernie Loosen, "It took the export market about fifteen years to wake up to the fact that the new German wines were crap."[30] Producers through to supermarket wine buyers were disinterested and uncaring. They had no reason to concentrate on quality or consider the overall impact on the image of German wine. Business is business. Supermarkets have to sell and there remains a large body of consumers buying the sweet and cheap offering. Producers are of the opinion that if the gap is there it should be filled. If they did not, someone else would. There was no long-term vision, nor a consideration of changes taking place in other producing countries. An industrial wine with an industrial approach in the most romantic of industries. Buyers were content to allow German wines to be represented by Liebfraumilch around the world. Consumer opinion saw this as the single offering from Germany at a time that exciting changes were taking place in the world wine industry and moved away leaving many industrial bottlers wondering what had happened.

Despite the fact that most German producers have realised the damage Liebfraumilch has caused their industry they have persisted with its production. The product fell into such disrepute that it became an industry embarrassment. Rather than eliminate its enshrinement in legislation or ban it outright the rescue plan has been an attempt to re-invent the Liebfraumilch wheel and target drinkers too young to understand the cringe effect the wine has on more senior drinkers reflecting on their misspent youth. Many new products from the same genre such as "Devils Rock" and "Bend in the River" are just cover versions of the same old tune. How many German wine consumers are seeing these products? Jazzed up bottles and labels. They are designed for export. Blue Nun and Black Tower have also been re-launched. Admittedly now the brands listed are actually decent drinkable commercial offerings. Like in most industries there have been some sackings. Blue Nun used to appear with a bevy of nuns on the label, now

---

[30] Page 64, Patrick Mathews, <u>The Wild Bunch</u>, Faber & Faber, London, 1997.

just Mother Superior is left to front the show.

Germany's prominent literature critic, Marcel Reich-Ranicki described good critics as ones who, "...always simplified for the sake of greater clarity."[31] Obviously German literature is a lot less muddled than trying to write a critic of their wine laws. The absurdity of Liebfraumilch's enshrinement is only part of the problem. The basic platform of how quality is formulated in German wine needs analysis.

As an overview, the first task should be a consideration of the different quality systems in Europe. The Italians have a very simple pyramid with categories of D.O.C.G, D.O.C, I.G.T, and VdT from top to bottom.[32] This system specifies the way in which blends must be composed and wines even made. The French use an *appellation contrôlée* system designed to protect the notion of terroir. The German structure takes this to supernatural heights by making their quality "pyramid" dependent first on ripeness and then having regional distinctions poured on top. Ridiculously quality is dependent not on terroir, vineyard history, or controls in winemaking, but on the level of sugar in a grape.[33]

It should be logical to even the newest wine taster that not all sites are created equal but this holds no sway in the quality regulation in Germany. Further, the level of ripeness has a name that is confusing to many even if you know what it means. Consumers often mistake the ripeness level terminology as an indication of final wine sweetness, which it need not be. The alcohol level is the key to understanding this but one needs to run the mental arithmetic.

For instance, *Auslese* wines are only sweet in taste if they are not permitted to ferment to dryness.[34] *Auslese* wine can be very sweet or it can be very dry. At the *Auslese* level the grapes have obtained a high level of

---

[31] p.310 <u>The Author of Himself</u>.

[32] The Italian pyramid has around 15 D.O.C.G. wines, or *Denominazione di Origine Controllate e Garantita*, over 200 D.O.C., or *Denominazione di Origine Controllate*, an expanding number of I.G.T., or *Indicazione Geographica Tipica*, and is lastly represented by the theoretically lowly V.d.T., or *Vino da Tavola*. Strictly speaking, it is not a guarantee of quality but rather one of establishing rules of production and composition were followed.

[33] In Germany, the indication or scale of ripeness is expressed in the *Oechsle* measurement. Quoting from the yet to be written Rough Guide to Winemaking, sugar is heavier than water and you can take the oft quoted *Oechsle* reading and divide by eight to get the likely potential alcohol in a wine.

[34] Fermenting to dryness means simply that the yeast has converted the fermentable sugars into alcohol.

ripeness and if the juice is not fermented to dryness the level of residual sugar will be enough to make this a lovely "sticky" wine. At the same time, if it is fermented to dryness we are going to find a *trocken* or dry wine higher in alcohol. *Auslese* is, or was, designed as an indication of very ripe grape material. If you decide to ferment it to dryness then you will end up with generally a powerful wine. If you do not ferment to dryness then you have more of an aperitif or dessert style wine.

This creates a minefield for the consumer. The level of ripeness defines the category. It is then up to the individual producer to stylistically decide how they present their wine from these grapes. It is too much to expect the consumer to understand. One time they buy an *Auslese* and it is sweet, the next it is dry and high in alcohol. We can see that the general impression the wine buying public has is that *Auslese* wines are sweet, whereas this need not be the case. Clear evidence of this consumer impression is seen by the fact that many German producers "downgrade" their wines to lower ripeness categories so as to fit into a bracket more known for dry styles increasing the sales potential.

For instance, producers will often "downgrade" their *Auslese* or *Spätlese* wines to the level of *Kabinett*. The public perceives them more often as being dry. One needs to look at the correlation to alcohol as well. Once one has their mind around this, then the confusion of region, districts, collective sites, and single vineyards comes into play. This is all very well if you happen to be a grape with an identity crisis, as you know perfectly well where you fit in. If one wanted to produce such a minefield of codified information would it not be better to barcode every vine?

German producers woke up sometime to the fact that all this gumpf was causing confusion and after considerable market research understood that this was fine for your great wine buffs but the normal consumer was plumping for something that didn't require ten minutes of study while one is being distracted by the screaming wife (and/or kids) in the supermarket. There was no clear idea of what an *Auslese*, *Spätlese*, or *Kabinett* wine was from a stylistic point of view. One producer's *Spätlese* was *trocken* and the other *halbtrocken*. It meant you could be in for a shock. Like randomly ordering a dish in a Hong Kong restaurant and getting puppy, you are not likely to make it twice. If the Germans could not get their house in order or even communicate a consistent style to the consumer then better to go for something which did not make one feel ignorant or disappointed.

This communication of style is the key. If the style in each category of ripeness had been consistent for instance;

"*Spätlese* = full-bodied "international dry" balanced wines" and;

"*Auslese* = late harvest = dessert style/Sauternes-esq/Sweet"

Communicating this to the consumer would have been much easier. As it stands there is no such structure and the differences, (a three-dimensional array) leave the consumer for dead.

Many wines were also labelled using gothic script, which aside from being hard for non-German speakers to read it tends to be rather threatening. This is where the theory that German wines suffered due to poor labelling developed. Certainly this was part of the problem and has been addressed by many producers. Even so, it was merely treating the symptoms rather than finding a cure. The core point remains that the shear volume of information is unnecessary and the entire structure of "quality" forces the theory that more sugar means better wine.

The background to setting quality based on sugar levels was derived purely from egalitarian motives. That is, you should not be listed as a first growth just because the old family has influence or a large estate. You should be judged on the quality of your fruit and wines. It sounds logical that quality should be dependent on the level of ripeness your the grapes achieve. The theory being, if you can get the ripest grapes then they must be the best quality. In a marginal winemaking climate this is not a bad foundation as poor sun starved sites are not going to be able to achieve sufficient ripeness to provide quality wine on a consistent basis. Even so, from a winemaking position the idea that the sweetness of juice alone determines the best quality is complete and utter nonsense. Why?

Winemakers are looking for is a balance between sweetness and acidity. The Australians adding tons, this is no exaggeration, of tartaric acid to their juices. They get high sugars from this sunburnt country but have little acid. Left alone the wines would taste of only alcohol be unbalanced and have a very short life span. If sugar level was the only determinant of quality, then this would be the only goal for the winemaker. Further, this balance can be achieved with a wine of say 8% alcohol or one that has fermented to dryness. The quest for sweetness probably also meant that good flavour producing but poor sugar producing Riesling vines were grubbed up, making way for such varietal stunners as Kerner and Müller-Thurgau. Müller-Thurgau produce large crops with the "right" sugar levels but tastes of, unfortunately, Müller-Thurgau. These sorts of production techniques rolled over hand-in-hand to the sort of marketing techniques generating Liebfraumilch.

Herr Reinhard Löwenstein of Weingut Heymann-Löwenstein described well to me the major fault with the focus on sugar levels as an aspect of quality. It means producers look to fitting their harvest around the sugar steps they must reach. Many focus on a certain amount of the harvest reaching certain levels so as that one can provide the number and types of bottles they need for sale. That is, a producer might need two thousand bottles of *Auslese* every year and as a result must hit this level in one of their wines. Vineyard management is then one of sugar production, something more efficiently done with sugar beet or cane. This means terroir is not considered and producers take their "eye off the ball" failing to consider what can be achieved in terms of flavours from their vineyards.

New World winemakers are concerned with the flavour potentials of their vineyards and how they will maximise those in fermentation styles. Part of the success of New Zealand's Sauvignon Blanc was learning to harvest a portion of "under ripe" fruit in order to achieve their distinct canned peas/asparagus aromas that disappear the riper the fruit gets. To do anything other is to completely misunderstand the concept of wine growing.[35]

We can understand that sugar level is the current official indicator of quality in German wine legislation. How does this transform itself into a quality pyramid? At the base of the existing quality pyramid are the lowly categories of *Wein* and *Tafelwein*. The former means that is what is in the box and the later that it is at least European in origin. Generally such wines are only German looking in their packaging. *Deutscher Tafelwein*, is the next step up and the "*Deutscher*" in front is a guarantee that the wine is of German origin. *Landwein* is another category and is effectively a German table wine but comes from one of 19 distinct districts. Do we really need to concern ourselves about regional characteristics in such a category? One could equate this category to the French *Vin de Pays* apart from the fact that their system can allow for the region to move up into AOC classification. Not so the German *Landwein*. The category is not transitional and this makes regional distinctions of no consequence.

At the end of the day, we can see the study of *Landwein* and *Deutsche Tafelwein* as somewhat pointless given their combined production accounts for around 2% of the industry volume. Why then has so much effort been expended on legislating and controlling something that

---

[35] Aromas and flavours are the key not sugar. Australia produces little in the way of aromatic interesting white wines except in its cool climate regions. The same is the case in Italy, where Süd Tyrol/Alto Adige and Friuli produce the best whites. To have adopted sugar as the quality determinant means abandoning the understanding of Germany as a cool climate wine region and trying to imitate warm climate results.

accounts for next to nothing of the total industry production? The answer to this is simply that the category was created in order to attempt to provide farsighted producers with a way of improving overall quality. The object of this category was to tempt producers into a category for their lesser wines, allowing them to be more selective with what they placed in the higher quality levels. From a winemaking point of view one is always trying to make a selection and one works from the top down, what doesn't make it into the flagship wine gets considered for the next level and so on and so on. In the end, a winemaker might be left with some liquid so unpalatable it is best sent for distillation.

If the *Landwein* category had been used as it was intended by the legislators some industry watchers estimate that it could account for up to twenty percent of German production rather than the pathetic two percent it blankets at present. Looking at this from the other direction this means that some eighteen percent of German "Quality" wine is really not. Consider for a moment, the quantum quality improvements that would have been seen in the next pyramid level if wines that were not quite of the quality to really be included were "de-classified" to the *Landwein* category. Part of this has to do with producers moving as a pack or an influential industry leader making the jump. If Hermann's mid level wine is only as good as Gunter's *Landwein* then Hermann has to either improve his mid level production or join in by putting out an equivalent quality *Landwein*. The problem is that producers have not embraced it as a concept. By now the consumer has accepted the category is only suitable for the guys sleeping on the park bench. Again this goes to show that all the will in the world in trying to legislate quality is not possible. It is like trying to legislate morality.

We can see an interesting parallel in the Italian industry. Italian wine legislators were embarrassed by the fact that the lowest category of their wines (*Vino da Tavola*) was often the best, at the cutting edge, and highest in price. The legislation had become the problem. Legislation had restricted innovation and prevented a producer from trying to do something new. Winemaking, like any industry, needs to experiment in order to advance. Be this experimenting with new technology, new varieties, or new blends of wines. Otherwise it is hard to advance wine quality. The administrators of the Italian legislation were inflexible and as a result producers used the only category of wine quality available to them for the release of these *avant-garde* wines. At the same time, there were millions of litres of your very average garden-variety *vino da tavola* being produced.

The situation became farcical with the release of the highest priced wines under the *vino da tavola* banner. These wines became known as the "Super Tuscans" and were rightly world-class wines. The administrator is a strange beast and decided the best way to curb this insult to their comfortable world order was to make it illegal to release a *vino da tavola* with the vintage year on the label. If you were producing a "Super Tuscan" this made things very silly. How could you talk about vintage variations or even let the public understand what year they were looking at spending big money on if you could not put the vintage year on the label.[36] Matters got to a point that legislators even granted a DOC to an individual vineyard in order to stave off their embarrassment. Naturally, the "Super Tuscan" producers were not without a bit of clout and basically forced the creation of a new quality category called *Indicazione Geographica Tipica* (IGT).

IGT is really a geographical nothingness and resembles the German *Gebiet* but allowed wines that did not fit into the scheme of things without a DOC to be included in something a little bit more refined rather than having to mingle with the rough-as-guts *vino da tavola* crowd. Italian *bella figura* was maintained. Largely it was an attempt to avoid foreign wine industry experts laughing and saying, "how Italian, your best wines are in your lowest classification". Upon commencement the IGT category had very very few applications for wine styles to be released with such a denomination. It looked a bit like the whole thing had stalled and would go the way of German *Landwein* until some of the bigger players started to use the classification. In a few years the use of the category has swelled and it is a pity the same did not happen for *Landwein*. IGT has become to be recognised as a category where a producer can release a quality wine without the image penalty of a *vino da tavola*. In fact, IGT has permitted varietal labelling and considerable winemaking experimentation. Further, we can see plenty of Italian *vino da tavola* running around in the market as well as plenty of French *Vins de Pays*. In contrast, there is virtually no German wine on the market tagged at a similar level, whereas there is certainly plenty of wine that matches their European neighbour's low level of quality.

The Germans missed the *Landwein* boat, which is somewhat symptomatic of the industry as a whole and unfortunate. It is one of the

---

[36] Many producers got around this in a very Italian way by using the required Lot Code as the vintage writing the required prefix "L" as small as possible. "L. 2000".

few things the legislators have done well. Few wines of any quality end up in this hollow category; with the exception of some wines that fail at the *Amtliche Prüfung* for lack of being typical, (some barrique wines for example). How is it that a nation of individuals such as the Italians are able to better function as a collective than Germans who have a reputation of doing things *en masse* very efficiently? The answer to this is a core problem of the German industry where big industrial bottlers strangled if not kidnapped the game for their own motives to the expense of the industry as a whole.

The next rung on the quality pyramid are *Qualitätswein bestimmter Anbaugebiete* (QbA wines).[37] This is the most important category if considered as volume of production in any given year. It accounts for some fifty to eighty percent of annual wine production. Why the massive variance in percentage production? This is entirely due to the fact that the quality pyramid is based on ripeness levels. In good years the level of ripeness will be higher and the greater the volume of wine that can "creep" up to the next level of the pyramid (QmP wines).[38] In poor years it means that many of the QmP wines are going to have to be dropped to the "reserves bench" of QbA; hence the variation in the percentage of wines released as QbA.

QbA wines generally equate to what New World producers would describe as their entry-level or estate wines. In saying this, often producers "de-classify" some of their potentially QmP wines to the QbA level due to their perception of being more commercially viable. It is also logical for producers to try to reserve the QmP category for their single vineyard wines thus attempting to confirm their status as estate reserve wines. Like most New World wines in this level of quality (QbA) many of these wines are fairly well manipulated by winemaking methods. QbA wines are permitted a level of chapitalisation or adding of sugar in order to increase the potential alcohol level in the wine. The residual sugar level at bottling can also be easily modified particularly with the use of *Süssreserve*, which is discussed more fully later in the text.

What the QbA category provides is a mark of certain "quality" levels having been obtained and that the wine comes from one of thirteen

---

[37] QbA; *Qualitätswein bestimmter Anbaugebiete* or quality wine from a designated wine region.

[38] QMP; *Qualitätswein mit Prädikat*, or quality wine predicated by ripeness. The level of ripeness is expressed in degrees Oeschsle and a minimum level required for each QmP varies depending or the region and the grape variety.

defined regions.[39] There are different levels of ripeness, which must be achieved in the different regions in order to reach the QbA level, and correspondingly the permitted level of chapitalisation that may take place. This is all very well codified and certainly controlled.[40] Heaven forbid that someone might add a gram too much sugar here or there.

QmP wines are top level of the quality pyramid. The "P" stands for *Prädikat*, which basically means that the quality level is predicated or ensured by the level of ripeness achieved. It is designed to stand for its purity in ripeness achieved and as a result no chapitalisation is permitted. Producers must give notice of their intention to harvest fruit potentially designated as QmP and the geographical area in which they are allowed to harvest is limited more than by the QbA category. This in turn suggests why many quality producers only release their single vineyard wines in the QmP category. QmP wines are allowed to have a *Süssreserve* addition in order to give the wines back some roundness and balance sharp acidity. In my opinion this is making a mockery of the imagined quality leap. On the one hand you do not permit chapitalisation in order to delimit "quality" between QmP and QbA levels but in the end effect you are able to add sugar (in the form of *Süssreserve*, back into the wine in order to give balance.

These wines should take their balancing of acid from residual sugar resulting from stopping the fermentation at the point where the winemaker judges the sugar acid balance to have been reached. To do otherwise is simply what commercial winemaking does and adds back palate fattening sugar to a dry wine. Certainly it is not easy to stop the ferment at the right point but the German climatic conditions are ideal for this task and with the level of technology at the *kellermeisters* disposal nowadays it can be done without excessive risk. QmP is meant to be a guarantee of top quality wine made from top quality vineyards and winemaking. Any use of *Süssreserve* on such wines is debasing the original intention for this category. Still, winery practicalities require it to be used and it is yet another example of the legislation missing the point.

In an attempt at summary, QbA wines are more generalised cuvees

---

[39] For a list drawing these regional aspects together refer to Appendix Two.

[40] All these categories and prädikats have, as mentioned, have different scales of required ripeness or sugar content. Matters are made more complicated as each region and grape variety has a different scale. This is logical given the fact that different varieties produce different levels of sugar and the difference from the warmer to the cooler areas in the potential ripeness that can be achieved. It is a large array of data and best confined to German winemaking texts.

and QmP wines are more vineyard and ripeness level specific. This is particularly so given that the QmP category blankets the "styles" of wines with particular names due to particular levels of ripeness or composition. There is effectively a ladder of ripeness within this blanket QmP category. Each rung on this ladder is representative of an increase in ripeness and a key to what has taken place in the vineyard. In essence, when used sensibly, it gives a very fast and general descriptor of what the particular wine is all about.[41] Running up the QmP ladder of ripeness we find *Kabinett*, *Spätlese*, *Auslese*, *Beerenauslese*, *Eiswein*, and God's nectar *Trockenbeerenauslese*.

With a little knowledge of German these become very easy to understand. *Kabinett* can simply be understood by virtue of the derivation of the word. *Kabinett* is like a special store or like most wine drinkers without a cellar in their villa, the best bottles are kept in a cabinet or cupboard! *Lese* means harvest, *spat-* means late, *aus-* means out, *-beeren* is berry, and *trocken* dry. As a result, you have late harvest, out of harvest, and individual berry harvest. *Eiswein* is something again easy to understand as the grapes are well and truly frozen when harvested. *Trockenbeerenauslese* (TbA) or dry berry out of harvest is also easy to comprehend.

Kabinett quality grapes must by definition be riper than those used for QbA. Immediately one can see why chapitalisation is not permitted for QmP wines as otherwise wines from QbA level could be "sugared up" to this quality category. Grapes at the *Kabinett* level may be harvested at any time during the picking season. Often when producers ferment and leave this dry (or *trocken*) it can be seen very much as the estate style and some writers suggest by implication it indicates the general style of quality German wine. In my opinion, it is the next category up the rung providing that indication.

Spätlese grapes are effectively tardy harvest. *Spätlese* grapes cannot be brought in until a minimum of seven days after the main harvest has begun. The sugar levels achieved really mean by international standards that they are merely just ripe rather than late harvest. Further, as this category is normally harvested prior to the onset of *botrytis* infection it gives the best potential for a producer to show with healthy ripe fruit the superiority of their terroir. There is a caveat, a wet blanket of course. The consumer impression or "style" which has been developed for *Spätlese* is

---

[41] Unfortunately, as discussed earlier in the chapter, using the example of *Auslese* there is no stylistic definition- either sweet or dry, meaning that as a descriptor it can only be used as an indication to what stage of ripeness the grapes achieved.

for the wine to be seen with varying degrees of sweetness. Historically, this cannot have been so and many producers spend a lot of time trying to convince customers that dry *Spätlese* are the true style the nonclamenture should indicate. The problem is the German consumer associates *Spätlese* with being left as a sweetish wine due to the efforts of some producers over the last fifty years. As a result, many producers that understand this perfectly fantastic category and the potential it has to demonstrate their terroir often move such wines down to *Kabinett* status.

Strangely *Kabinett* has developed a reputation for generally having dry wines and in doing so the belief is re-enforced. Things just go full circle and it must be incredibly frustrating for good producers to persist in releasing Spätlese wines. Again it all falls to the individual producer and unless you know them you are walking into a minefield of differences despite the over categorisation and legislation. Again, legislation was an attempt to make logical compartments but has merely resulted in consumer confusion without giving any reliable guide with what to expect.

Auslese wines are generally going to exhibit some influence of botrytis infection. They can come in at any time during the harvest as long as they have sufficient ripeness. All diseased and unripe grapes must be taken out. That would suggest that *Auslese* wines can only be harvested by hand as with machine harvesting if would be impossible that the diseased berries were not also collected. These wines are very serious gear and many producers will harvest at this level so as to ensure a crop, otherwise it is a decision/gamble to hold grapes out there in the hope of hitting *Beerenauslese, Eiswein,* or *Trockenbeerenauslese* levels. As one can easily imagine, there is a great risk of the weather combining to provide the correct circumstances. It means setting aside a years vineyard work in the hope that the right climatic conditions materialise. It is a simple financial fact that to produce the maximum amount of crop one goes for *Tafelwein*. As you go up the scale it increases the risks from the elements and the crop starts to dwindle.

Beerenauslese is effectively a Sauternes style and may require many passes through the vineyard to individually harvest berries, which must be affected by *botrytis*. Full-blown *botrytis* affected wines like these see a loss of 40% in the liquid content of the grapes. Not only has, by this stage, the crop dried and shrivelled up like an old kangaroo's scrotum but it is expensive to harvest and to find victims willing to stand out in the German weather hunting for such grapes.

The system is fraught with quirks. Producers might need to

"declassify" so sending theoretically higher quality (due to higher sugar) wines to lower categories as they need wines in the lower brackets to sell. Winemaking considerations come into play as well. It is surely better to have a delightful *Spätlese* wine rather than something that just scrapes into the *Auslese* bracket. There are also some inexcusable practices, if this so-called quality scheme is meant to be so, where a technique known as "face-lifting" takes place. Simply, a producer can raise a *Kabinett* wine up to the level of *Spätlese* with the blending together of an *Auslese* level tank. Quality huh?

Amazingly, *Eiswein* seems to be the higher category sweet noble wine that the public drool over. Certainly this has to do with the marketability of the harvesting story. From a winemaking point of view this is a curious oddity. It is an exciting idea that the frozen grapes extract only pure juice but we can see that those sites, which often are susceptible to deep freezing, are often on lesser vineyard sites. That is, these vineyards are often low lying and produce no great wine if harvested during the regular vintage period due to the fact that they receive less heat and thus produce lesser quality grapes (lower sugar, green flavours, and high acid for example). Leaving such sites to fall victim of Mutti Nature producing conditions for *Eiswein* elevates production to an international oddity with excellent public perception and demand. Germany needs to convert its *Eiswein* image to the other wines in its true quality range.

In looking at such sites in isolation, we would be unlikely to classify them as great. Even so, part of the skill of the winemaker is to assess all his or her sites and select over time, and in some cases generations, as to what is the best variety, clone, and destination for fruit produced off that site. We must not imagine that sites are never replanted. An effective economic lifespan for a vineyard is around 30 years and sometimes less.[42] Thus, we can assume that in every generation of winemaking within a family it is likely that they have been making decisions about replacement plantings. Things change as does the stock of vines from which one can select their plantings. If one's site is prone to certain diseases then you are likely to select a vine/clone next time around that has some resistance to

---

[42] Economic lifespan is considered based on the years it takes to grow to a fruit producing level and producing such fruit which is not too green/unripe. That is, in the initial few years of fruit production the grapes are generally unbalanced. In the range of 8 to 15 years the vine is at its most productive and gives the best yield to quality ratio. As the vine material gets older the crop level is lower but the intensity or "wisdom" of the fruit becomes more complex. If a producer is able to command high prices for "old vine" wines then the economic lifespan of the vineyard is naturally prolonged.

such problems. The same goes if the winemaker decides that looking at the soil a certain grape variety might do better in that site. It is not set in stone with what the vineyard should be planted and nor is it set in stone the destination wine resulting from that land. Trial and error can find the right mix of variety, clone, and wine style to elevate a site to greatness once the combination of all factors click.

If a winery understands that a certain site is one that can produce a top quality *Eiswein* from time-to-time and then if the winery dedicates this site to such production what is stopping it from being seen as a great site for such production? The vineyards of Chateau d'Yquem might produce a perfectly terrible Syrah if it was so planted but no-one could argue the quality of its Sauterne. Even so, from a winemaking point of view, *Eiswein* seems to have been elevated by the consumer to sit on the top of the pyramid and this is no doubt due to the romance of its harvest and production. The greater the public fascination for this wine the more important it will so become.

Eiswein now thankfully has its own *Prädikat* and required level of ripeness, which stands, at the same level as that for *Beerenauslese*.[43] *Eiswein* is certainly not something that can take place except in rare circumstances. There needs to be an infection of botrytis and in effect the period for *Beerenauslese* harvest is upon the vineyard. Then what is required is a great freeze, through snow or better by a severe hoar frost. In some of the worst conditions, the harvest takes place by what look like bundled up vibrant coloured Michelin men. It is important that the grapes arrive at the winery as soon as possible in their frozen state whereupon they are pressed. Naturally, only the water inside the berry freezes and this is easily separated. The resultant juice is so thick and concentrated it is a wonder to behold. The press juice has to be at -8 C$^\circ$ so you can imagine that one is looking for grapes out in the field of around -15 C$^\circ$ to ensure with handling that a true *Eiswein* results. To get grapes at -15 C$^\circ$ really means that the outside air temp has to be completely bloody ridiculous and it is a silly thing to do around Christmas time when anyone sensible would be locked up next to the fire drinking a fine Barolo.

It is tremendous that the *Eiswein* harvest can often actually take place in January. This means the vintage takes place in the New Year. Due to the fact that the growing season is from the year before it takes that year's

---

[43] I am not even going to touch on the craziness that allowed *Eiswein* to be attached to other *Pradikats* where one could then end up with *Auslese Eiswein* and *Beerenauslese Eiswein*. This was even too much for the Germans and they thankfully abandoned it around 1982.

vintage. Yields are naturally pathetically small. From a sizable part of a hectare which has been set aside one can expect only a few litres, making the opportunity cost enough to make the firm accountant turn blue.

Eiswein production is given a bit of a helping hand nowadays. In the early 80's plastic sheeting began to be seen cladding vines. The idea was to prevent wind and rain attacking the fruit left in the hope of a harsh frost. The problem was that this non-porous film created its own humidity leading to the wrong sort of rots and moulds. Gradually a film was developed with micro pores, so allowing the gentle penetration of airflow, decreasing humidity, but not permitting water to enter. With a massive drop in temperature the must weights and acidity increase[44] and it has been found that the new protective film also assists with the creation of the right conditions, (i.e. healthy *botrytis*) for both *Beerenauslese* and *Trockenbeerenauslese*.

There is and has only ever been one true "ice wine" made in the Southern Hemisphere and that took place at Chard Farm in Central Otago on, if I recall correctly a hoar frost morning in 1992. This is one of the most talked about wines in New Zealand. Canada is the only other region that can make *Eiswein* using the "German" method on a regular basis. We can compare this to the use of the German *Reinheitsgebot 1516* beer brewing method. One could argue that German beers are among the best in the world and this has a lot to do with the retention of this brewing art that adds nothing but water, barley, yeast, and hops. Anyone around the world can use this method and many do in order to also make stunning beers. There is no natural climatic limitation on the use of *Reinheitsgebot* whereas there remain few places on earth where the conditions are right for the production of *Eiswein*.

Realistically, *Trockenbeerenauslese* is the greatest card in the German wine pack. It can only be made from a truly great site where optimal ripeness is reached prior to the onset of infection by *botrytis cineria*.[45] The king of all white wines is the *Trockenbeerenauslese*. The berries must have turned to raisons and when they are brought into the cellar they must have a potential alcohol of around 22%. This wine results with a colour and

---

[44] At a harvest temperature of −10 C°, I am aware of a harvest taking place giving a must weight of 170 *Oechsle* (potential alcohol 22%) with 17 g/L acid. The wine eventually fermented out to 7.5% alcohol, (recall the high concentration of sugar inhibits/kills the growth of yeast), giving a residual sugar level of 240 g/L. Having tasted the wine, I can report it to be completely balanced and with an aging potential that should certainly out see me.

[45] Referred to as *edelfaul* in German.

consistency of cough mixture, (they can range from a deep orange to brown colour), and I have tasted examples of more than 30 years of age that are still vibrant, intense, and the most complex of wines. In my opinion they are more of an oddity rather than something that can be readily appreciated as who can afford to do it often. *Eiswein* and *Beerenauslese* are more approachable but it is nice to have been able to try such a miracle of nature on a few occasions in a lifetime of wine tasting.

Before we consider complicating matters, we should also pass attention to the fact that wines must be labelled as to the level of residual sweetness they have. The terms *trocken* (dry) and *halbtrocken* (half dry) are terms used to given an indication to the consumer as to the residual sweetness of the wine. The borders for these sweetness levels are strictly delimited.[46] As stated above, the level of residual sugar is an indication but not necessarily gospel as to how the wine will taste given a good helping of acid in the wine. Readers might be surprised to learn how much residual sugar Australian red wines are sent to bottle with but this is less to mask acid, which many of them have had to add, but to create a feeling of big, round, and full wines in the mouth.

We can think of the foregoing QbA/QmP pyramid as basically a simple-ish guide to the ripeness level and after some consideration it is not too hard to come to grips with if one thinks of it as a ladder of ripeness. Nothing is ever perfect and the "styles" that have developed within those categories with their resultant anomalies are hard to reconcile. As I stated one needs to know the individual producer to get an idea of what he or she is really doing within those categories. This posses no hardship for the *cognoscenti* but for the regular wine consumer it is nothing more than a minefield.

A series of tinkering with laws to try to bash this all into shape has only resulted in further denying the obvious which has been pointed out to the authorities by a series of wine producers and writers for numerous years. The most complicating factor, with German wine sets in not at the regional classifications such as the Rheingau or Pfalz but at the further

---

[46] *Trocken* wines may contain up to 8g/L residual sugar and halbtrocken between 9 and 18 g/L. Given the level of natural acidity which gives German wine its structure, longevity, and compatibility with such a diverse range of foods the level of *trocken* at even 8 g/L of residual sugar is barely detectable and sometimes the wines are still noticeably acidic. Readers might be surprised that many commercial branded Australian Shiraz wines are released with 6 gm/L sugar and no one is suggesting that they are approaching half dry!

division and dilution of this. The next stage to consider, if anyone is still reading this, is the breakdown of regions into different areas and single vineyard sites.

This chapter has nothing to do with sausages but for all the good the German wine laws of 1971 did it may as well. In the late 1960's or 70's the nations within the European Economic Community had to bring their food and beverage laws inline with that of rest of the EEC. Beer, sausages, and wine were all included. The German brewers fought to maintain their beer purity by ensuring that their beer must still be made in accordance with the *Reinheitsgebot 1516*. I am not sure about the Bratwurst lobby but if what I have tasted is anything to go by, these guys certainly knew their sausages! Wine law was no exception and by 1971, German regulations needed to fall into the EEC. It would have been an ideal opportunity to tinker, if not drop a new engine in the machine. What resulted was the worst law quality producers or consumers could imagine and perhaps it would have been better to call in the Sausage Society lads for help.

The German Wine Law of 1971, set up the system of quality being dependent upon grape ripeness. The foregoing chapter discusses this "quality" pyramid and this is essentially the structure around which the law is framed. As we have seen, unlike any other European wine law it makes no consideration of terroir as an aspect of quality. A golden opportunity was missed to create a system of wine laws that protected quality. Blame it on the 60's? In short, those who were able to lobby pushed forward the notion of egalitarianism that was running riot like the students in Germany at the time. The theory being that it did not matter what pedigree the site had, anyone could make great wine all you needed was high sugar content. This was a concept welcomed by the ruling socialist coalition of the day.

At the time of the 1971 Law there were over 30,000 *Einzellagen*.[47] This had a sound historical basis and was largely founded on the concept of terroir and the ancient taxation structure. It surely should not really matter how many einzellagen there are. In theory, if a site is good enough or has some aspect of terroir that separates it from the rest of the vineyards around it, then why not have a name. The premise is that each and every vineyard site has a particular microclimate and as a result exhibits a certain style of wine which can differentiate itself from another due to a combination of variety, soil, and aspect (light, wind, heat

---

[47] *Einzellagen* means a single vineyard or individual vineyard site with a geographical and/or historical name.

retention, drainage, slope, root depth) and the like. The number of them is, therefore, immaterial. Even so, 30,000 were over the top and unworkable not to mention the fact that if everyone has one then it is not a special distinction anymore. Here the aims of the legislation were sensible in trying to reduce this number, which it did to around 2,600.[48]

As an aside, we can see the proliferation of single vineyard names in the New World. Each vineyard site there seems now to have a name. Church Block, Cricket Pitch, Graveyard Block, and so on. The names might sound strange to some Old World ears but so do translations such as Sack Drager (*Sackträger*) or Golden Hole (*Goldenes Loch*). Due to the fact that these names are not so tied to a town and district they appear to be less complicated. Their aim is the same, the identification of a plot by a "historic" name. One wonders in 20 years if wine industry experts will be asking the Australians to reduce the number of single vineyard names they have. I cannot imagine it and each producer would say that it is their right to identify their site with whatever name they chose.

Single vineyard sites were out of fashion and this was partly supported by the wine world witnessing the rise of "egalitarian" concepts in the New World. New World winemakers were generally anti-terroir and appeared to demonstrate vineyards with no providence could produce quality wines. Off they went with the most basic of climatic and soil information, planting vineyards that produced very drinkable and saleable. In general New World winemakers were very dismissive of terroir and their theory was further supported by their concepts of blending. Their concern was that releasing a wine from a single vineyard might often mean a bad wine in a bad year or even a lesser wine by virtue of not having blending options. New World wineries strove for consistency both in terms of quality control and in ironing out the bad year "bumps" so as that the public always could purchase a solid reliable wine. Part of creating this is managing vineyards via irrigation in order to give as constant a fruit ripening profile as possible, dripping in water when it is needed. After vintage, blending from different sites irons out problems and is know as "blending away". This is the blending of various attributes from different wines. Sometimes you are doing it in order to hide undesirable aspects and other times you blend in order to compliment/accentuate attributes from various wines so as that the sum

---

[48] This is much like the situation in Italy where a single vineyard site must present itself and also demonstrate some form of historical documented name. In the end the customer decides as to the worth of the single vineyard name. These are clearly indicated with the term vigna/vignetto preceding the named site.

is better than the parts.

The top Australian wine, Grange "Hermitage"[49] was and is blended from a number of different vineyards. For effectively the only "premier cru" wine from the Southern Hemisphere it is remarkable that no marketing noise is made whatsoever regarding the vineyard sites. In fact, the reverse is the case and is akin to Petrus declaring their grapes are from somewhere in France. The end result is the product and this is what the consumer sees. There are no real restrictions in the New World and the entire wine legislation fits within a few pages, controlling what chemical additives can be made and basic food hygiene assurance. If you were to blend so as to iron out some problems in Europe you would become a criminal. It goes on. It is not difficult from a winemaking point of view to change where the wine in a tank "comes" from. It is certainly happening in Europe and with commercial pressures why is anyone going to release anything less than the best that they can from their most marketable named sites? Who can afford to put out a bad wine from their best marketing named vineyard? The abuses of the system are probably the lowest in Germany and highest in Italy.[50]

Taking the moral high ground must be cold comfort when having to fight in the wine world with one arm tied behind your back. No one is going to put food on the table or being able to tell their kids that the rest of Europe might cheat like mad in order to compete with the Australians but not us. Surely it would be better to modify the laws to reflect practical realities.

Aside from the fact that the 1971 law established the level of obtained sugar as the determining factor of quality worse aspects were enacted. Reducing the number of Einzellagen was an effort at consolidating matters, and rightly so. Where the mistake was made was to try and compensate for this loss of a "marketable" vineyard name by completely throwing the baby out with the bath water and allowing the Einzellagen names to be "diluted" to cover an area of up to 5 hectares. So, wonderful specific plots that once been just a few rows of vines now covered for marketing purposes an expanse of land that had little connection with the original named site. Tom Stevenson correctly states, "…the legendary quality of the individually named vineyards, or true *Einzellagen* no longer

---

[49] Now known as Grange, as if the Australians wish to export it they cannot use the term "Hermitage". They persist in terming average locally produced sparkling wine as Champagne.

[50] Comment justified from personal knowledge. As with most European rules the Germans studiously follow them. In Italy and France there are a lot of grey areas.

existed after 1971."[51]

In his excellent and recent work, Stephen Brook, has described the 1971 laws as, "the upshot of adoption of famous names to identify a large characterless region was not only to confuse, and no doubt con, the consumer, but to wreck the reputation of both (*sites such as*) Piesport and Nierstein.[52]

We must also think that the land parcels due to their division over time were often small 0.2 hectare lots. To flood this out to something that covered 5 hectare is patently retarded and could have only been dreamed up by those with vested interests and permitted by politicians having their hands held or palm's greased. Walking through a vineyard will make this plainly obvious. Take a small site on extreme calcium based soil jutting out on the edge of vineyard land. For many years it has been noticed that the wines from those few rows, where the soil is noticeably different, produce a really interesting mineral wine. So, you start to make the wine separately from it and find that it is a very good wine. After some vintages clients seek the wine from the vineyard you have now called "Hundegraben". If you were lucky enough in 1971, that the name was not one of the 27,000 or so culled but you might now find it expanded to include all the side of the hill, some 5 hectares, not just the few rows of vines on that special soil. The vines on much of the 5 hectares are tended by a bulk wine merchant with little interest in quality. At the same time, he is very interested in the fact that he can now use this name, which has become associated with quality built up from wines off a small part of the site. It is obvious what is going to happen here. The name is destroyed as is the public's confidence. No longer does the public see the use of a single vineyard name as something indicating quality and the name is perhaps associated with dross.

Not content with reducing the number of *Einzellagen* and destroying the concept of it by permitting its expansion to cover undeserving terrain, the law created a new geographical "appellation". We can easily understand the simple concept of 13 wine producing zones such as the Rheingau or Franken. These were sub-divided with two regional descriptors added (*Grosslage* and *Bereich*) which do nothing but further dilute the reputation of German wine. They could have quite easily been disposed of in the "reforms" of 1971 but they were not. In fact, unless you live on the particular vineyard it is often difficult to ascertain if a

---

[51] p.262 Tom Stevenson, <u>Sotheby's Wine Encyclopaedia.</u>
[52] Stephen Brook, <u>The Wines of Germany</u>, Mitchell Beazley, 2003, my italics.

Grosslage name is an *Einzellage*, (single vineyard) or not. There is no way to tell them apart.[53] A *Grosslage* is by definition a collective site and effectively a very large coverall geographical blanket; a wet one at best.

The fact that the actual term *Grosslage* does not have to be used and the fact that there is no way to tell if it is a single vineyard name or not, leads to consumers gaining the impression that such wines are from single vineyard sites. They may well be, if followed by the *Einzellage* name but who can tell the difference? In the ideal world where all the wine was glorious then this would not present a problem. Great single vineyard wines do the *Grosslage* no harm but the reserve is the case. Surely the point to having a single vineyard name is to demonstrate the unique nature of its place in the scheme of growing things. By mingling things with the *Grosslage* name, one is only diluting further the value of the *Einzellage*.

Bereich is the German term for district and is not even as specific as a suburb. Effectively if you see this term it just means that the wine comes from within that district. In its favour, at least if it is to be used then it must be on the label. That is, you have to write the word *Bereich* followed by the particular zone name, for instance, "Loreley" or "Burg Cochem". Even so, this is small payment for all the rest of the confusion that is created and in truth, the level of wines that are generally released as Bereich wines are not being bought by people with any knowledge or desire to know anything more about the wine than how to operate the cork.[54]

Ironically the wine control and laws are in place to ensure that fraud does not take place whereas the greatest fraud has effectively been enshrined within the law! The trade off for reducing the number of *Einzellage* was to allow their dilution by using that same name to cover a greater area. It means *Einzellage* became meaningless terms and certainly no guarantee of quality. Further, it is nothing short of "passing off" when one allows *Grosslage* to be used in the way that makes them look like a single vineyard name.

By the time the 1971 law was done and dusted, the German industry had moved from one on a par in terms of eminence with that of France.

---

[53] *Grosslage* is often known as *Grosslauge* by Germans which means "big lie" in English.

[54] Even in the event that one was to persist with the unnecessary terms of *Grosslage* and *Bereich*, it would have been possible to place some degree of separation or distinction between the *Grosslage* and the *Einzellage* simply by making it a requirement that the word *Grosslage* was used on the label. It is a requirement that *Bereich* be on the label so would it have not been logical to require *Grosslage* to have also been written on the label when used.

Further, the wine quality that had defined Germany at the upper levels was absolutely world class. The small quality producers releasing wines from single vineyards and estates were what with Germany had made its fame. Riesling was seen as the most noble variety and the German expression of it the supreme example of single vineyard terroir superiority. Post war, the Liebfraumilch situation struck and by the time of EEC conformity the large bottlers had won. Their wine was the one generally seen around the world as representing Germany. With the 1971 law, they all of a sudden had access to names of villages and vineyards that bore little if any relation to the *schrott* they were producing. It allowed them to marry into respectability but at best it was a shotgun wedding for the quality producers.

It became well know that the foregoing aspects were major flaws in the system and a source of considerable confusion for the consumer. Concerns were repeatedly raised by international wine journalists and by the general public. Quality orientated producers also knew that this was creating confusion among their clients, even German ones. The Germans were unable to come to grips with the need for simplicity and had built a system with ever decreasing circles within circles being passed off as assurances of quality, the end result being that the customer ended up dizzy and unfortunately not from drinking.

There was no shortage of knowledge that the system did not work just a shortage of anyone willing and able to do anything about it. Much of German politics and union wrangling is based on a system of non-confrontation and consensus. This is nice a neat and there are no busted heads on picket lines. It is much better to do dirty deals in private.[55] The same thing happened in the shaping of wine laws. Those who wanted to talk about it were shouted down and many merely did not want to make a scene thinking that they would just get on with it and make their own good wine. The camel is a beast designed by committee. It is just in this case that the reigns to the camel were also held by the powerful private and co-operative bottlers/producers .

There are sufficient examples in German history where the omission to act created a worse situation and a defence of not directly being

---

[55] As an aside, at the same time that we are seeing a move in Germany by quality producers to take back control of their industry and stand up for themselves we are also seeing a decline in the use of consensus labour bargaining/politics and its distortion of the market. Like the egalitarianism/socialism of the 1960's that ushered in the 1971 laws, we are seeing political parallels with increasing privatisation and the rise of elitism as an acceptable face within the German wine industry.

implicated. This state of affairs persisted for over 20 years whereby the wine law in Germany was so obviously flawed and the collective German wine house close to burning down. Powerful co-operative bottlers were sufficiently close to the blaze in order to pour petrol on the flames. Small quality producers and journalists had finally enough. The Phoenix that rose from the ashes was a movement to re-classify German wines based on a system of terroir.

Chief protagonist for this was English wine writer Hugh Johnson. For many years he had been making the point that the legislation, as we have seen, is basically a denial of geographical facts. On the one hand you cannot argue terroir and the site importance and then permit the name or designation of this particular site to be used for wines from within an expansive un-particular region. It has been Englishmen who have campaigned most strongly for the righting of the German flagship. In around 1987, as the story goes, English wine journalist Stuart Pigott found a land tax document in the library of the Loosen Estate in the Mosel. This document, from 1901, clearly demonstrated the rates due from various vineyards. The logical conclusion is that the better estates were able to pay higher rates. From here one could construct a hierarchical table of vineyards and thus as system of *grand crus* and so on. There was no shortage of Englishmen campaigning for this, to quote Tom Stevenson, "...If the Germans ever conduct an official classification, it would probably consist of no more that the best 250 Einzellagen and only the top ten per cent of these would be required to create the sort of international reputation that Bordeaux's First Growths have so effectively achieved."[56]

It would be wrong to suggest that this move was limited to the efforts of a group of English journalists. Around this time, there was a move in the Rheingau to create a different quality structure called Charta. This was based on the desire to present wines in the true style of Rheingau Riesling. There were various quality parameters, regulations on levels of residual sugar, and use of a common bottle shape. It was effectively the forerunner of the VDP system of terroir classification. Charta as a concept did not really succeed but gave birth to the idea that there was a movement of quality orientated producers looking at defining a style for wines within a framework of terroir. It will be discussed in greater detail later in the text.

The core theme to this book is that Germany can regain its wine

---

[56] P264 Tom Stevenson, <u>Sotheby's Wine Encyclopaedia</u>, DK, 1999.

reputation, the wines are certainly good enough. In order to do so there must be a return to an understanding that quality is predicated on terroir. Charta was the foundation of this seemingly logical idea. Focusing on the great vineyards will give a trickle down effect. How do you focus on the great vineyards? Simply, they need a name and a defined place in a quality pyramid. Once they have a name they can go about earning a reputation for style and quality. Elite it may make some estates. Even so, a short examination of the various wine guides gives an indication that "blind" tastings by experts are enough to determine there are better estates, vineyards, and wines like in any other industry. The various efforts at rebuilding the quality notion of German wines are considered in Parts Three and Four.

Part Two

Modern Talking[57]

---

57 As an aside, Part Two shares its name with a former German pop group of extremely doubtful talent. One of the members has gone on to further infamy, chiefly due to various antics reported in gossip press, the *piece de résistance* being caught out having sex with the sales girl in an Oriental rug shop. German wine clearly needs more Modern Talking.

Revolution: Who Let the Dogs Out?

We have heard from the wine press (no pun intended), of a "wine revolution" in the last thirty years. As far as revolutions go it has been relatively bloodless, unless you happen to have inherited a non-competitive wine estate. There is no debate that there have been radical changes to the industry in this time and largely as a result of the New World wine influx onto European markets. The European Union as a protective trading zone was, and continues to, unproductively produce masses of un-drunk and in some cases undrinkable wine. Much of this excess goes off to be turned into heavily subsidised windscreen wash so keep this in mind when you are racing down the highway past vineyards of little distinction. This is only set to escalate with the EU expansion of 2004. You can start to clean the screen with some vintage Bulgarian gear.

Despite the active protectionism of the European Union, wines from the New World were entering into the common market. At the same time, changes to the demographic base and a shift in tastes/aspirations made wine reachable by a new group of consumers who were happy to buy their wine in supermarkets rather than from some pompous Rupert wine merchant. The "hinge factor" was probably when wine writer Steven Spurier was able to demonstrate New World wines could cut it and in fact be seen in "blind tastings" to be better than some great names from the Old World. This was back in 1976, where Spurier put together a tasting for some fifteen French wine critics with Chardonnay and Cabernet Sauvignon. France versus California with the latter coming out on top. Naturally the French cried foul but to their consummate distaste subsequent re-runs produced the same result. The French reaction was to bury their collective head in the sand but the English press latched onto this humbling of the French as one would expect. The English market was a prime target for the wines from the New World not only due to language and historical ties.

The English started to look further a field for their wines and this was at about the time significant volumes of Australian wine became available for export at a realistic price. The tidal wave on which the Australians then surfed into markets has not looked at breaking yet. Once Apartheid ended in South Africa they joined the swell as well. Only 10 years ago, (when Australian wines had already made a significant impact) French, German, and Italian wines made up over two-thirds of UK imports. This has now slipped to well under half and sadly the largest backwards step has been with German wine. As a very broad generalisation the French were partially protected by having the same varieties as seen in the New World wines, the Italian numbers remained up due to rapidly adapting and the high volumes of "plonk" that remained being consumed in the numerous Italian-esq restaurants, but Germany had no protection of an internationally desired cuisine or a grape variety in vogue. In addition, German representative groups failed to quickly grasp their wines were ideally matched with Indian food, something that boomed around this time in the UK as well.

Most overviews of German wine point out the importance it once had at various royal courts and how it was always acknowledged as superior in the world of white wine production. They then go on to blame Liebfraumilch for the creation of the "sweet and cheap" image that it maintains to this day, and blame the Australians for developing technology to create wine consistently like Coca-Cola, so spelling doom for German exporters. The heydays of Liebfraumilch were also the time of flared trousers and the drinking of Chianti as an unfortunate means to a trendy straw covered candleholder. All three of which could have in turn killed the reputations of their respective industries. This is probably unfair to flairs, given that the fashion industry is notoriously fickle anyway.

Chianti and the Italians in general were required to bring themselves into the modern world. The Italians did not have the lofty wine reputation of the French. This permitted a flexible approach, ideally suited to the Italian character. They were able to embrace technology and concentrate on lifting overall quality without affecting price in general. They quickly realised the need to focus on the desirable image of Italian weather, history, *la dolce vita*, and general lifestyle. At the end of the day, these changes allowed them to consolidate their traditional export markets in the lower price brackets and to continue quenching the thirsts of tourists. Further, they faced little attack on the domestic front given the provincial loyalties of their domestic wine drinkers.

Super Tuscan wines also brought considerable attention to the Italian industry as one doing new things and at the top quality level. Their aim was to stay close to tradition but basically avoid having to put white wine in the Chianti blend. The mind boggles when it thinks of what quality orientated German producers could have done if they had effectively protested the 1971, law by saying the elastication of the *einzellagen* is so illogical that we are releasing our greatest and most expensive wines as *Deutsche Tafelwein*. What would have been the result then? Would it have meant that a handful of producers like in Italy attracted all the attention for what great wines they were making? Would it have meant that the public would have, like with the Italian wines, been happy to pay the highest prices for super-Rheingau *Eisweins* released as *Deutsche Tafelwein*? Would this have created a small elite group of super regional wines like as in Italy's 100 best reds? We will never know.

Time stood still in France, where a reliance on name, growth, and inherent wine snobbery was assumed sufficient to carry the day against the upstarts from the New World. Much like at Agioncourt, pride comes before a fall. In recent years we have seen the French scramble to use New World "flying winemakers" and join with New World companies to turn some of their lesser regions into New World styled Old World wines. The French, with or without outside assistance, continue to produce good wines the only real result has been the satisfaction in seeing the French brought down a peg or two. Their industry was too large for the New World to "defeat" it but major inroads have been made and things have not been easy for many French producers.

Like the Italians the French are very inward looking with their wine consumption and have little use for imports of New World wines. [58] On the other hand, Germany is now importing more than it consumes of domestic production. The Italian and French industries might have taken a hit in their export markets but their parochial domestic consumption patterns have largely protected their producers despite a trend to drink less and of a better quality. The reverse is the case for the Germans. Their domestic market needs convincing as to their own wines and it has become fashionable to drink wine from *ausland* rather than the domestic drop. Germans are generally widely travelled and the wealthiest areas are near or in wine country. They were familiar with foreign lands and had often experimented with local wines when travelling. Wine imports from Italy, Spain, California, or Australia presented no great unknown when they started seeing them arrive on German shelves. The German industry was highly exposed to entry from foreign wines.

The French were willing to let their great estates provide the cache of a quality wine producing land. This is something not happening in Germany. This has a lot more to do with merely the influence or reputation from the great estates. In general terms the quality of the average industrial/commercial wine from Germany is probably poorer that those commercial wines from Bordeaux. Why? This has a lot to do

---

[58] Australia also imports very little wine (5% of consumption), most of which is very cheap or Champagne.

with winemaking and climate. In Bordeaux the level of cropping will likely still permit good ripeness and there is not then the need to manipulate wines. Importantly the grapes inside the commercial Bordeaux are going to be the same varieties as what goes into their famous regional brothers. In Germany, the cropping level of industrial wines leads to so much removal of acid and addition of sugar that the grape is rather an unwitting journeyman in the process. Further, what go into these industrial wines are things such as Kerner and Müller-Thurgau, not Riesling.

Germany, on the other hand, got caught with her collective pants down. Her traditional export markets were being feed with Liebfraumilch in all its spine chilling kitchness. There was no eye on the weather rail looking for what was coming from overseas. As I will point out later, the so called New World technology was really not so but the Germans did not see the need to change and not only did the New World hit with something different but they timed it right, brought in new drinkers, and landed the brand generation. The German reaction was to drop the price of their wines and continue to find ways of producing it cheaper. This only exacerbated their image problem because it stereotyped all German wines as cheap and nasty.

In general terms "flying winemakers" had the edge in terms of professionalism and understanding of what were the new consumer tastes. The former is starting to be redressed but the latter sadly is a long way from being understood in the Old World. It is hard when bound by tradition to change things radically. No one taking over a multi generation estate wants to be the one in the family history who lost the lot and as a result conservative inaction is the norm. The reverse can also be true. A complete abandonment of tradition can lead to the loss of markets and also destroy an estate. This sort of thing is obviously a very fine line. My argument, contained within Part Four is that tradition needs to be harnessed correctly and the industry strengths utilised in order to match the market success of the New World. There also needs to be a radical reconsideration of what markets traditional German producers should be targeting.

The wine industry's focus, in the last twenty years, has shifted dramatically away from the Old to the New World.[59] More importantly,

---

[59] The publication of winemaking research is overwhelmingly done nowadays in the New World. Further, this research is more often than not done in wineries on a very large scale or even in a dedicated experimental winery. Call it applied science but it builds

the focus of the wine consumer has also shifted in this direction. One needs not to be drowned with industry statistics in order to confirm this fact. A visit to your local supermarket sees the shelves awash with wines from overseas and far away. Why have Europeans, with their own wine lakes to subsidise from their taxes, sought wine from Australia, South Africa, the USA, South America, and New Zealand?

Coinciding with the export boom in New World Wines or the so-called wine revolution Germany used Liebfraumilch as her flagship. At the same time as Germany was shooting itself repeatedly in the collective winemaking foot, Italy was inventing the Super Tuscans as a way of getting their world class products to market without them being associated with wicker covered Chianti bottles[60]. Herein resides the key difference. Tuscan wines ranged from the cheap mass marketed rubbish to the top level. The products were well differentiated. There was no confusing wicker Chianti with Super Tuscans. It was clear that if you wanted a great Italian then you went with the latter but if you were looking for just a glugger then the average Chianti could help wash down a cardboard Pizza bought on the way back from the pub. There was an acceptance of this fact without negative impact on the top-level wines.

Germany faced the same situation. Top flight Rieslings and at the other end "sweet and cheap". Why then could not Germany deliver itself from the "sweat and cheap" evil? Italy was being lead by a group of individualists each doing their own thing and striving to be individual, this was ideal from a winemaking point of view. World-class Italian wines made by people with an individual story to tell. The German scene was being lead by powerful co-ops and the individual "stars" were content to let them run the group marketing whilst they just got on with making great wines overwhelmingly for the *cognoscenti* in the domestic market. This is where Germany got left behind. The wine laws and lack of consistent producer to producer styles in the various "quality" steps made it impossible for the consumer. Super Tuscan was simple. It was great wine, rare, reassuringly expensive, and all you had to know was that it was from Tuscany.

Further, German wine PR communication was left in the hands of the large players who, in their interest, wanted to only portray themselves as

---

a culture of up to the minute use of findings rather than the production of knowledge within university halls well insulated from the rough and tumble real world.

[60] As an aside, the main component of Chianti is Sangiovese. Many Super Tuscans also rely partly on this grape variety. The noble Riesling appears in the best of German wines as well as the sweet and cheap.

what mattered in the industry. The drinkers of Liebfraumilch were happy as it was flowing in at a better price. It in turn created an image of "sweat and cheap" which did not stack up against the New World fruit packed, dry, well marketed, and well presented wines. The Italian individuals were concentrating on the export market realising that showing the best to wine writers meant good write ups also for the "value for money" producers. There was a distinct trickle down effect from all this publicity. Customers who could pay did. There was always a collectability/rarity factor. It was not everyday drinking stuff, but that was available at the next step down in good value for money, attractively packaged wines. Germany did not, and still struggles, to provide something in the middle making it hard to up sell from "sweet and cheap" or to drop down from the elite when not a special occasion.

The Italians had to be outward looking in order to sell expensive wines. The opposite was the case in Germany. The wealthy lived right on the doorstep of the great wine regions and it was only a few minutes drive to the best-of-the-best. As a result, individualistic and what would be iconic wineries anywhere else in the world were able to sell their product with no problems to the beneficiaries of the German *Wirkschaftwunder*. The top producers were able to survive in a world where there was little competition from outside. More and more imports came to Germany until the present situation where imported wine accounts for over fifty percent of German wine consumption.

Former comfortable export markets were in decline for the top producers due to there being more choice, more easily understood, and better marketed wines on the shelves in those markets. Meanwhile the DWI were working on ways to sustain the pushing of Liebfraumilch around the world as a means of keeping their co-op member power base happy with little concept that the wine consumer was looking elsewhere. New World offerings gave fruit, were not masked with loads of cloying sugar, and had street cred.[61] People might buy an Australian wine once

---

[61] One of the greatest "crimes" committed against German wine was the copycatting of German wines around the world. In Australia, and the United States, we grew up with the inbiquidous original Liebfraumilch but also with very poor quality Australian/American wines sold in Germanic style packaging under the names as Hock, KaiserStuhl, Moselle, and use of the term Rhine Riesling to denote the Riesling grape variety. These wines were sweet, cheap, and highly sulphured local versions of Liebfraumilch but released with the good sense not to taint local wine reputation but served to reinforce the idea that this was a Germanic style. As a result, this perpetuated the negative image of German wines in the New World without the German industry having had anything to do with it.

because they think kangaroos are cute but they will not buy it again if they do not like the taste. Australian wines have benefited from a consumer perception that they are fruity, powerful, easy drinking, and consistent. All of these factors can be a plus or a minus depending on what wine style, consumer, and price level you are targeting.

New World wines also trained consumers to buy and drink upon purchase. With at least a six-month advantage in the vintage date, a wine from Australian vintage 2001, tastes ready to drink when a European wine of the same year starts to ferment. Be that as it may, New World wineries understood the trend towards supermarket consumption and that the new consumer bought to drink immediately. This new consumer likely had no cellar in which to mature wines until they were hitting their best. A consume now age was upon us. Great German Riesling was not suited to this sort of market. It is often unapproachable for a number of years. Wine merchants were not going to take the costs of holding stock of wines that were long from hitting their prime drinking window. This trend is now so well established that it will be hard for German producers to redress.

There will be greater pressure on them to release wines ready for immediate drinking. This will mean detraction in the style of great German Riesling if not handled correctly. This could result in wines that do not show the best of what Germany has to offer being released in order to meet the drink now demand. Supermarkets have encouraged this with requiring a high turn over rate and wanting the new vintage on shelf as soon as possible. A disturbing trend is where consumers start to look at older vintages and assume that it has been unsold, sitting on the shelf for a long period of time, and not worth buying because it is either dead or ruined. It is not the same for reds and a challenge for German producers will be to make both early drinking styles at the entry level and to educate the consumer that their better wines need age. Here is a great opportunity, all the same, for a winery willing to restructure their product range and winemaking styles.

There was no refuge in mid-price level wines. At the mid level, things were too complicated. The New World boom came and this was all very simple for people that had no interest or financial freedom to drink something other than the entry-level wines. Vintage variations are difficult to explain to a mid level customer from a land with little, if any, heritage of winemaking or wine. Poor labelling made it difficult to comprehend in what had become an increasingly simplistic branded world. Less time and less information, combined with the journalistic barrage that came from the New World served to hamper Germany's efforts. Those efforts were also communicated very badly and in some cases neglected. Journalists have often cited the New World varietal revolution, whereby wines were labelled with what was in them rather than some style or regional denomination like Chablis. The consumer knew immediately what was in the bottle and if they liked Merlot or Chardonnay it was easy to find. One needed to know nothing of Bordeaux or Burgundy to understand this.

New World winemakers have been credited with creating a so-called varietal revolution, largely in California. Clear they did not have a region with a known name and thus really had no choice but to label the wines with the varieties contained within them. It has been said that Australia's debt to Bordeaux goes beyond varieties such as Merlot and Cabernet. It extends to the fact that, like in Bordeaux, Australian winemakers seem very comfortable in formal evening attire! The original varietal labellers were Germans. The grape variety was always required by law and if not by law then by traditional use.[62] It might have been hard to find in amongst a string of geographical references and ripeness indications but it was there. Where was the DWI publicity machine when all this was going on? Many years of poor results could have been avoided by the DWI proactively campaigning. It is only recently that we have seen the understanding of this and its implementation. Too little, too late.

Could the rot have been stopped by the wine authorities in Germany requiring an export certificate? That is, prior to any wine being exported it must undergo a process similar to what the Germans already in place with their bottling approval system. This would have been possible even within Europe and in an ideal world could have been expected to ensure certain minimum requirements were met prior to the product being permitted to leave the country. In Germany an export certificate system would have meant only a basic modification of the existing wine approval regulation. Even so, an export system is only as good as the standards set and their application. Granting an export certificate based purely on numbers rather than a sensory examination in this day and age is relatively pointless, given the fact that very few actual faulty wines will end up being presented.

We can see what presently gets through on the *Amtliche Prüfung* includes the most embarrassing of German wines, which are generally so technically manipulated that they numerically acceptable, and as a result

---

[62] The birth of varietal classification, i.e. the sale or description of wines based on the type of grape, emerged in Germany from the start of the 18th Century.

the sensory evaluation for export would need to be tightened.[63] I am certain that this would have been an anathema to the German wine authorities as it would implicitly imply exported product had to be potentially better than what was available for the domestic consumer. There is no way that the producers of bulk industrial wine would have permitted an export certificate to be enacted. Further, the sensory examination boards are notorious for their composition based more on influence rather than an understanding of winemaking or the future direction in which the industry should head.[64]

A far more useful means of trying to redress the entry level wine image would have been to concentrate, as previously discussed, on the use of the *Deutscher Tafelwein* category as a robust entry level product where "sweet and cheap" and innovative blends could have been effectively relegated to something above *vino da tavola* status, removing the connotation of quality wine. Further, this would and permit styles/varieties more suited to this market segment be included.[65]

If there has been any revolution, it has been in the fact that the New World, without a lengthy history of grape growing being able to select winegrowing regions less based on the cultural history of transportation and rather regions better suited for growing consistent quality grapes. This might not give the climatic vintage of a lifetime but with healthy ripe fruit there is more a winery can do to improve the wine rather than just try to rescue it through winemaking intervention. Less poor vintages and generally excellent ripe fruit means consistency and predictability, two of the factors ideal in commercial winemaking.[66]

New World winemakers had everything to gain. Any mistakes they made were seen as trial and error rather than a potential disaster for the

---

[63] Who controls the controllers? Who is the arbiter of taste? I am reminded of the New Zealand industry, where an export certificate exists, concerns a wine that was rejected based on the sensory examination. That wine went on to win wine of the year in an international wine competition held in Europe.

[64] Old farts with nothing else to do.

[65] With Deutscher Tafelwein you are permitted regional labelling, varietal declaration, and a vintage year. Despite sounding like *vino da tavola*, it actually works more like the Italian IGT.

[66] We can see the ongoing process of "discovery" of suitable vineyard land in the New World. New areas are being opened up and often demonstrate themselves as better than the original regions cultivated in the New World. The Hunter Valley in Australia is a case in point where easy transportation access to Sydney provided a major wine-growing region. As time goes on we see the region is prone to rain during harvest and many of the wineries based there resort to bringing in fruit from regions with less climatic problems such as Mudgee and Orange.

family estate. The overwhelming percentage of industry production passed into the hands of a few major players making unified marketing possible. Their industry was fresh, vibrant, and had a confidence growing from international success. Flying winemakers began to find that their production of commercially successful wines could take place by transporting their methodology to any wine producing country. This has meant for a great transfer of technology and is the subject of the next chapter.

Canned Winemaking: Vorsprung Durch Technik

The overwhelming mass of wine available today is produced by industrial methods that mirror petrol refining and in some cases taste like it. Many winemakers like to term their work "commercial winemaking". You can substitute the word industrial and it means the same thing. Commercial winemaking is basically the globalisation of wine production through multinational companies and the ready transfer of technology largely led by what are termed "flying winemakers". Often taste-the-same wines result and the additives come out of a can. This is due to the winemaker using a pre-written script with no understanding of the terroir. The winemaker is more likely to spend his or her time driving between wineries rather than flying.

In the simplest form a "flying winemaker" is a migratory creature that follows the vintages between the Northern and Southern Hemisphere. The species evolved due to Old World wine producers having the words, "why don't you make it taste like the Australians" rammed down their throats until they gagged on lashings of *querous troppus*.[67] Many old world cellars went off in search of this magic wine-buyer pleasing ingredient. Cheap enough to find, willing, and not scared of getting their hands dirty it did not take long for "progressive" Old World cellars to be hiring New World winemakers. Thus, the "flying winemaker" was invented.

From personal experience I have been fortunate to work in both sides of winemaking. For much time I split my involvement between elite production and commercial winemaking. Effectively half time I was an artist working on the cellar floor, (often literally making it shine) in order to achieve the best I could from a given harvest. This effort was rewarded by wine judges and gave a warm inner glow, which partly helps one when standing in a cold cellar. The other half of my time was spent putting together wines for the supermarkets. Here one is doing a job and always guided by the commercial nature of it and there is no shame in that. In

---

[67] Much of the oak flavour generated in modern New World wines has to do with the use of oak chips. These are small pieces of toasted oak or toasted powdered oak and effectively are mini barriques. They are added to the wine during fermentation or ageing and leech oak flavour into the wine. Given that a new oak barrique takes months to do this and costs around €550 with an effective life span of 3 years it is little wonder that oak chips at a few Euro per kilo are used to give commercial wines some oak characteristic. They do not give the elegance of good barriques and their use is questionable/illegal in Europe. This just means that wine cellars are importing a hell of a lot of "garden mulch" and it is not to make the rose garden near the tasting room look cute.

fact, there is a lot of job satisfaction in putting together good, drinkable, very enjoyable wines, at a certain price. There is no reason why each income level of drinker should not receive the best value for money wine and this is largely through the skill of flying winemakers who, like the aims of their Antipodean society, end up producing very egalitarian wines.

This flying winemaker species, with tannin stained hands, living mostly on beer, and wearing things such as steel toed Blunstone[68] boots, and calling everyone "mate" had a killer instinct for the production of commercial wine. The effort and professionalism they dedicate to the production of wines at the lower price levels continues to shock European producers. They were convinced that their production methods were the way to make wine and took a certain pride, verging on arrogance, in showing everyone's grandmother how to suck grapes. The Ozzies hopped around the world sprinkling their packet yeasts and talking about fruit driven wines. Soon after along came the Kiwis…a much less arrogant breed, (and deservedly so) but prone to catching the wrong trains, never remembering their wallet, (very handy when it comes to paying for anything), and generally having trouble sussing out that a watch was for more than a handy tool for helping to boil an egg.

Critics of this methodology insist this makes for most wine at the same price points tasting the same around the world. Differences in wines began to narrow and wines that stood out from the taste the same pack really only resulted when someone wanted to launch a product, take a loss on it the first year, and then hope to continue the sales. Taste-the-same drool from every country on the planet soon hit the shelves, which was lapped up by a consumer looking for fruity wines with the production consistency of Coca-Cola. This trend was purely customer driven. Wine writer Patrick Mathews describes this fruiting up of wines and making them non descriptive of their terroir as being given the "Australian Veneer".[69] Overall, there is some substance to this view but in the defence of flying winemaking, many winemakers do apply their skills to improving what is available from the local terroir.

Flying winemaking in hand with major multiple outlet traders, (especially supermarkets) have made entry level inexpensive wines predictable and depending how you feel about it, taste the same no matter where they originate. That is because there is a common thread. The

---

[68] A Tasmanian manufacturer of protective work boots which are highly fashionable in London with a price that makes their very cheap hardware store purchase in Tasmania all the more enjoyable.

[69] Patrick Mathews, The Wild Bunch, 1997, Faber & Faber, London.

consumer is demanding wines that have a certain taste and so the wine buyers in the supermarkets have a duty present what sells. Their job is to fill the shelves with things that move off them, not with wines that require the public to demonstrate too much understanding. Why do people buy the wines of Gallo? Winemakers have to ask themselves this question. Either a vast proportion of consumers do not understand the industrial scale of such production despite the efforts of marketing gurus to attempt to associate it with romantic notions of winemaking or they just do not care. The wine is fault free with flavour aspects the consumer enjoys and it provides a completely un-complex purchase decision.

The holy grail of commercial winemaking is to develop a Coca-Cola-esq product where the product is completely consistent vintage to vintage and purchased based on brand recognition without any need to put the vintage year on the label. Brand marketing then takes place with various psychological props for the consumer convincing them that they are a certain type in buying the "Marlboro Man" wine.[70] It works in all other consumer good sectors and has come to wine with globalisation. Wine I snow a commodity to be traded. One can see the increase of breweries that have invested in the wine trade and their aim will be to use their marketing, branding, and distribution skills in order to sell wine like they do beer.

It is largely through technological advances and a greater understanding of winemaking methods that such work is possible. There was a *"vorsprung durch technik"*[71] and the rumour has it that all this technological driven winemaking was invented by Australians. This is as accurate as the myth of Dom Perignon "inventing" the champagne process. You will not find Australian winemakers correcting this mistake largely due to the fact that most young winemakers now are convinced that the reason for the Australian success stems from home-grown technical innovation. In reality, large German companies were responsible for most of the technical advances. Technology was harnessed by industry and resulted in industrial wines. The large wine firms and cooperatives of Germany were actually the first to harness the use of temperature control in fermentation and the use of particular yeast strains in order to accentuate/de-accentuate different characters in the fruit. Further, without sterile filtration technology there would have been no

---

[70] It is now standard that large wine sales companies train their sales team to look at various end customer profiles with brands suited to certain types; "the Chardonnay girl", "the Entertainer", and the "Easily Pleased" are ones I have heard.

[71] A quantum leap forward brought on by technical innovation. Apologies to Audi.

way that the Germans could have ever released their "sweet and cheep" wines. Without sterile filtration there would have been the risk of a re-fermentation in the bottle when yeasts began work on the residual or added sugar. Poor initial grape material required a sack of winemaking tricks to produce drinkable wines. As a result, the first commercial wines were actually from Germany rather than the New World. Like in so many things the Germans worked the technology out first, but it was seriously applied in Australia by winemakers not bound by tradition and who saw it as a means to provide better commercial wines rather than as a salvage solution to poor vineyard material.

Commercial winemaking is a straight manipulation of the wine or must. It involves the correction of the grape must in terms of sugar and acid levels. "Squeaky clean" equipment and the use of inert gas blankets protect the loss of fruit aromas. Oxygen is the enemy and clean equipment the ally in this winemaking battle. The raw material of grapes has acid added, concentration to remove water content, tannin additions from various sources, grape must concentrate added to boost potential alcohol levels, and oak chip flavours to mimic the taste from barrels. Ferments are run to dryness ensuring no complications in storage. If you want any sweetness in the finished wine you just add sugar into it before bottling.

Flavour additions and so on are happening as well but this is still considered dirty pool. It is like doping in sport. Where do you draw the line in remaining competitive? Suffice to say, commercial winemaking is here to stay. For German producers, the former kings of mass-produced wine, this is somewhat ironic. They now have to decide how to compete against this flood of wines. The only difference is that the basic material used for German commercial wines cannot compete with that of New World regions due to their marginal climate. Commercial wines from the New World and even the warmer regions of Europe have more fruit and body than your thin over cropped German offerings.

As in any winemaking process it all starts in the vineyard. In the New World vineyards are often set up with drip irrigation and moisture probes imbedded in the soil. These are able to give the vineyard specialist an idea of how much water is needed. Some winemakers suggest drip irrigation is like force-feeding a goose. In reality it is merely a farming technique to iron out vintage variations. Further, considerable work goes into ensuring vineyards are sprayed with crop treatments and at the right time. Weather prediction is a major factor in minimising the levels of sprays required rather than merely preventative over application of chemicals. Saving on sprayings is environmentally as well as economically beneficial. Artificial electronic bunches are being developed to hang in the fruit canopy and record the real time climatic conditions the grapes experience. With computer modelling spray programmes become based on science rather than feeling you should be spraying because your neighbour is out doing so.

Sunlight interception in the fruiting zone and considerations of how much vegetation is required at various stages of the season also play a major role. Many of these vineyard management factors are also applicable to elite grape production, often better done by having a higher cost benefit. Still, it is done with a different focus. The commercial side will look to maximising the crop yield without diluting flavours and avoiding rot. The elite side will often look to minimising crop yields in order to boost flavour components and a level of rot might add some complexity to the wine. At the end of the day it is a trade off in terms of price received for the wine as to what aims are set in vineyard management.

A feature of commercial winemaking in the New World is the trucking in from around a nation grape must rather than working in a small delimited zone. As previously mentioned this is a means of ironing out the bumps in a microclimate or region's growing season. The New World, without restrictions, takes advantage of this in order to produce more consistent wines. Have a go at doing this in the Old World and you will end up in goal. Mechanical harvesting is something not isolated to the New World and is a distinct feature of all commercial winemaking. Without this in Australia there would be little Australian wine. The cheap German wines also need to use machine-harvested fruit.

Single yeast strains are used to ferment juices in commercial winemaking. These come out of a can and were developed in Germany but embraced by New World commercial winemakers. What are canned yeasts? These are "active dried yeasts" or ADY. They are strains of yeasts that have been isolated and then grown for production on an industrial scale. There are always naturally occurring yeasts in vineyards, on grapes, and in cellars. These tend to mutate and thrive under certain conditions, be it in vineyards or wineries. The result is each individual yeast has a characteristic that provides flavours in the resultant wine compounded by the temperature at which fermentation takes place. The concept is to take yeasts that give what we see as positive characteristics (structure, fruit expression, or ferment characters) and use it with certain grape varieties. Often the winemaker is looking for a type of yeast that has a known tolerance to sugar, alcohol, or temperature. They provide predictability in winemaking as well as a means of attempting to influence the flavour development in the wine. In order to use them the winemaker must first re-hydrate them as they arrive in a granulated form. Once they have been re-hydrated they need to be multiplied and gradually acclimatised to the juice they will eventually end up fermenting. Generally, they tend to be aggressive yeasts that kill less rigorous naturally occurring vineyard yeasts (not always a positive thing) and spoilage yeasts (always a positive thing). A small winery operation can afford to closely monitor natural yeasts and often derive exciting flavour differences resulting in far more complex wines. Commercial winemaking cannot run this risk. Slow, sluggish, or stuck fermentations are a commercial winemaker's nightmare and thus canned yeasts provide security.

Temperature controlled fermentation was also developed in Germany. It was more as a means to ensure wines fermented to dryness by keeping the tanks warm but New World winemakers faced the problem of needing to keep fermenting wines cool due to the hot vintage temperatures. As wines ferment they create a massive amount of heat when grape sugar is being converted to alcohol. It was noticed that if a ferment was run at different temperatures then different characters resulted in the wine. Generally the cooler the ferment the greater the retention of fruit aromas in the resultant wine. This means winemakers will often have some warmer fermentations in order to gain more complex ferment notes in the wines and cooler ones in order to maintain the fruit characters. Generally, the aim with commercial winemaking is to maximise fruit flavours and subsequently refrigeration is of major importance to any winery. When cooling fails, chaos results. Fermentation temperatures can climb out of control.

Reverse osmosis is a technique used to extract water from the wine or juice. It boosts the level of concentration, alcohol, and flavour a wine will have. It gives wines of greater strength and returns a lot of what has been removed from the grapes by over cropping. When over cropping has not taken place it provides wines with greater fruit and structure intensity. Some grape varieties respond better to it than others and there is still some speculation on if it means treated wines have less aging potential. As one of the aims of commercial winemaking is to produce ready to drink wines, reverse osmosis is a winemaking asset and the question of aging does not really become a concern.

Micro-oxidation is a relatively new technique. Despite the fact that in commercial winemaking oxygen is the enemy, it is well understood that barrique aging of wines provided both oak flavours and an improvement in wine harmony brought about by the gradual absorption of oxygen into the wine through the pores in the wood. Micro-oxidation is a technique to basically achieve this desirable slow level of oxygen absorption in tanks. At the end of the day it makes for softer tannin structures and means that the wines are ready for sale far sooner than would have normally been the case. To soften the tannin structure in big red wines was normally a product of time but nowadays it can be effectively mimicked with the use of "Micro-Ox". This has been a boon to all red winemakers, especially in regions such as Southern Italy where harsh tannins are characteristic of some of the native varietals. With micro-oxidation, rounder wines result being easier to drink earlier.

Sterile filtration has been mentioned in relation to the production of Liebfraumilch and it was probably the Seitz organisation in Germany who first commercially developed this technology for winemaking. New World winemakers embraced it more for getting wines to bottle sooner without running the risk of a further fermentation, (malolactic or secondary) in the bottle so as to provide a sterile, stabile, clean product. It means protecting the wine and getting it to market quickly.

Many of the foregoing techniques are also applicable to the production of elite wines. It is the focus and the use to which they are put more readily with commercial winemaking where we see their greatest impact. Frankly speaking, Flying Winemaking has provided real benefits for the consumer and progressive wine cellars. Making an improved product at a very reasonable price, especially when the style of wine produced is actually what the consumer likes, is commendable and there is nothing wrong with producing something that sells. It was and remains a consumer led means of production. The consumer of entry-level wines today is receiving a far better quality of product than 15 years ago, making wine enjoyment possible for a wider social spectrum. This has obvious health and cultural benefits.

Further, it has made many co-operative cellar able to sell their production at a price permitting investment in technology and better winemaking. Many co-operatives faced ruin or at best government bale out until their winemaking was modernised by flying winemakers. It is not uncommon to enter a wine region where one co-operative is profitable and the neighbouring one making a loss. The only difference has been the intervention of a flying winemaker cleaning up the wine styles and gaining a route to market. Profitable operations have then been able to invest in plant and equipment leading to the bottling of their own product with further value adding. Such cellars and their members understandably offer no criticism of flying winemakers.

There will always be a pelatron of these sorts of commercial wines. No one ever lost money on underestimating the taste of the wine buying public. Perhaps it can have a benefit and mean people will start to trade up. I am certain that this is the case. If you speak with general wine consumers, they find a starting point and move on from there. This can sometimes mean that they hop about at their initial level or they begin to trade up, learning more about wine, seeking more individual products. The challenge is to bring people from beer and spirits to enjoy the diversity and health benefits of moderate wine drinking not to mention the improved social aspect.

Commercial winemaking is not sitting still. It has understood the problem image of taste the same and is starting to look at a greater "injection" of local character into the wines. This is to ensure a point of difference and provide something new for the jaded drinker. In commercial winemaking there are important gains to be made in fusing the two winemaking worlds. There is a rapid transfer of knowledge nowadays and this means few secrets in winemaking. New World winemakers had to travel in order to gain experience. It provided them with a continued refreshment of ideas and they must be careful not to think that they have done everything right and be complacent. Many might but the intelligent ones understand the next level to which they must take these commercial wines. Already wine buyers are starting to complain of "taste the sameness" and flying winemakers will need to adapt if they wish to maintain their market strength.

Wine is now a commodity and is traded as such. Stuart Piggott in his recent work, <u>Shöne neue Weinwelt</u>, describes in excellent detail how this has taken place and the spread of quality wines around the world. It is unfortunate that such a wonderful campaigner for German wine uses his chapter on Germany to describe more about what the winery owners are clothed in rather than their chances to remain individual and rebuff globalisation.

We can see that commercial wines and their flying winemakers have provided numerous benefits to the entry level. If there is a downside, their wines can tend to be taste the same. For the German industry the impact has been massive and will force a complete rethink in the way wines need to be produced. The German industry has to decide how it will tackle New World commercial winemaking. Unfortunately for German producers, their problem was compounded due to the fact that their commercial wines as well as their middle level production suffered a decline brought about by the New World revolution. As a result, they do not just have to repair the situation with their commercial wines like the French and Italians.

Great German Riesling;
World Famous in Germany

There is no right way to make wine. There are, unfortunately, a lot of wrong ways to go about it. Despite the scientific basis there is still an aspect of art. Each vintage is different. The good, the great, and the downright ugly. Winemaking is an attempt to lift the bad years, and maximise the brilliance of a great year. It is a mixture of science and passion. In the difficult years all your skills and cellar tricks are called upon whereas in the great years the fruit does most of the work, not that it seems like it at the time. Graduates from winemaking universities come to grip with this fact in their first real harvest after study and the smart ones soon realise that often good winemaking contains a lot of hard won experience. Experience is something you don't get until just after you needed it. In winemaking terms that means waiting for another harvest in which to apply matters learnt.

Viticulture and winemaking techniques do not differ greatly around the world. Many of the modern techniques and tools of winemaking were developed in Germany as discussed. Even so, many of the styles of German wine are dictated by the wine regulations rather than by what the customer has demanded or what can be achieved with technology. This is due to the fact that levels of ripeness for the different "quality" categories are codified as are critical aspects regarding the making of the great sweet wines. There is no room in the regulations for doing something different, even if it is known that it will result in a better wine. German wine consumers can rightly feel short changed in this regard.

Germany is at the climatic limits for viticulture. It remains to be seen if the Greenhouse Effect or climate change is going to continue a string of warmer seasons for Germany. Even so, marginality tends to produce the best expressions of style, such as in Champagne or Burgundy. Germany faces risk from spring frosts and has a high risk of rot. Through chemical sprays the risk of rot can be lowered. A better understanding of grapevine diseases and weather modelling permits growers to make informed decisions regarding protection programmes. At the same time, total organic production is very difficult in Germany. At the end of the day, the best vineyard sites are ones less prone to disease and frost. Again, terroir comes to the fore. Limiting the crop yield is essential. Be it through the soil structure, close planting of vines (so limiting the zone in which the vine can push its roots), minimisation of leaf canopy, and level of pruning. Generally speaking lower crop levels mean that the grape bunches are filled with more of what the vine has to give. It is a bit like one really big expensive Christmas present or lots of little ones.

The vine requires certain specific aspects of location and climate in order to be able to survive. We can see that the differences in all these aspects make up a large component of the terroir concept. As a result, it is worth briefly considering some of these aspects.

The location of a vineyard, in terms of world geography, determines the general suitability for growing grapes. The world's quality vineyards are located in temperate climates and we can consider Germany as such despite a harsh winter it has a continental climate generating a sufficiently warm summer and enough sunlight hours in a year. Viticulturalists talk about sunlight hours and heat in terms of degree-days, but with grape growing the heat aspect is more important. The aspect in which a vineyard lies is also a factor contributing to quality. We can see the benefits in Germany of having a site protected from cold winds and having a Southerly exposure to maximise the reception of sunlight. Further, by having a sloped vineyard in Germany one increases the interception of light, due to the fact that the midday sun is rarely directly overhead. This can sometimes be enhanced by the reflection of sunlight off the rivers into the vineyards.

Rainfall is a significant factor. Grape vines require water and rain timed at certain intervals. Rainfall is not really a major concern for German producers whereas being prone to frost is an important one both for the potential damage to the vine and certainly to the crop during the growing season.[72]

We can expect that Germany, like most European countries has a suitable band of the foregoing in order to produce wines. Unlike some of its warmer neighbours, its conditions make it more suitable to the production of fine delicate whites rather than the production of red wines.

The crucial aspect to a consideration of terroir is the soil composition and structure. The vine root system can penetrate very deeply in search of

---

[72] Many marginal viticulture areas in the New World will use a combination of "frost pots" which are basically large diesel burning drums and helicopters to save a crop from frost. This works by having temperature sensors in the vineyard linked to a pager or mobile phone so just as you have managed to get to sleep it rings. You then race back to the vineyard, igniting the diesel, and get the helicopter pilot to hover over the vineyard in order to churn up the air. This reticulates the air around the vine, which is being warmed by the frost pots and generally saves the crop. A very expensive but effective method.

water and nutrients. Vigour of the vine can be limited by containing the space in which the roots can source food. Spacing of vines, working the topsoil, and the underneath soil structure tend to provide the best ways of limiting the rooting zone. In wet areas, good drainage can also set sites apart, stopping the vines from becoming water logged. Soils with good heat retention characteristics, such as gravel, sand, and loam are assets in cooler climates. In many cases, gravel soils and slate surfaces as seen in the Mosel provide a heat reflector and considerably modify the vine microclimate. Clay soils tend to be colder and as a result contribute less to the microclimate but act as a holder of water. Soils that have a high level of chalk are alkaline and contribute to high acidity in the resultant wines.

Riesling is a highly versatile grape variety. Like Chardonnay, it has travelled the world. It is such a terroir specific grape variety that despite the best efforts of flying winemakers, they have not managed to produce taste the same wines with it unlike what has taken place with Chardonnay. This fact should act as a wonderful defence mechanism for German producers who are able, therefore, to market their distinct version. We can see a similar factor with Nebbiolo, the grape component in such Italian greats as Barbaresco and Barolo. Nebbiolo has been planted in the New World without finding an expression as it does in these very special terroirs. The varietal versatility of Riesling extends in its ability to provide great wines from dry to lusciously sweet[73] and have the capacity to age so brilliantly.

Riesling, and nothing else, is the most noble of white wines. This is without dispute among wine lovers, experts, and journalists. No other white wine can provide such impact of flavours and aromas, intensity, and structure. Riesling provides the white wine with the greatest ability to age. No other white variety has such a great characteristic to remain fresh, fruit driven, and develop complexity after lengthy bottle aging. These characteristics stem from the varietal natural helping of acidity, which remains even as sugars concentrate when the grapes are attacked by *botrytis*. The key to great *Beerenauslese* wines are found in the fact that the sugar and acid levels remain in balance. This is not something that can be said for other white wines when made in a dessert, *passito*, or late-harvest style as they tend to be "sticky" or cloying.[74] Many Rieslings do not even start to come into their "drinking window" until they are over 10 years of

---

[73] Lusciously sweet is the term used by the VDP in their classification of such wines.
[74] Such dessert wines are generally made from Chardonnay or local varieties, none of which have an acid structure to provide the longevity such wines made from Riesling provide.

age. Try that with a flabby New World oak driven Chardonnay, but only with salad.

Riesling vines are incredibly robust. The fact that it flowers late can mean spring frosts are avoided but late ripening means by harvest the weather can have turned decidedly foul. It expresses clearly differences in soils and microclimate meaning it is a great exponent of terroir. It has a tremendous fruity nature as well as plenty of natural acidity. It can be cropped relatively highly without detracting too much from the overall wine quality. Even so, better wines will result from lower yields. It can produce wines with tropical and exotic fruit notes despite being a long way from where such fruits grow. The push in the past was to find clones that were able to produce higher yields but quality growers have realised this is not the best direction and are replanting with better material. Clonal selection is the best method for finding the right vine material for the particular site in terms of flavour profile, disease, and frost resistance. German scientists are likely to want to work with genetically modified material in order to speed this process of natural selection. It remains to be seen what the consumer response is to GM work with vines will be.

Vineyard yields are an essential aspect of quality winemaking. The best producers are self-regulating and often undertake crop thinning, despite the fact that they have likely pruned to only a few buds per cane in any event. All these things affect direct costs in terms of labour and opportunity cost with lower juice yields. Imagine what costs are involved when a bad season ruins all this minimisation and thus attempted concentration of crop. The irrigated areas of the New World must seem like paradise to many an Old World producer. The lower the yield the more energy the vine is able to place into that fruit it has, so concentrating flavours.

Terroir is a subject worthy of complete book. I have referred often to it in the foregoing chapters. New World winemakers often refer to the French emphasis on terroir as, "SCAM, (Soil Climate Aspect Mystique), but in public they use the word terroir". For many years New World winemakers have insisted that terroir is merely a means of artificially demanding high prices for wines based on non-existent site-specific nuisances. Marketing dream or reality? Terroir is a reality but unfortunately someone told the marketing department who then proceeded to wax so lyrical it has been debased. It should be a valuable tool to demonstrate wine differences to the consumer. I feel there is no reason for a wine to have a distinct village or vineyard name attached to it unless there is some discernable taste that requires such geographic pinpointing.

Rather than make my own long-winded case for terroir I would simply turn the Australian's[75] argument around. Australia is a big country and few wine consumers realise the differences between the zones due to unfamiliarity with its regions. Australia rarely suffers a bad vintage and this is not only due to weather, irrigation, or as many winemakers would like to believe great winemaking. The key to their consistent performance is that they have learnt very well to blend and their willingness to use material from widespread regions. There is no legal structure preventing this as in Europe, despite the fact that the continents are roughly the same size. Europeans will well know that a disastrous year in France can mean a great vintage in Italy but one can hardly imagine Rhone Syrah being beefed up in a bad year with material from Sicily. To do so would mean the final step in the "CocaColalisation" of wine and a trip to where soap-on-a-rope is a smart thing to pack.

Vintage variations take place in Australia as well. A poor season in the Hunter Valley can be offset with using fruit from the McClaren Vale. You will still see Hunter Valley on the label. The "anti-terroirists" in Australia have to only answer one question. That is, if terroir does not exist then why are you blending from different regions? It is not just to balance a bad year as it takes place in every season. They blend from different regions because those regions clearly give different characteristics. Terroir exists and it is proven in every bottle of fruity Australian wine. These wines are an assemblage of different regions to ensure that they give the balance of desired characters. If it were not so they would merely use fruit from one region. Trucking costs money and it is not done without reason.

The terroir specific nature of Riesling makes generalisations difficult as to what it is like. Within Germany, climatic variations and changes in soil structures make for great differences even within regions. These aspects will be considered in later chapters where the individual regions are considered. Even so, some generalisations are possible. Wines of the Rheingau, where the vineyards are exposed to the South and benefit from heat reflection off the Rhine, are generally characterised by their fullness with spicy, honey, and flowery fruit notes pushed with robust acidity.[76] In addition, the proximity of the vineyards to the river provides conditions

---

[75] Australian winemakers have been the most aggressive in their debunking of terroir but this is an obvious generalisation as many well-travelled Australian winemakers are passionate advocates of the same.

[76] To immediately qualify this statement; the wines of Lorch- at the top of the Rheingau dogleg show a relationship to the wines of the Mittlerhein.

suitable for the creation of *botrytis* or noble rot. These wines have force and generally are a richer golden colour. Even within this region the soils vary to such a degree providing wines of distinct differences in character.

Wines from the Pfalz[77], a warmer region, are more fruity in their structure and some examples are similar to what better New World Riesling producers can aspire to emulate. Lighter soils are better suited to commercial wines whereas more clay or calcium based ones tend to give more mineral and structured wines. It comes as no surprise that the Pfalz is known for some of the best Rieslings and for the source of the most commercial given that both soil structures exist.

The high natural level of acidity in Riesling can be balanced with sugar. Sugar is most effective in masking acidity and as a result many Rieslings tolerate a high level of residual sugar without making them tasting sweet. The use of residual sugar to balance acidity can make for a more harmonious wine. Wines with a residual level of sugar are at risk of re-fermenting at a later stage as yeasts remain in the wine unless removed by sterile filtration. Post World War II, producers realised their wines were more attractive when the acid levels were offset somewhat. As technological changes took place producers were able to utilise sterile filtration and bottling techniques which permitted wines with residual or even added sugar to be released without risk of re-fermenting in the bottle. Quality producers were able to avail themselves of the technology to produce better wines, which is what technology should be used for. The downside to the masking quality of sugar is that unattractive components in a wine such as bitterness or notes of rot can also be "hidden" with high additions. Volume producers could take the fruit from an over cropped vineyard yielding thin faulty wines and mask these problems with sugar. We have seen how the use of such technology by volume producers effectively destroyed the reputation of the industry with the release of oceans of Liebfraumilch.

Due to cellars being very cold wines often stopped fermenting of their own accord before reaching dryness. Nowadays, there is far more intervention from a winemaker who wishes to retain natural sweetness. Chilling, the addition of sulphur dioxide, and filtration will arrest fermentation and by using one or all of these techniques a winemaker is able to halt fermentation when he or she feels the right balance between fruit flavours, alcohol, acid, and sweetness have been reached. Subsequent

---

[77] The Rheinlandpfalz or Pfalz is often termed the Palatinate and some tourism efforts label it amusingly as the "Deutsche Toscana", which is particularly unfair given that the natives are unlikely to charge excessive prices for food, hotels, wine, and souvenirs.

sterile filtration avoids the risk of re-fermentation. This is the quality way of achieving residual sweetness.

From a winemaking point of view it is much easier to control fermentation by allowing it to run to dryness. In New World regions where dry wines are desired, a fermentation that "sticks" or stops is a winemaking nightmare and considered bad fermentation management. As alcohol level builds and sugar levels fall a hostile environment is created for yeast. In order to restart fermentation considerable work is required in acclimatising a new yeast strain to ferment in a hostile medium especially when cellars are cold, vintage work is ongoing, and demands on tank space are at their highest.

The development of *Süssreserve* allowed easier winemaking, particularly for volume winemaking outfits. *Süssreserve* is unfermented grape juice, filtered and then stored appropriately for later addition to dry wines in order to give the balance provided by sugar. This meant producers were able to just let wines ferment to dryness under constant temperature control and at a later stage add back a portion of *Süssreserve*. There are a number of regulations[78] regarding the use of *Süssreserve* insomuch as that the reserve should be from the same material it will eventually be added back to. A boon to producers one would think but as with any easy system there is often a quality trade off. Top producers and the better wines are made without *Süssreserve* but with the stopping of the fermentation at the correct point of balance.[79] Volume producers were able to gain their masking sugar addition, (up to twenty-five per cent of a wines volume), with relative simplicity.

One can see the natural balance being achieved in the wines of Weingut St Antony (Nahe), demonstrating the combination of winemaking methods. Here the best use of both winemaking philosophies is combined. Their designated dry wines, (entry level) have both yeast and nutrients added. This is to ensure that the wines go to dryness and that the fermentation runs as smoothly as possible. In this regard they are searching for a yeast that even in big years such as 2003,

---

[78] Much abused but this is merely a matter of paperwork. A wink is as good as a nod to a blind horse.

[79] A natural balance achieved by stopping the fermentation is far superior. Roughly speaking ripe grape juice has its sugar composed of equal parts glucose and fructose. The glucose portion ferments prior to the fructose and thus at the point where fermentation is likely arrested the natural sweetness is generally composed of fructose. Fructose has a different taste and is far more delicate. *Süssreserve* is overtly glucose in its taste and thus when one is striving for every factor to obtain top quality it is preferable to understand when to correctly arrest fermentation.

can tackle the sugar, handle the cold cellar temperatures, and ferment out to completion (dryness). To their mid and upper level wines they do not make any additions, (yeast nutrient or ADY yeast). The wines were permitted to ferment with the naturally present yeasts. In general, these yeasts are not as strong as ADY and have a tendency to be much less easier to control. In this regard we can also consider that the fermentations are more likely to "stick" thus leaving the wines with random levels of unfermented sugars.

They then describe these as "naturally sweet". Having tasted the wines I would tend to want to describe them as "internationally dry" trying to avoid the "s" word in any context. Given the levels of acid, which have been retained and subsequently balanced, by the level of residual sugar the wines do not have a sweet taste to them. This is something that other German wineries would do well to note and many of the elite estates work in exactly this way. "Internationally Dry" is a silly term but conveys the correct message without referral to the term sweet. Most New World efforts at Riesling have an amount of Residual Sugar added back in order to give the best balance rather than meet a labelling requirement. At the end of the day, Weingut St Antony have made wonderful wines with a direct example of letting the ferment control the level of residual sugar rather than add it back later after the wines have gone dry. Much harder winemaking indeed, but the harmony is evident in the exceptional quality of the end product.

In some years the level of acid can be oppressive. A certain amount of acid can be removed by adding calcium carbonate to the clarified juice but any resort to acid removal is going to affect the overall quality of the wine. Potassium bicarbonate can also be used after fermentation to bring about a reduction in the level of acidity. Both methods are limited in the amount of acid that they can remove. Both these systems basically precipitate tartrate. They are of limited help when spring frosts have affected the ability of the berries to assimilate malic acid. As the calcium carbonate and potassium bicarbonate methods work on tartaric acid, they can be of little help when much of the acid level in the berries is composed of malic acid. In this case a technique of "Double-Salt-Deacidification" can be used as it also precipitates malic acid.[80] When a

---

[80] For those who are interested, Double Salt Deacidification works by taking a portion of the juice (called the aliquot) and adding a calculated amount of Calcium Carbonate slowly to this aliquot whilst maintaining a high pH, otherwise the correct crystal budding of malic and tartaric acid will not form. This results in a black juice which is then filtered back into the mass, producing an overall lowering of the acid (both as malic and tartaric).

variety such as Chardonnay had a high level of acid, the solution would likely be running a malolactic fermentation.

Malolactic fermentation is a biological fermentation that generally happens after the alcoholic fermentation and converts malic acid into lactic acid. It is characterised by giving a buttery character and can be offensive if used unsparingly. Any wine with malic acid remaining in it can go through "malo" at a later stage, (often in the bottle) and does occur when wines have not been sterile filtered. Some wine styles respond well to full malolactic fermentation whereas other wines such as Riesling and Champagne tend to avoid it as the flavours are undesirable. It tends to make Riesling flabby and suppress varietal fruit. This is not to say that some Rieslings are not put through full or partial malolactic fermentation but it does not tend to marry well with the wine and thus is not a suitable method of acid reduction. Blending component wines that have had malolactic fermentation with those that have not introduces a risk of inoculating the mass. I am yet to meet a strong advocate of full malolactic fermentation for Riesling. Even so, there is the possibility of working with a strain of malolactic bacteria[81] which works prior to the alcohol fermentation and in fact is killed as alcohol levels rise. This strain does not impart a diacetyl or butter character but it is difficult to work with and is highly sensitive to sulphur dioxide which generally has had to be used in order to maintain clean green fresh fruit, thus conflicting with reductive winemaking.

The best results for Riesling are from long slow cool ferments of clean clear juice.[82] This is not a hard and fast rule as many winemakers prefer some grape solids in the juice feeling that it gives wines of greater longevity. Too much in the way of grape solids means the possibility of Hydrogen Sulphide being produced. This rotten egg smell will tend to kill fruit aromas if not checked early on in fermentation by the addition of a yeast nutrient. The best and softest method of obtaining clear juice is from pressing whole grape bunches and then cold settling. An efficient cooling system on tanks speeds this process as does the addition of the

---

I have worked with musts that despite having acids of 16g/L, most of this was malic acid (12g/L) and in order to remove this we had to add tartaric acid prior to DSD in order to maintain the balance. Australian winemakers would think you crazy adding acid to a juice with already 16g/L.

[81] Malolactic fermentation usually occurs with a strain of bacteria *Leucanostoc Oenos* the strain I refer to here is *L. Planterum*.

[82] Whole bunch pressing leads to cleaner initial free run juice. A school of thought says it is only necessary in years where there is considerable rot.

appropriate enzymes. Completely clear juice for fermentation can easily be achieved with a centrifuge but this is more suited to volume wine production. The centrifuge is simply a way of spinning the juice at high speed resulting in a separation of clear juice from solid material. Most quality producers are looking for some sort of middle ground and will tend to include a percentage of unclarified liquid in what they transfer to fermentation. Like many aspects of winemaking the percentage is determined by experience, desired wine style, and the vintage.

There is much debate between winemakers over the methods of maturation prior to preparing wines for bottling. Some will want to use old large wooden casks in order to give a fine slow micro-oxidation. Others swear by stainless steel. Still others are trying the use of barriques. During the maturation phase, there is also the question of if you allow the wine to remain on its fine yeast lees. In doing so you create another layer of complexity in the wine. If you are doing extended lees contact then storage needs to be in oak casks other than in stainless steel. If extended lees contact takes place in stainless steel then you stand to develop reductive aromas leading to H_2S or rotten egg smell over time. Here with Riesling we are talking the need to use neutral wood rather than overt barrique oak notes. This is to provide a long slow micro oxidation that comes by letting air in through the pores in the wood. The winemaker's enemy is generally oxygen but not in this case. Some producers are using barriques in order to give oak flavours to their Rieslings, but I do not feel that this is the direction to go. To do it in one of your wines and to do it with the right oak and toasting is something that can be beneficial, otherwise the flavours are inappropriate to Riesling. In unripe years time in cask can help due to the gentle oxidation rounding out the wines. Very delicate wines do not benefit from overt wood notes whereas richer wines are able to support it.

Weingut Molitor in the Mosel has been a great success. He follows a process of crushing fruit unless it is "problematical" as he terms it. What he means is when it is full of *botrytis* and thus under such circumstances whole bunch pressing is used. Clarification is by sedimentation and he ferments with "natural" yeasts. He ferments partially in wood and is a firm believer that high quality wines should receive some oak treatment. His wines undergo an extended period of lees contact.

What should Riesling taste and smell like? We should note that there are some general varietal characteristics and aspects, which are accentuated given a particular vintage. For instance, in a warmer vintage we might see greater notes of honey, spice, citrus, and toast aromas. The

Deutsche Wine Institute (DWI) has produced a wine aroma wheel in conjunction with the Association of German Oenologists and the respected lecturer Dr Ulrich Fischer. This is a derivation of the classic and now famous "Wine Aroma Wheel" as developed by Dr Ann Noble of USC-Davis. The DWI correctly credit Dr Noble on their wheel. A wine aroma wheel is a device divided into a number of key segments around the inner circle. The initial aroma keys or tastes can then be subdivided into more specific descriptors. Figure 1 is the DWI version and Figure 2, the more widely used "Aroma Wheel" from Dr Ann Noble. Despite some minor differences in the method they use, essentially the wheels provide primary, secondary, and tertiary aroma terms.

On the rear of the DWI version, they list the suitable terms for describing German Riesling. These are; "vineyard peach, apple, grapefruit, rose blossom, honey, and cut green grass". We can see from Figure 1, that there is no mention of petrol notes. I fail to understand why one of the first and most important descriptors of classic German Riesling is not listed by the DWI as one of the key descriptors nor even does it rate a mention in one of the sub-categories. The best information I can receive from the DWI is that petroleum notes are not seen as something positive. It appears that the DWI feels this to be negative and wish to sweep such descriptors away from consideration in their effort to spin the Riesling bottle. Yet again, the DWI fail to understand their own product and the fact that many consumers of Riesling enjoy this characteristic and even if they do not it is a persistent undeniable varietal characteristic and mandates a listing.

Whether petroleum notes are a positive or negative attribute is merely subjective. It is a characteristic as sure as any of the other key aromas and thus should have been included. We can note from Figure 2, that Petroleum notes are considered a key aroma ingredient worth mentioning and this original "Aroma Wheel" is designed as a general device for wine descriptions, not one specifically for Riesling. It is a little bit like the Champenois producing a Champagne Aroma Wheel and omitting a section on "bread aroma", something which is a key characteristic resulting from the contact of the yeast with the wine after the secondary fermentation within the bottle. The DWI should have made their wheel square.

One cannot avoid using petroleum as a key aroma term of Riesling. In fact, this note often tends to show itself with greater age in the wines. Hugh Johnson describes this note lovingly as, "the wiff of the forecourt". Despite the serious omission by the DWI, their aroma wheel is a very good device with which to apply to Riesling in general. I would suggest the following modifications. A new section of "Petroleum" should be added, (between "Smokey" and "Microbiological"), with "Petroleum" on the inside ring and "Diesel", "Kerosene", "Paraffin", and "Petrol" on the outside. On the outside ring under "Microbiological", certainly "Sauerkraut" should be added, despite its unpleasantness as a descriptor one is too close to home to neglect its inclusion. Under "Citrus", certainly "Lime" and "Orange Peel" should be added as should "Lychee" and "Passion fruit" in the tropical fruit sector. "Lavender" should be added to the "Pungent Flowers" sector and "Fig" to the "Dried Fruit" portion. "Vegetative" should include "Potpourri" and "Capsicum". In the "Oral Perceptions" category, surely "Steely" should rate a mention for Riesling.

FIG. 1: DWI Aroma Wheel[83]

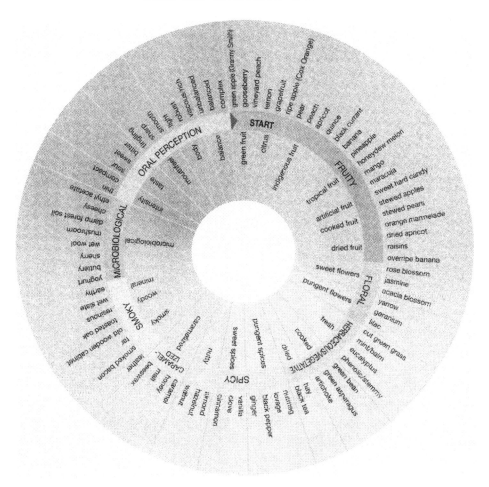

[83] I should note that if you want posters or any promotional material such as this wine wheel from the Deutsche Wein Institute you have to pay. This is an extreme case of shooting yourself repeatedly in the foot. With an industry in freefall one would expect that you fall over yourself at the thought that someone might even just maybe perhaps be untrendy enough to want some of your gear! If you pass by any Chianti display there will be a minimum of two scantily clad promo *"Vellini"* handing out badges, notebooks, and booklets. None of them, unfortunately, have ever wanted to make note of my address or bank details in exchange for such material. Come off it DWI, do you really want €2 for a wine wheel? Is it going to break the bank? (As an act of moral protest and in true Tasmanian tradition, I stole mine when the Rottweiler guarding the information box was distracted).

FIG. 2: Dr Ann Nobel's Aroma Wheel[84]

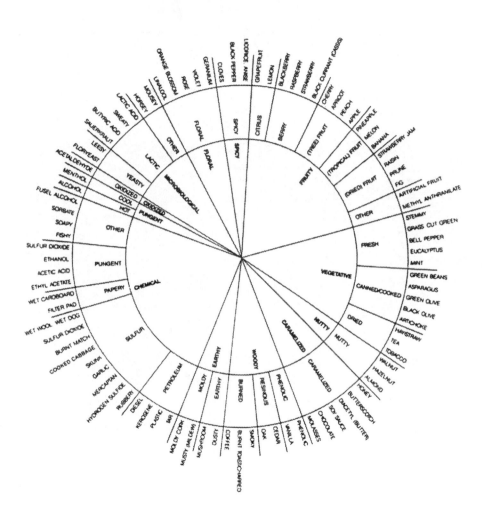

[84] Dr. Ann Noble, Am. Journal of Enology and Viticulture, Vol. 38, No. 2, 1987.

Tilbert Nägler runs his family estate Dr Nägler in Rüdesheim am Rhein in the Rheingau. It is an operation of only a few hectares but provides wines of exceptional value for money. Tilbert is a highly reserved young man who likes to let his wines do the talking. Shaking his hand you understand immediately that he works the vineyards as well and is no stranger to hard work. We have discussed petrol notes on a number of occasions and he feels that these are tertiary aromas that come out with age. He states that some of the 1989, wines he has are now showing these sorts of notes. Drawing him out on this he also feels this is accentuated in years of low acid. I generally push the line of water stress and he counters it with asking why it is generally not seen where vineyards are over cropped and have low water retention in dry years. Good point.

It is very interesting is to take the wines from the Hessische Staatsweingüter Kloster Eberbach. This estate has an excellent array of wines from over diverse terroir in the Rheingau. My discussion with the winemaker some time ago was regarding the high level of petrol notes found in the Berg Schlossberg vineyard in Rüdesheim. He is particularly concerned about this and did not seem to like the aromas. Personally I found them to be most attractive. His response was that the vineyard is prone to water stress and this brings on the "problem" as he described it of petrol notes. Tilbert Nägler from Dr Nägler also has vineyards on this *Erstes Gewächs* site and he also notes the lack of water holding capacity. That factor influenced his decision to use the site for *Klassifizierter Lage* wines rather than push for *Erstes Gewächs* status, as he could always get riper fruit from his Berg Rotland site.

If water stress is the key, then unfortunately we are likely to see less of this intrinsically wonderful characteristic in the Berg Schlossberg wines from Kloster Eberbach due to the fact that from 2002, there is the possibility of irrigating their part of this site. My tastings of the 2002, confirms this. The wine is now far more fruit driven and does not have the force or big structure behind it. The wine is still good, but for me it has changed direction, towards a style that I prefer less. This is a pretty fast and practical indication of water stress helping give rise to the petrol note in the wine.

Stefan Ress of Weingut Balthasar Ress feels that the petrol notes develop over time, in addition he finds that it is an intrinsic and appropriate part of Riesling. I agree.

We see little of petrol notes in New World Rieslings. Is this due to the fact that the majority of their vineyards are irrigated? Tim Adam's Clare Valley Riesling has this classic "wiff of the forecourt" and his feeling is that oxidation provides the source of this character. He feels slow controlled oxidation over time via aging of the wine gives this note. At the same time, his vineyard is not irrigated. Brian Croser, a doyen of the Australian industry and making some of its better Riesling wines at Petaluma Estate, says he does not exactly know where the petrol note comes from. His feeling is that it might be pronounced in very cold years and might have something to do with oxidative handling of the wines.

Science has had a look at this debate briefly via MS-GC (mass spectrometer – gas chromatography). The cause of the petrol note is a compound known as 1,2,6-trimethyl-1,2-dihydronaphthalene, or TDN for short. Generally this is seen at higher levels in aged wines. TDN is released by acid hydrolysis from intermediate, carotenoid derived compounds during wine aging. The precursors for this are found in riper grapes and those that have had greater exposure to sunlight. The scientific analysis also indicates that a decrease in wine pH results in an increase in the rise of TDN. So what does this mean to anyone without a higher degree in organic chemistry or practical experience in manufacturing Class A drugs at home?

We should set out from the start that the levels of TDN are highest in Riesling and thus it can be seen as a peccadillo of the variety much like the methoxypyrazine content of Sauvignon Blanc which leads to a freshly cut grass aroma. A year with full sun exposure and very ripe fruit is likely to give higher potential for this characteristic. In years where the acid is higher, thus giving a lower pH, there will also be a greater development of the precursors for TDN. Now if your vineyard was well exposed to sunlight and had low water holding capacity you would likely find a level of water stress in dry seasons which in turn would increase the potassium levels in the grapes, so lowering pH whilst not assimilating acid. Vineyard yields will also have a major impact on this and we can see that many of the top wines with high levels of petrol notes have come from vineyards with very concentrated yields, whereas the mass commercial highly cropped wines demonstrate little of this. Yields in Australian vineyards will generally be much higher, given the use of irrigation permitting a greater level of crop without too much reduction in fruit flavours.

At the end of the day, TDN is the cause of petrol notes and it is likely accentuated by water stress. Further to this, the conversion pathways would mean that given slow controlled oxidative aging process petrol notes would develop more noticeably. If the TDN levels are not there to start with, then the oxidation/ageing aspect is not going to produce overt petrol notes. We can likely assume that Riesling has a base level of TDN potential, and thus this is why in most Rieslings after lengthy ageing a petrol note will become apparent. This also solves the issue of why wines that have been reductively made, (i.e. not an oxidative handling process) and are still very young also can demonstrate this petrol note.

There is a tendency to see a lot of New World Riesling with very green or even unripe flavours because they are trying to ape German Riesling. At the same time, German producers will need to learn that their wines need a fuller, fatter mouthfeel, more fruit, and balanced acid.

There are plenty of other potential descriptors for Riesling but these are the core flavours and aromas. Learning to use such an aroma wheel and descriptors can make the experience of Riesling greater. The more one knows about characteristics the more one is able to gain an appreciation of a winemaker's style and the type of fruit their different vineyards produce. Providing a wine description is like that of a movie critic, what is right for one is wrong for another. Matching wines to food is the next step, something to which Riesling is ideally and enjoyably suited.

The DWI, have taken their charter of looking after the education and explanation of the German wine situation and produced a comprehensive CD ROM entitled the Deutscher Weinatlas. This gives stunning graphics mapping out the vineyard surface and breaks down all the *Einzellagen*. They deserve to be given credit for putting together something, which in all honesty does give the best possible picture of German wine split into *Anbaugebiet, Bereich, Grosslage*, and *Einzellage*. It had to be done, and with German precision it has been done well by the DWI. The plethora of geographical and quasi-terroir divisions needed to be encapsulated somewhere and this atlas does it very well.

Even the most willing and enthusiastic consumer is only ever going to recall a few names and seek those wines out on a repetitive basis. We come full circle to the argument that by inundating the consumer with over 2,600 *Einzellagen* their use becomes meaningless. Moving towards a reclassification so as that there are only potentially a few hundred *Einzellagen* makes more sense.

From time-to-time I start to wonder if great German wines are a secret that only after some sort of rite of passage do you begin to really discover. France achieves its wine fame from the five percent of great wines it produces, whereas German gains its image from the ninety-five percent of *schrott wein* it exports. This is what leads me to describe great German wine as being, "world famous in Germany". Looking to the French, we can see that the great wines have enhanced the reputation of regions and let average wines bask in their afterglow. In Germany the situation is reversed. The low quality *schrott wein* producers have, with their efforts, dragged down the name of quality estates that used to receive prices akin to those in Bordeaux. Pick up any English or American wine magazine and there will always be articles on Italy, France, and the New World but generally once a year there is a token article on German wines. The argument can be made that this is due to relative market importance or interest but in truth magazine editors believe it is too difficult to explain in a short space.

To fall into the clutches of a German wine enthusiast should be a wine lovers dream. It is an enthusiasm that is hard to contain when guests are stunned by the flavours and quality of German Rieslings. Associates and colleagues of mine are often astounded of how little they know or hear of German wine particularly after they have participated in a tasting.[85] Great German wines are a hand sell product. Producers have to open their wines and present them in order to convince a sceptical wine public before that public will change its preconceptions. This will take a long time and I hope it co-incides with the efforts of the new generation German winemakers who are taking the right decisions to make their wines fashionable again. At present, in order to find such wines it is often necessary to visit the winemaker directly. This means a level of knowledge or recommendations from the *cognoscenti*. When you do visit a quality producer you will discover in a matter of minutes that few sweet wines are on offer and what is tends to be stunning. Visitors asking where they can find the wine distributed in their home region are often informed that the producers sells mainly to private clients, the wines are generally sold out quickly, and the price is laughable by world standards for such quality. Not sweet but cheap, keeps going around in my head.

Great German Riesling, be it "World Famous in Germany" or not, needs explaining. Terroir, vintage variations, styles, excessive use of "vineyard" names, and all that bloody gothic script make things more difficult but not impassable. The key to German Riesling's greatness can

---

[85] An annual gathering of friends in the villa of one of Barbaresco's best estates is more of a competition to see who can bring the most interesting wine with which to stump the others. All wines tasted blind until the tasters drift this way themselves. The group of wine buffs/winemakers bring some hideously expensive wines, (mostly liberated from museum stocks of where they consult). All wines have to be revealed and the prices paid for them as near as can be remembered or reckoned. On one night of the most enjoyable wine was revealed as a Hessische Staatsweinguter 1989 Heppenheimer Centgericht Riesling Auslese bought for the princely sum of €7.40

be found in the terroir and the understanding of the transformation of its fruit into wine by talented winemakers. Nowhere else in the world can produce such complex Riesling. The Australians produce an interesting style and are not short of winemaking smarts but one cannot substitute the natural balance of terroir-produced acidity with bags of tartaric acid. The New Zealander's have a high level of natural acidity, but they have a long way to go in terms of flavours and comparative value for money.

A famous advocate of Riesling, in particular the German version, is Jancis Robinson MW. I was delighted to see an article in the Financial Times where she describes a blind tasting of international Rieslings. This blind tasting reflects the effort made by Stephen Spurrier in his Paris Match to convince the sceptical French about the quality of New World wine that basically started the ball rolling for New World recognition. Robinson MW states, "…a blind tasting of 36 top Rieslings from around the world…was instructive. Although there were only 15 German wines in the line up, five out of six of my favourites were German." (The sixth was a £30 bottle of Austrian Riesling).[86] Where were the New World wines in this line up? The facts are that they did not appear in the top six. In no other blind tasting of world wine styles that I am aware of is there so often a complete shut out of the competition from the New World. This should spur German producers and their representative bodies into action.

Robinson MW also lists five "Rieslings for Chardonnay drinkers". Is this dumbing down the argument, or taking the focus away from Riesling as being Riesling? I do not believe so. Such attention can only be beneficial to Riesling and in particular German Riesling given the fact that all five suggestions were German. To suggest Rieslings for Chardonnay drinkers is an interesting strategy. First, the wines suggested are likely in mid price brackets and in direct competition with equivalent priced Chardonnays. It is important for German producers to bridge these consumers to their product. Half the job is done. If they are buying Chardonnay they are firstly selecting a white wine and secondly, more likely to be drinkers looking for up front fruit characters. There is also a solid swing away from overly oaked Chardonnays which can be witnessed in the glut of this on the US market. Furthermore, there is a swing in consumer tastes towards ABC (Anything But Chardonnay).

Many German Rieslings provide exactly these characters and it is a

---

[86] Jancis Robinson MW, "A smell of success for the noble Riesling", Financial Times, Weekend XV, March 29 2003.

perfect opportunity to provide a Chardonnay alternative and convince consumers by trying for themselves the wonders of German Riesling. Presently the upwards trend in white wines is for Pinot Grigio/Pinot Gris. Dropping the "Pi" from the front of the variety name might make things more technically accurate given the dubious content of some bottles. When well made Pinot Grigio tends to be slightly aromatic, have a good minerally flinty taste, and have a refreshing acidity. The better examples are grown in cool climate winemaking regions. So how far away are we in finding a description of a simplistic Riesling? This trend should demonstrate that German Riesling can be an alternative for people who are comfortable with a certain wine style and permits them to be a little bit more adventurous without the risk of spending money on something they might not like. It is not a strategy for selling the classic complex Riesling but provides a sort of insurance policy to the regular Chardonnay consumer looking for something different. If well teamed with food options, this can be a prime outlet for entry level Riesling. Marketing action is needed.

German producers have to take their inspiration from articles such as Jancis Robinson MW and develop a strategy to present their wines to the public. Without doing so, they will face increased competition from New World Rieslings and run the incredible risk of permitting the Australian industry to kidnap the consumer's concept of what Riesling should taste like. If they are not proactive, the public will start to drink more and more New World Riesling that makes its way onto shelves in the slipstream of the success from other New World wines. If the public starts to take to these wines and associate Riesling with the style they present then the situation will be very bleak for the German producer. The major threat from the New World is an Australian industry dominated by a few major players with a lot of power and the drive to make money. They will be forced by their shareholders to make a success of Riesling. It will not be good enough just to beat them on taste every time. At the same time, New World Riesling appearing on the market will tend to raise the profile of the grape and this looks good for the German producer.

At the moment, an eminent wine writer such as Jancis Robinson MW has no room in her top five wines for anything from the New World. This suggests the wine journalists understand that it is the maximum expression of the style but for how long and will it remain so if German producers do not manage to communicate this fact to the consumer on a more direct basis and soon.

The Rough Guide to Counter Revolution

If there was a New World Wine Revolution then there certainly can be a counter revolution. For any revolution to succeed it needs successful management. In the German terms this revolution management is in the hands of representative bodies such as the Deutsche Wein Institute, Verband Deutscher Prädikatsweingüter, and the producers. I will address in Part 3, the efforts being made by the DWI and the VDP in bringing about a counter-revolution. The Old World can fight back but they have to be proactive rather than continue to watch shelves in wine outlets gradually change to only being stocked with New World offerings. Only part of this fight back is going to take place in former export markets. The other battle will be domestically for German producers to stave off the attacks their domestic market will come under from New World producers.

It is clear that part of the success of Australian wines has been the development of "Brand Australia". This has a lot to do with the work of the Australian Wine Board and with the fact that producers are speaking with one united voice about what they are trying to achieve. This sounds like a contradictory statement but in fact it is what occurs. They found for their industry the right direction in which to head and pursued that aim, in different variations on the theme, but with the same overall goal in sight. This gave them their individuality but a unified core promotional position. This does not yet happen in Germany but maybe it is starting from the initiative of private membership groups such as the VDP. Such groups are always going to be limited by funds as to what they can achieve. It is a pity that the overall industry representative body, the DWI, has not monitored more closely the work of successful bodies such as the Australian Wine Board or even the work of their Austrian "cousins" who have brought much attention to Austrian wines in recent years and greatly redressed the disastrous reputation they had after the glycol scandal.

Producers lump their lot in with the association, rightly believing it is the association's job to promote generically their wines. This is fine if the group has a strategy. A strategy of nothing is working therefore we must do something radical is merely an over-reaction and a sign of not really having looked at the issue from a distance. The end results are confused marketing attempts and not well thought out packaging recommendations, something that will be looked at more closely under consideration of the DWI's efforts with "Classic" and "Selection" in Part Three.

The United Kingdom market, for various reasons, has taken to New World wines. Their is now well entrenched. New World wineries are starting to look at continental Europe as an interesting export target. This is unlikely to affect Spain, France, or Italy as they are very parochial in their wine drinking, in many cases exceedingly provincial. Germany, despite being a major wine producer, is also a major wine importer. A few years ago, for the first time, more foreign wine was consumed in Germany than the domestic stuff. For instance, Australia has undergone a major expansion in its plantings of vines to the point of now being a bigger producer than Germany. It has a relatively small domestic population and thus must focus on export in order to survive. One wonders in the future if the Australian industry will not be attacked in the World Trade Organisation for dumping if some of their selling practices continue.[87] It is likely by now that Australia has more or less reached its peak in the UK industry. The number of places available for their products is at saturation point. Australian producers are looking to take share from other Australian producers now rather than remove Old World wines as they initially did. They have developed very aggressive discounting and marketing techniques, the likes of which are only understood or adopted by a few Old World producers.

The world wine industry is now fully in the grips of globalisation. This is particularly rife in the New World. The rapid expansion in their industry has meant a series of buyouts and consolidations of winery groups. Beer groups sought out and purchased wine companies and have not hesitated in wanting wine to work like their beer marketing. Naturally, such industry players are aggressive in terms of export tactics and generally have access to worldwide distribution networks allowing their investment in brand driven marketing. The rise of brewery investment in the New World wine industry is direct evidence of multinational drinks groups adding a division to their operation and distributing the products accordingly. This becomes a circle which generates itself like in any form of industry globalisation. Big distribution networks require big clients and thus we have seen the rise in importance of supermarket chains selling wines. This factor is probably best represented in the United Kingdom, where supermarkets or what are termed major multiples of around a thousand outlets or more are able to buy wine as they do any FMCG (fast moving consumer good). Their margins and buying price dictate large

---

[87] The cost and selling price for a wine can be worked out. Under international trade laws it is an offence to "dump" products, whereby they are sold well under cost price.

supply volumes in order to mean profitability for a producer. This in turn means a producer needs to reach certain economies of scale, production volumes, and cost savings. Pressures on costs must have a trade off in quality.

An interesting parallel to the history of the German industry development can be seen. Germans developed the first industrial scale wines and rather than merely turn marginal vineyard material into drinkable wine with technology they also drove the price of that wine down and continued to drop their prices in order to generate sales. The New World, Australia in particular, has built its commercial industry success on technologically driven winemaking. We are now seeing a rapid fall in the average price of Australian wines. There are pressures to sell and this can lead to severe discounting. The consolidation of the Australian industry in the hands of a few major producers/exporters only accentuates this fact. Further, they rely on winemaking technology to produce their wines. The German mistakes should be a cautionary tale for Australian producers who rely on adding acid, taking it out, adding tannins, keeping oxygen out, putting it in with micro-ox, adding oak chips, and using reverse osmosis to concentrate the wine. There is the potential for Australian wines to become world famous for providing good value for money commercial wines. Consumers looked at cheap German wines and began to associate the industry with such wines. Many years ago no one would have thought German wine would largely be associated with commercial dross. In the near future, could Australia develop a reputation for making excellent commercial wines but little else? Another parallel from the past is the exposure the commercial/industrial German producers had to the export market. The Australian domestic industry is too small to absorb anywhere near its production. Time will tell. We are already seeing the release of high residual sugar (up to 12 grams) red wines from Australia. Red Kangaroomilch?

In reality, the Australian industry has managed to achieve a reputation for the production of top quality commercial wines and very good mid level offerings. Not so at the elite level. Trying to come up with a list of potential First Growth wines from the New World is exceptionally hard. One might be able to list five from Australia, five from California, and two from New Zealand. There are some producers in Germany with five wines in their portfolio that could rightly be described as First Growth, such as Weingut Dr. Bürklin Wolf. This should set alarms ringing for German producers and representative bodies. If the New World can produce cost effective products then let it do so, but defend the elite nature and aim for quality in the domestic industry placing the publicity emphasis on the First Growth level.

Supermarkets and major multiples will continue to grow in their share of global wine sales. As a simple matter of convenience and consumer buying trends indicate this will be the case. Further, the importance of a brand for the consumer and for the supermarket makes them an ideal partner with the global commercial producer. Consumers have less time for purchase decisions and desire one-stop shopping. Supermarkets love branded products. They come with support in terms of money for listing, promotions, and are advertised without them having to pay a cent. POS, (Point of Sale) materials, promotions, and in-store tastings are all paid for by the wine producers and their representatives. These are simple and very effective ways of generating revenue.

The task of buyers in major chains is to meet sales targets on floor space to profit ratios. It is no good for them to have the most exciting, diverse, or eclectic range. They need what the public will buy. The item that can generate volume sales without either the wine buyer or customer thinking will always get to the shelf first. German wines are hard to explain, especially the elite which require hand-to-mouth selling. Stefan Ress of Weingut Balthasar Ress feels that the greatest opportunity for the elite wines is within the United States restaurant market where the sommelier can talk to the wines.

Many wines of small and mid sized producers, despite their quality, become un-commercial in this sector. Uncommercial is not the same as making wine which is uncompetitive on a world quality scale. At the same time, we can see in general terms the consumer is beginning to tire of taste the same commercial wines. Commercial high volume producers are attempting to address this trend by increased efforts to buy wines made in sufficient volumes but still remaining representative of the region from which they originate. It remains to be seen if the customer will accept this or demand more individual products. It is most likely that there will be a gradual evolution of product rather than a wholesale backlash against this sector. At the same time, such a trend means an opportunity for both the volume German producer and the boutique German winery.

German producers have to ask themselves if they want to be in this market sector. Naturally some will. Some are forced to remain in this sector. We can see in the New Zealand market that many wineries are starting to try to produce greater volumes and try for export market critical mass so satisfying global plans for distribution. There are a number of German producers who can aim for this market sector, unfortunately there are also a number of German producers who hold onto a dream that they will reverse their fortunes by gaining a supermarket contract. As a brief diversion, let us look at the prices producers must sell their product for in order to reach certain price points.[88]

Table 1: Indicative United Kingdom Supermarket Cost Price[89]

Retail Price GBP £	Buy Price (Unnamed High Street Shop) in € ex-cellar.	Buy Price (Unnamed Supermarket) in € ex-cellar.	Average Buy Price of UK Supermarkets in € ex-cellar.
£3.99	0.60	1.65	1.12
£4.99	1.25	2.65	1.95
£5.99	1.95	3.40	2.47

Price points (retail price level) are what drive the United Kingdom industry. If a producer wishes to enter the market they must ensure provision of an ex-cellar price that means once all the transport costs, taxes, agents commission, and the profit requirements of the supermarket are added the product is able to be retailed under say £4, £5, or £6. Logically, the higher the price point the lower the volumes one can expect to sell. By way of explanation in the foregoing table, I have included the buying price of one High Street wineshop chain. Their price demand is always the lowest and their profit requirement always the highest in the UK market. The second column showing the buy price of one particular supermarket is generally the highest buying price in the UK market. This is due to the fact that they offer to their clients an everyday low price and they do not promote wines at lower prices giving the producer a consistent buying price with which to work. The last column shows the average buying price in the UK market.

There are in the UK, a considerable number of taxes imposed and

---

[88] For those not overly familiar with the UK retail wine market, wines are generally saleable as they fit within certain price levels. For instance, there are cut off points at £2.99, £3.49, £3.99, and so on. In buying a wine the decision is often made if the wine tastes suitably to compete within one of these brackets. If it does it will need to meet certain cost levels in order to enter and compete.

[89] These figures are from the author's industry experience.

middleman costs which inflate the price. Tax is the overwhelming inflator of the price ex the producer and distributor margins can often be as low as those of the producer. Supermarkets or major distributors, through their buying muscle, demand anything from a 28 to 40% profit margin. Most products in the UK market will need to be promoted in any number of ways. By this I am not referring to direct publicity, but offering to the supermarket/major multiples a price less that what you see above in order to permit them to offer deals to the consumer such as "3 bottles for 2", "£1 off", or "3 for £10". The supermarkets try to keep their margin but sometimes lower it by 10%. Some years ago it was realistic to expect that some 20% of your product would need to be sold at promotional price; nowadays that number is often around 80%. This means that a producer has to ensure that they are able to make some profit given that the prices listed in the foregoing table are likely the best case scenario and that this will apply to only some 20% of the product they are selling. These prices are for a finished bottled product. The basic costs of materials, (dry goods) such as cork, bottle, and label. A bottle can cost €0.13, bottling costs €0.10, closure €0.13, labels €0.08, carton €0.06, and totally around €0.50

One can see at the lowest priced level there is not much money left over for wine. With this the winery had to pay the grape growing, chemicals, administration, amortisation, winemaking products, winemaking, refrigeration, filtration costs, and so on. We must also understand that as the price of the wine increases there are greater expectations in terms of product presentation meaning higher priced dry goods (better bottle, cork, and label). Producing wine at the lowest price points if fraught with risks for just a few cents profit. Wineries working in these sectors will hope only to supply a volume of their product to the lowest category. Generally, not until the wines are being sold at the retail price of £3.99 to £4.49 that the winery can expect to sensibly make some money. This is partly due to the greed of the UK taxman and the need of supermarkets to allocate floor space to products giving a certain return. If wine cannot do that then the floor space logically has to be given over to other products such as cell phones, meat, or clothing.

UK supermarkets are dealing with producers who need to sell at these price points. With a wine lake behind them and seemingly endless competition from overseas, producers are not in a position to argue. One can also imagine the risks and pressures on maintaining low prices. In such a price sensitive market producers quickly fall off the shelf if they increase price not to mention the risk of being "de-listed" due to the buyer finding something more interesting. The competition is always pushing. With any increase in tax and movement in the price of the Euro against the Pound, producers are generally asked to shoulder the burden. Producers look to the UK market with little real affection other than it is a prestigious high profile market and a way of moving large volumes of wine in a few orders. Other markets provide a better rate of return. This being said, with globalisation, when will other markets tend towards using the UK market buying tactics?

Can Germany really consider competing in the lower price categories given the costs of production and likely returns? New Zealand for instance cannot and has not tried largely to focus in that direction. They have attempted to maintain their image of quality and as a result achieved a higher average price. There are some immediate lessons for the German industry here. From an industry image point of view there is more to be gained in producing better quality wines. If you can make those wines at very good prices then you have the foundation for attracting custom. Germany does this but needs to get the message out.

New Zealand has a limited area climatically available for vineyard planting and a very small domestic market. Given their high industry costs and limited production space, they are not the ideal world supplier in terms of volume business. The interest in their wines is such to bring some of their more commercial offerings into supermarkets/major multiple distribution but largely they must concentrate on specialist retailers and restaurants. Given the prices they can achieve at home by sales to private clients and within their oft seen vineyard restaurants they must reach these prices before considering export. Why would you sell abroad for substantially less than you can receive at home? As a result, the shelf price you will see for New Zealand wines is higher than most other wines from around the world. All well and good for the Kiwis but what are the parallels to the German industry? First, there is a focus on the elite producers. These are the ones written up in the wine magazines so showing the entire industry in a positive light. Second, they have understood that they cannot compete in the volume wine game. Thirdly, they have promoted their "clean green" image to the world. Germany has percentage wise, more biodynamic growers than anywhere else in the world but of this we hear so little. The potential lessons from New Zealand are considered later.

It appears the wine market is starting to polarise. At one pole there are the commercial volume wines and at the other the most elite products. There are everyday drinking wines, easily obtained from a supermarket and the special occasion wines which are generally sourced from specialist negociants. There is also a polarisation in the price of products. Jancis Robinson MW states[90], "The difference in price between the world's most expensive and cheapest wines has widened to such an extent (ironically at a time when the gap in quality is probably narrower than it has ever been) that I shall probably never feel able to buy the seriously sought-after wines again. Farewell First Growths, Grand Crus, Penfolds Grange, and top Italians." No mention of top German wines here, despite the regard with which Robinson MW holds them. Is this simply due to the fact that the best of Germany's wines from the small private estates provide the world's best value for money wines?

It is important to look at the current market trends and how, if German producers look closely enough, they will see how many of these trends are actually reflecting assets their industry already possesses. When the so-called varietal revolution hit they already were the specialist in this type of nonclamenture for wine but they did not capitalise upon it. If they harness their assets they will be in a prime position to force either a counter-revolution or at worst an increased level of success for their industry. There are some wonderful opportunities if things are well managed. We can see most of the current trends in the wine industry have to do with the New World starting to mimic aspects of the Old World and herein lies the key to why there is a potential counter revolution. New World producers are not mimicking aspects of the industry that they do not think are providing wine quality, complexity, or marketability.

New World producers have managed, for some reason to escape the attention of the wine public and journalists for their lack of focus on terroir. This certainly has to do with the historical development of the industry and the lack of geographical familiarity most wine consumers have with the New World. It is all out there somewhere far away. The concentration journalists seem to place on the production styles from various Old World regions is very rarely replicated in a consideration of the New World. Is this because journalists feel the consumer does not care, so re-enforcing the idea that terroir is a misplaced concept in modern day wine buying? Is it due to the fact that journalists have understood that regional differences are meaningless in industrial scale New World wines given the fact that most wines are a blend of various regions? You are far more likely to read wine tasting notes that state, "typical Australian Shiraz" but what can be more unspecific given the

---

[90] Jancis Robinson MW (1997), <u>Confessions of a Wine Lover</u> (Penguin).

growing regions for Shiraz probably are as widespread as from Spain to Southern Italy? It is akin to stating, "typical European Cabernet" which we know varies greatly. For whatever reason, New World producers have been let off lightly and this has suited the generalism of current consumer buying patterns and the importance of brand development.

New World producers are realising the fact that many of their offerings, particularly in the commercial sector, are falling into the category of taste the same wines. As a result, there is a major push towards appellations of origin in the New World. We can see the New World is now trying to distinguish its wines. There is a well developed movement to create appellations. This is an interesting change from the assertions in the past that terroir did not exist except as marketing fantasy. Regions such as Coonawarra, Margaret River, and the Hunter Valley are trying to define boundary limitations and so distinguish their wines from the others.[91] There is a purely commercial reason for doing this just as there are many producers in those regions who understand fully well that the wines they produce from different soils and microclimates result in different wines. They wish to differentiate their wines from others and this is particularly due to the fact that there has been a heavy reliance on the use of varietal marketing. This being the case, people drink Chardonnay or Shiraz and each wine region is trying to demonstrate that they should be buying from McClaren Vale, Hunter, and the like. Of crucial importance is that this immediately defines terroir. If people are saying, I would rather try a Mornington Peninsular Pinot Noir than one from Central Otago it is because they are finding something as a common theme with Mornington Peninsular wines that they enjoy.

Terroir is perhaps also a hard concept for Australians in many ways. This is due to the fact that the climate is not a marginal one for grape growing. Considerable amounts of sunshine and you just turn on the irrigation tap to ensure that the grapes reach their optimal point for harvest at rather high crop levels. This is an obvious over simplification but the kinks in the Australian season are far easier to iron out. There are less vintage-to-vintage variations. Given also that vineyards are much larger they tend to flatten out the differences. It is hard to find in a single 10 hectare plus vineyard subtle differences and unlikely that separate fermentations will result. Terroir is something that is going to take a long

---

[91] Note as an aside that an appellation can also turn sour. It is only as good as its members and what they want to do. A poorly run appellation can quickly position itself as being a region of low quality wines. Think of the reputation Frascati has.

time to demonstrate itself fully in Australia.[92]

The test for the development of appellations in the New World will come with how well they are enforced and followed. Australians pride themselves on the ability to produce wines to the same standard without vintage variations. Their Valhalla is the production of a wine with the consistency of Coca Cola marketed under a brand name around the world. What will happen in bad years? The present practice of trucking in fruit from regions not suffering from a bad season will not be possible under an appellation system. Commercial producers, more often than not run by accountants, are not interested in hearing a winemaker talk about a bad vintage. It is not something easily communicated to a client on the other side of the world and if such wines are released there are plenty of products willing to substitute. The customer is not going to stick with you through a patch of bad seasons. They are looking for consistent quality. This does not run with globalisation of a brand. No winemaking company wants to release a product less than what it can produce in a good season. Appellations are meant to mean that the fruit from that region is the one that ends up in the bottle. Breaches of the denomination will make an appellation worthless overnight with a corresponding perception in the market.

New World winemakers are starting to look at production methods in the Old World in a new light.[93] This is in the top wine categories rather than the commercial sector where New World winemaking methods, with some modifications, are here to stay. New World winemakers are looking more closely at the concept of complexity. It is a natural progression.

---

[92] Further we can see that the concept of terroir is better understood in both Tasmania and New Zealand. These regions are merely a drop in the Australasian wine bucket but at the same time have a higher proportion of vineyard owners who are less likely to be sheep farmers converted to grape growing but more likely wine enthusiasts who look to European wine styles for their inspiration. It is easier to see in a small area such as New Zealand and Tasmania dramatic climatic differences between vineyards in what are marginal climates for grape growing and how the orientation, drainage, and slope of hills affect the crop. At these Southern outposts of winemaking there exists a far greater respect for terroir and it is well understood as a concept.

[93] As an aside, Australia's greatest wine, Grange resulted due to the perseverance and European study tour carried out by Max Schubert in the 1950s. In order to gain more complexity New World winemakers use their overseas vintages as a means of gaining experience in winemaking and more complex styles of wines. Happy to make the commercial wines whilst travelling many discover the styles of wines, like Schubert, that they would like to return and make in their home countries under their own labels. Such wines, like Grange, are achievable given the right winemaking and the finding of the correct terroir.

When the New World industry "grows up" and stops trying to gain attention like a teenager clamouring for compliments with their overtly fruit driven wines they will start to produce interesting wines. Certainly this is taking place as there are a number of boutique producers who understood the need for greater complexity.[94] They have always been seen as somewhat eccentric and serving a niche market in their home nations.

In Europe, there is a far greater understanding of the essence of not meddling in the winery; of not correcting the must too much and letting the vineyard make the wines.[95] It is becoming a tired cliché now but one can see during a visit to a vineyard if this is the case or not. Crop yields are the key. New World wineries are far more likely to manage vineyards based on the yields they feel they can achieve without a detrimental affect on fruit quality for the price of resultant wine. Vineyard irrigation is particularly controlled and as a result more consistency across vintages is achieved. In the winery there is a move to handling ferments in a more "traditional way". Open topped fermenters, warmer ferments, and spontaneous fermentations are starting to gain currency. Old World producers have probably tended to rely on tradition for traditions sake. Traditional methods, such as large oak casks rather than the rush to barriques are an important step in producing wines that are not overly oak driven.[96] The better winemakers will look to what tradition and technology in combination can provide for them in terms of wine improvement. There are more "fusion" wines being developed. That is, adopting the good things from both the Old and New World in ones wines; giving both fruit and complexity.[97]

Wine drinking habits are changing. There is a continued noticeable move from beer to wine, a product associated with a greater level of sophistication. The breweries have attempted to redress this balance by releasing more "sophisticated" premium beers and with some success. Drinkers making the move from beer to wine are likely to start with less complex and more fruit driven wines. In addition, there is a new

---

[94] As in Europe, it is not a given that merely due to being small better wines will result. There are a lot of really bad wines made out there by small producers as well.

[95] This concept can also be abused as an excuse for laziness, poor hygiene, and unprofessional winemaking. I refer here to producers with a correct concept of minimal intervention and excellent quality fruit.

[96] In my opinion, the use of new barriques is inappropriate for the Riesling variety.

[97] On a personal note, many people cannot understand that as an Australian you do not make wines that taste like Australian fruit bombs. For me, there is a great importance to understand the history of the estate, the region, and form an opinion as to the style of wine which is suited to that site.

generation of wine drinkers without any preconceptions about German wine. In the past German wines were generally seen as poorly packaged and could not compete in the new "branded" market. The New World had also employed someone other than the kids to design their label.

One should never judge a book by its cover but the fact of the matter is that people do. Poor packaging was often backed up with overly sweet poor product. We can be realistic and understand that the over use of heavy gothic script did not help especially when there were more light hearted offerings from other nations on the shelves. The products looked old fashioned and were. A traditional look has its place, as I will discuss later. Increasingly, in a conspicuous brand world one is defined by the products they associate themselves with. Turning up to a party with a bottle of Blue Nun is not a way to pick up chicks; not at least the ones you want.

The domestic German market is presently highly focused towards red wines. Given a history of red wine production of light colour a dark red is seen as one indication of quality. To this end, there have been many plantings of varieties such as Dornfelder in order to obtain good colour. Dornfelder translates as the "smell of wet cardboard". It would be very short sighted to remove good Riesling vineyards in order to meet this present demand for reds. If on the other hand it is removing poor quality vineyards that were normally providing wines to the sweat and cheap sector then perhaps it is not such a bad thing. It would mean less volume and better quality of material available for good Rieslings, tending to avoid the gloss being taken off the variety with poor examples. Certainly drinkable reds are being produced by German wineries but generally at silly prices. With the European Union expanding to the east and the increasing globalisation of wine distribution it will be very hard for German producers to compete in the red wine sector anywhere other than by selling to their increasingly disloyal domestic market.

Increasingly the next generation of wine drinkers are starting with products called alcopops. These things, which are enough to make a brown dog ill, are often loaded with sugar. Notice that they do not mention they are sweet and no one is the wiser. They are merely a variation on the theme. There is a great potential for wines that are clean, fruity, and with a slight hint of residual sweetness to meet the demands of such markets. A successful image change in many of the old German standards of Black Tower and Blue Nun may prove that there is life in these old brands yet. Effectively they were really the first attempts at branding wine. Why are they products causing a cringe factor with older generations of drinkers? Is this some form of guilt by association…not being able to recall what one did when under the influence of the Black Tower or some unspeakable abuse of the Blue Nun? Brands such as these are key in some market sectors by attracting the young consumer to try German wines. There is nothing wrong with them. They are honest products and the approach of wineries nowadays means that good winemaking skill is often used in their production rather than it being blended from what remains. In fact, by making an entry level wine one is able to entice consumers to trade up and investigate wines of greater complexity once they have isolated components they enjoy.

Other attempts at this sort of thing are Bend in the River, Devils Rock, and wait for it…Reh-Kendermann are putting out a "Terroir Series" of "Super Premium Rieslings". Fire Mountain is another offering along these lines. The name is likely a direct translation of *Feurberg*. This is a *Grosslage* near Bad Dürkheim and can be seen as one drives past the rubbish dump on the way into town. Many of the *Weissherbst* (blush style) wines from this site over the last years have had a distinct note of burnt plastic bag. Not Fire Mountain; it certainly does not come from *Feurberg*, but is a blend of wines from the Pfalz. With wines from other lands such as Italy, packaging efforts such as these strangely do not impact on the overall impression of Italian wines. The state of the German industry image is so fragile that the same might not be the case.

Very few of us are drinking what we were fifteen years ago. Part of the game is also making the wines trendy for a new age group of drinkers. These wines sit in their price range and this is the way to start. They will then tend to move up. At the entry level we have to be careful to make the packaging uncomplicated. This does not mean vomit coloured labels but needs careful consideration of what attracts that market sector consumer. Unfortunately, often in Germany poor labels result due to lack of correct market research. Much can be learnt from the Italians here, who have made new drinkers move to their products successfully. University towns in Italy have a high level of new styled wine bars. Key is that the target customer lacks a high level of disposable income, has little expertise, and does not have a high tolerance for embarrassment in selecting the wrong wine. They want some level of tradition, sophistication, and an image that is not projected with overly gimmicky labels.

Packaging must be clean, easily understood, and provide some credibility. This group, strangely in some ways, tends to move towards modernised "traditionally" packaged products. Successful producers have revamped their image without abandoning the traditional look. Some German wineries have started to do this. Wineries such as Reichsrat von Buhl, Bassermann-Jordan, Bürklin Wolf, and Langwerth von Simmern are cases in point, of a modernised traditional look. Other producers whom have attempted to mimic the highly coloured animal themed Australian labels are trying too hard and in the wrong direction. It is a bit like dad trying to be cool at an 18 year old daughter's birthday party by disco dancing.

Customers start to worry when they see "old" wines on the shelf. This is due to the fact that New World wines at the commercial levels are designed for early drinking and the fact that their wines have six months on them before the same European vintage is underway. As a result, a 2003 white from Australia tastes fresh and ready to drink at Christmas 2003, whereas an Old World wine has just finished ferment. The implications of this are obvious. The solution is found in competing in this sector as best as possible with one's own new releases and trying to educate customers in the mid to upper brackets that better Rieslings require time in bottle before release. This can only be done by the industry setting compulsory release dates. Italian and French appellations do exactly this. At the time of writing you will find 2000 Barolos on the market and the wine buying public has been made aware through lengthy efforts in education that this *is* the current release. Ok, it is easier with reds but the same should be done for great Riesling.

The rise of quality food movements is a wonderful trend. This is seen in the plethora of fusion restaurants and quality small eateries emerging around the world. The most notable of such movements commenced in Italy under the name of Slow Food. It had its origins in fighting the opening of yet another branch of the "Scottish" Restaurant in one of Rome's most beautiful areas, the Piazza di Spagna. From these beginnings at the end of the 80's a complete rejuvenation of what is artisan or quality hand made foods took place. This has now become a worldwide movement and the same people who are looking to get away from a life of pre-packaged foods are the same that embrace the differences that can be found in terroir specific wines. German elite producers need to be closely associated with such groups. There is a Slow Food movement in Germany, with groups in most major centres. They are surprised at how little contact they have with local producers.

German wines should be ideally placed to take advantage of this trend. They are ideal with food. The problem is that traditional German cuisine has as bad a reputation around the world much akin to that of English food. Bratwurst in a bread roll is not something that is going to set the world alight despite how great it tastes at the rugby. Understandably, great sausages are washed down with lashings of great beer as anyone who has had a *weisswurst* and *hefeweiser* beer for breakfast on a Sunday morning will attest. With a natural acidity, Riesling is a perfect partner for foods. Key outlets for Riesling, and especially the great ones, should be top restaurants. Further, the foods that go well with Riesling are those I would term PacRim (Pacific Rim). These are fusion foods found in West Coast USA and East Coast Australia. Asian and PacRim foods need wines which are refreshingly crisp, dry, and fruity. This seems to fit the Riesling bill perfectly. Seafood matches are also the way to go. "Food Friendly" wines are a market sector which should be targeted by Riesling producers. The New World already are doing so with their Rieslings. Marketing needs to be geared towards this.

The Asiatic kitchen is influencing all western kitchens. This has become the modish way to eat. We have seen the restaurant scene transform, including Germany. The English contribution to food can traditionally be seen as roast beef, soggy chips, mushy peas, and battered fish. Germany with her *sauerkraut* and *bratwurst* hardly looks like much of a traditional rival in terms of their fare. There has been a vibrant gourmet revolution around the globe with fusion influences from the Mediterranean and Asia. The Asiatic influence means that Germany with her Rieslings should be in ideal place to enter the restaurant sector. It is a very hard market with delivery, late payment, non-payment, and the like but at the same time the exposure one gains is priceless end customer advertising. In addition, few restaurants wish to offer wines on their lists that are available to the public in wine stores or supermarkets, lest mark ups become too transparent. German wines have little worry in this regard, especially their better estate offerings. They are unlikely to be found in stores. At the same time the public needs to be made aware of why they should select such wines from the list. Asiatic foods require wines that are dry, crisp, fruity, and luscious. All these things can and do describe Riesling. German Riesling is unique in that it can navigate through an entire menu.

As wine lovers we have no doubt heard of the "Three B's" in the Pfalz. This refers to Bürklin Wolf, Bassermann Jordan, and von Buhl. As far as the world of cuisine sees it the "Three B's" for Germany are *Bratwurst, Brot,* and *Bier.* German wineries will not start a counter-revolution by trying to convince the world that their kitchen is anything other than best enjoyed in Lederhosen. There are enough problems trying to convince the public regarding the wines. German wineries if they wish to embrace the food scene as a means of demonstrating the value of their wines will have to adopt the fusion scene food and find opportunities to demonstrate the perfect match they can present. This is an expensive exercise and requires considerable effort. Unfortunately, the DWI is not geared to understanding this as a concept and like most things in the German industry any advances in this direction will have to come from those producers who are up with the play.

Initiatives in this direction have been shown. To cite an example, Wein Gourmet / Der Feinschmecker magazine as well as the Jeunes Restaureateurs d'Europe have linked together in order to present *avant-garde* German chefs with correspondingly excellent German wines. It is a private initiative, as are most things of any intelligence in German wine marketing. All the same the DWI could understand the success of it by having visited the temporary restaurant they built at VinItaly, the heart of the Italian wine scene, in 2003 and try to build a similar operation. Five different menus were offered and 15 to 16 wineries present around 4 wines, which sommeliers then recommend in relation to the course you have chosen. It is an ideal way to demonstrate the food and wine match.

With all these factors, wherein lies the chance to produce a counter-revolution? Like any situation, if you only concentrate on the fact that something is wrong you are not working on developing a solution. There has been a rush in Germany to rightly decide that something is wrong and the only way to solve it is to mimic those things in the New World which have been demonstrably successful. This is out of date and fire fighting management. It gives no credence to the assets the German wine industry possesses. The key is to study the direction the New World winemakers are moving and get there before them or at least be ready to counter in force with publicity demonstrating those aspects that already exist in the German wine industry. It is no good working oneself up to making a lot of changes when you are targeting what went on or what was trendy years ago. The challenge is to predict where all the changes and demographic demand shifts are moving and develop a strategy for this.

To give a direct example, I had drawn to my attention a cheap UK weekly glossy *Hausfrau* magazine with all the usual food news parked in the back. There is a wine recommendation and it goes something like this, "a screw cap superstar from Down Under, this scrumptious Aussie Riesling is chock-full of lime cordial flavour with tinges of grapefruit round the edges. It's the absolute business with a summery salad or barbecued seafood, and I'd even be tempted to serve it up with spicy Thai stir-fries. The screw cap, of course, means that this is the ultimate picnic wine, as you don't even have to remember to take a corkscrew with you."[98] One has to imagine that this very fluffy wine review is pitched appropriately at the reader but it does set out a few interesting points. The first are the food matches cited and second the use of screw cap closure.

Removing the words Down Under, one could well imagine that it is a description for a Riesling from the Pfalz. Why isn't a German wine under review there? What is completely ironic is the fact that the packaging of the product goes against all the present offerings of the German marketing gurus. It is released in a screw cap bottle of dark brown colour in the old hock bottle format. Here is a direct case of the New World winery giving tradition credence to their version of Riesling whilst German wineries are falling over themselves not to use either screw caps or the brown hock bottle! The wine is being sold at £6.99, so we are talking ex cellar prices that are certainly within reach of German wineries and well above the average mass export price of German wines which hovers around €0.90 per litre. I know the wine recommended, Leasingham Bin 7, and it no where near compares in quality to say a Kurt Darting wine from the Pfalz which would retail for less than £5.99. German wineries dream of getting a listing at the £6.99 price point.

The good news is there are a number of trends developing in the UK market. The first is the demand for exclusivity. There is a demand to find wines that are not available on a mass distribution basis. Naturally, this is not at the entry level and there is a very nice trend towards people wanting to be supplied by wine brokers who can deliver to them the same sort of wines they would find by going to the cellar door when travelling. German wine producers should be quick to spot this trend as a great potential market for themselves. It is really not a major mental leap. German wineries have well understood cellar door sales and the "*weinprobe*" deal better than any other nation in the world. It is a perfectly normal thing in Germany to travel to the *Weinstrasse* and taste wine. These things have been copied in the New World and even in Italy. The stuffy wood panelled Tyrol mountain hut looking *probezimmer* is so out of date for the new generation of wine buyer. To see the combination of modern and tradition one only needs to call in at Weingut Dönnhoff in the Nahe. It is little wonder that their estate attracts both foreign and younger

---

[98] I am unable to track down which magazine this came from, likely due to the fact that I tore the page out of the magazine, but the words are accredited to their wine "expert" Natasha Hughes.

German visitors.

German wineries are very much geared for selling to private clients and many in fact exist from this very front door trade. It is not unusual to see a German winery sell between 30 and 90 per cent of its wines in this manner. A figure of 25 to 30 per cent in the New World would be greeted with the popping of Champagne corks and bonuses all round. German wineries make good use of their client database and with some lateral thinking it is not hard for them to reach this to clients in the UK, even if they have to go via a middleman. Further, all German wine estates will have someone who speaks English working there and the fact that the cheap airfares revolution become a normal part of life means that for less than a tank of fuel one can be immersed in the heart of some of the most hospitable and enjoyable wine regions in the world without any great culture shock. More promotion in this regard is needed. Get people to the region and they return knowing more about the wine and searching for it at home. Certainly Germany has a short tourism season, but the weekend break market is an expanding sector. Hotel packages with gourmet dinners and wine tastings are not that hard to develop.

It is essential to focus on the elite producers. With some 10,000 winegrowers it is impossible to draw attention to the industry by lumping for some sort of middle ground. People might drink an everyday Bordeaux or Chianti but the French and Italian industry push forward the names of their great Chateau and Super Tuscans respectively. The public relations push needs to be made on the group of great producers in Germany. There seems to have been a fear in Germany of creating some sort of elite. Winemaking is by its very nature an elitist game. The history of wine is predicated on the fact that it was the drink of the elite, drunk at royal courts whereas beer and gin were the drinks of the Northern European less well to do. Even in cultures where wine is the national drink there were and remain different levels of quality available to those who can afford it and the rough peasant red shared with a hunk of cheese.

It is hard to understand why this fear of elitism seemed to exist in the wine industry and was not present, for example, in the automobile industry where German cars have for many years been seen as luxury models. Whatever the reasons, it is high time that they stopped having fear of putting their hands up and saying, "these are my wines and they rank among the best in the world". Creating cult wines or an elite only serves to focus on what the industry can achieve and sets the image for the industry as a whole. In addition, very few wineries in Germany have understood the marketing points or selling differences that can be achieved by making noise about either the particular vineyards or the winemaker, who in New World countries is generally part of the marketing.

Further, what is needed is a better understanding of what the consumer wants. There is an elite sector, middle, and entry like in any industry. There is nothing wrong with the entry sector wines looking closely to the packaging and styles presented by commercial New World wineries which have proven that they understand eminently well this market sector. The elite sector is the main chance to set the industry standard for what is uncompromising top quality Riesling. This is what all in terms of Riesling should be compared with. Look to Burgundy and Champagne. Many excellent Pinot Noir and sparkling wines are produced around the world but these regions retain their image as the benchmark of the style due to the fact that a few great wines are their flagships. Champagne and Burgundy will retain their level as flagships given the image development that has gone in on their behalf despite great wines being produced elsewhere around the world and in some cases surpassing them in quality. This is where the German elite producers have a great opportunity in order to reinforce to the wine drinking public that great Riesling comes from Germany and nowhere else.

Large producers need to look to fighting the New World, whereas the small need to understand the role of tradition, terroir, and uncompromisable quality. If German winemakers wish to tap export markets more successfully they need to become outward looking. One can see that they are starting to understand the need to modify their styles for market demands. This means producing entry level wines in a manner that they would currently describe as New World. Using a reductive style avoiding oxygen pick up retaining fruit flavours are ideal for commercial wines. When one visits many German producers they will often show you wines that they describe correctly as being New World in style, even if they do not personally like that direction. It shows that this style of wine can be replicated and often has more complexity given that it comes from older vines and true Riesling terroir. Here is a chance to provide effectively commercial style wines made in a reductive style but that have a greater level of complexity than found in wines pitched at the same audience from the New World. In effect, raising the bar over which other wines have then to jump. Use the Riesling trump card.

The mid sized German producer must attack the New World and say, okay nice stuff and well done, good rounded fresh fruit, but wines that have tartaric acid thrown in, chips thrown in, concentrate, and the like are never going to yield the balance and desirability of proper estate wines. It may be that many consumers are plumping for the industrial stuff from the New World at the moment but there is going to be a big New World wine lake and it is all very similar. It has taught the consumer fruit and consistency. These people are now looking for something better and the trend will be to trade up to more complex wines.

The average willing to spend, as I will call it, is increasing. The value in German exports has climbed some six per cent in the last year. This means that there is growth for demand in the middle sector price bracket. The consumer here is looking for something more than just the basic commercial wines. Something a little more special and interesting where there is room to have an interest in the story behind the wine. There is serious potential here for German wineries and I sincerely hope producers are pushing their representative bodies to develop marketing and sales promotion plans which are proactive. Past efforts were very much a fire fighting style of management or more correctly merely letting the opportunity burn.

German wineries are often family run. This means that there is someone behind the label and the more exclusive products at a good price the more likely that professional people and wine enthusiasts will want such products. The foundations for this exist. The communication of the story and distribution of the wine is the difficult part. Good producers have enough on their hands with day-to-day running of the business and cannot be expected either to afford the specialist for each market or be able to do it themselves. This should be the focus of industry promotion by a representative body, not trying to convince journalists that the old sweat and cheap wines are now not so nasty. Better to say, those wines have improved but now let us look at what is really happening in the sector of the industry that employs the most people. It is a direct push against globalisation and the representative bodies must understand the majority of their members do not have the size to take on the global wine businesses. They are better to prepare a plan of attack which permits them to demonstrate an alternative to this feature of world wine marketing.

In the final analysis, the counter-revolution must be a grass roots one. It must be led by quality producers understanding the changes they must make and be willing to implement those strategies. In addition, such producers will need to push their representative bodies in the direction they see as delivering this change. A representative body is, at the end of the day, only as good as the group of people it represents and the tendency in the past has been for elite producers to remain silent and not gain the representation from the DWI that they deserve. If they come to the conclusion that the DWI is unable to work in their interests then they have to accept that this body is nothing more than a representative of the big bottlers and a statistical collecting service. If so it means they will have to pay extra to be a member of a private representative body that looks after their future rather than dwells in the past.

In the foregoing I have used many examples with reference to the UK wine market. This is due to familiarity and due to the fact that the UK market has historically been the most professional and diverse wine buying market in the world. Through long tradition the UK market is the one which sets the pace in terms of wine buying trends. Post war, the UK market took to the sweet and cheap wines. One might find this strange, given the recent hostilities, but a key factor in the rapid acceptability of German wines was the fact that they were handled by agencies with names such as Hallgarten, Sichel, and Loeb. The founders of such firms had been Jewish émigrés from Nazi Germany.

At present, the US market is leading the way in understanding the outstanding value of German wines. The English should be rightly miffed that Americans are getting first grab at the best Germany has to offer. The exports to America have risen some 20% in value recently, it remains to be seen what effect is caused by the present tendency for the Euro to remain strong against the US dollar. This latter point demonstrates the fact that markets are now global and subject to far more influences than merely wine quality or image.

At present over 99% of German wines sold in the UK are retailed at under £5. The good news is that the average price is increasing but the bulk of German wine (some 62% of sales) remain in the under £3 bracket. We have seen what this means in terms of the price for the producer not to mention that this firmly sets the image of German wine. The UK market is in a rut of chasing rather than leading, looking for commercial wines and continual variations on a theme such as the Pinot Grigio trend.. Varietal labelling remains important in such markets as it gives an immediate style classification for consumers. As stated in the foregoing it is highly important that German producers let it be known that the style of Riesling to set all benchmarks should be theirs and not allow it to be kidnapped by the Australian industry.

At the same time, the domestic German market is changing. The most encouraging trend in the German market and the key to the counter-revolution is the new generation of winemakers. They have seen the hard work of their parents but have the confidence of youth on their side, having accepted the situation the market finds itself in and looking forward for a solution. Largely they will find the solution through better winemaking, lower yields in the vineyard, and concentrating on understanding the appropriate market sector. These young winemakers have gone out to the New World and seen what is being done, returning home impressed with some things but also understanding that given the right management they know they have the foundations to make more interesting wines and the tradition behind the family estate which can be turned into a marketing positive.[99]

---

[99] Some few years ago it was a laugh to think that a European winemaker would send curriculum *vitae* out looking to do a vintage in the New World. Nowadays firms are flooded with applications from Old World kids trying to get some experience Downunder. Australians generally like to think that this is someone coming out to see how things are really done, but in reality it is more of a reversal of the sort of sabbatical the great early post war winemakers from Australia undertook. They came to see how things were being done out of interest. They did not then go home and say everything is wrong, but they took things they had seen and harnessed them to the industry requirements in Australia. The same is happening now in Germany. The young winzer goes off to make an experience and comes home with plenty seen and done. I would hazard a guess that the feeling on the plane on the way back home is one of seeing fantastic opportunities for their own home estate.

Part Three

Steps to Renaissance

Is the Deutsche Wein Institute Fiddling While Riesling Burns?

I do not want to be seen as too critical of the Deutsche Wein Institute (DWI). They have their responsibility and do exactly what their charter describes. I am sure that it is a tough and thankless task in many ways. Their approach, in my assumption, has been that the laws are the laws and in a very Teutonic way their role is to educate people as to the laws no matter the flaws. I may be completely wrong and they may well think the laws are completely brilliant but my attempts to gain such information from them were met with sending me just another set of the annual statistics. Given the fact that they have worked very hard to produce two new categories of wine, namely "Classic" and "Selection" one must imagine that they also understood that the rot had set in and German wines were becoming harder to sell than pork chops outside a synagogue.

German wines are not solely represented by the DWI. There are a number of producer associations, marketing groups, regional forums, and the like. Chief among these groups is the Verband Deutscher Prädikats und Qualitätsweingüter (VDP) which is a private confederation of leading wine estates who work together on marketing and representation. Both groups have had a long process of inward inspection, talk, and debate on the issues facing German wines and despite my analogy of fiddling while Rome burnt; it is true that it was also not built in a day. Both bodies require time to try their respective approaches to reverse the situation. Far be it from me to criticise anyone who is having a go at trying to fix the situation, any attempts are better than none.

Both groups have come to the same conclusion; simply if it was difficult for producers to understand then it was certainly a minefield for consumers. It began to sink in that one of the reasons that German wines might have lost their edge and certainly market share was in some part due to this complex, confusing, fuddle that exists.

In 2000, the DWI launched their new wonder weapon to take on the world, "Classic" and "Selection". It was built from the ground up. That is, it worked on providing so called simple categories or classifications for entry to mid level quality wines. The concept eminently suited the mandate and purpose of the DWI.

If you have had a few German wines in your time, how would you go about defining the terms "Classic" and "Selection"? My first reaction would be to think that each variety has its own classic style and each region has its own classic expression of that variety. We are not going to see something that is generic to German wine. Classic Rheingau Riesling is going to have a slight petrol aroma and crisp acid structure. Classic Pfalz Riesling is going, in my opinion, to have more fruit notes whilst still being crisp. It would be fair to assume that a group of experts could come up with a general description of what they found to be "Classic" in each region regarding different varieties. The general consumer, on the other hand, might very well have a different idea about what they think is "Classic". When I have asked general wine drinkers not particularly familiar with German wine what they think by the term their opinions range from "old fashioned" to "traditional". This is probably not what the DWI or wineries really have in mind or what they would like to communicate. Rather they wish to communicate the applicability of this category or style to the modern day consumer. One would expect that the DWI undertook a wee bit of market research in their main markets prior to selecting the terms but if they did they are being very tight lipped about it.

"Selection", well sounds more like some sort of winemaker choice to me. Something the cellar selects from various sites in order to compose a cuvee. If I had been asked as a consultant winemaker to come and make a "Selection" wine, I would have expected to be given free hand in the cellar to put together a blend that reflected my interpretation of the variety, terroir, and winery style. This is much like a house cuvee in Champagne. One of the big criticisms of German wines from outside winemakers is the obsession on keeping each separate vineyard's production separate all the way to the bottle. From a winemaking point of view, it is merely a liquids control exercise to demonstrate all the grapes from a certain patch of paddock end up in a bottle as a wine. It well may be that a particular site gives a certain style of wine and there is a market for that style. At the end of the day this is the essence of the terroir concept. At the same time, one element to the art of winemaking is the use of one's skill in blending to create a wine that is better than the individual parts. For non-winemakers it is probably hard to understand that a few percent of one wine can radically alter the aromas and flavours of a blend.

The use of the term "Selection" conjures up ideas of wines that are designed to maximise their flavour expression through a cuvee. Each estate or even winemaker will have their own "signature" selection. There is nothing wrong with such a thing in fact it is one of the wonderful things about wine. As long as there would be no attempt to say all Selection wines are of a similar style then there is nothing wrong with drawing up a term which sets certain quality parameters and leaves it to the estate to show what their selection within those parameters. It would be a benefit to many German estates to be able to get away from the rigidity of the current laws and just concentrate on making cuvees without having the market penalty of effectively making *Tafelwein*.

But, as can be imagined, what one would think from the use of the terms "Classic" and "Selection" are far from what the rules describe. The basic definition of "Classic" is that it is a dry-style classic from a particular region. "Selection" is a dry style from a select or declared site.[100] Hmm, there is enough room to turn a London bus around in these definitions. In order to try to tighten them up, a more expansive explanation is contained in the following table.

Table 3: Summary of DWI Classic and Selection Rules

	CLASSIC	SELECTION
Regional Origin	• One region which must be specified. • Individual wineries permitted to use a district name but no other appellations such as village or vineyard name can be used	• Wine from an individual vineyard site in a specified region.
Permitted Varieties	• Traditional varieties as so set by the region, to be used with the word Classic. • A blend of two or more varieties is not permitted, except where this is a traditional wine style.	• Traditional varieties as so set by the region, to be used with the word Selection. • A blend of two or more varieties is not permitted.
Min. Potential Alcohol	• Min alcohol of 12%, except in	• Minimum harvest level of

---

[100] There is winemaking dry, tasting dry, and legal dry. They do not necessarily mean the same thing.

	Mosel-Saar-Ruwer with 11.5%	90 degrees Oechsle or to Auslese level of ripeness.
Vineyard Restrictions		• Maximum Yield of 60hl/ha with only hand harvesting permitted.
Wine Style	• Described as "harmoniously dry" which translates as a maximum residual sugar level equal to 2 times the acidity level with the cut off level at 15g/L.	• Wines must conform to trocken style of under 9 g/L residual sugar except for Riesling where the sugar is permitted to be 1.5 times the acid level to a maximum of 12g/L.
Quality Controls	• For estate bottled wines (Guts or Erzeugerabfüllungen the term is permitted without further restrictions. • If the grower and bottler are not one and the same, then the parties must register with the authorities their contract to produce a Classic wine and the amount of grapes, must, or wine that will be received.	• For estate bottled wines the term is permitted without further restrictions. • If the grower and bottler are not one and the same, then they must register as for a Classic wine the only difference being the deadline is 1 May before the harvest and not 1 July as for the Classic.

		• The appellation (vineyard name) of a potential Selection wine must be registered with the wine authorities.
Sensory Controls	• Sensory controls only as normal for gaining an AP Number.	• Sensory controls as per the AP Number application and an additional sensory control to permit the use of the Selection name.
Label Information	• Region, grape variety with word Classic and vintage.	• Region, grape variety, vintage, and vineyard site name. • Not permitted terms such as trocken/dry or halbtrocken/off-dry (this takes affect after vintage 2003).
Marketing Restrictions		• Wines cannot be released until 1 September the year following the harvest.

Many wine buffs will have seen estates use the terms "Classic" or even "Selection" on their wines for many years. Any trademarks that existed prior to the 6th of December 2000 now can only continue to run until the end of 2010. This means these terms were already in partial use by producers. Now they mean something else.

Do these terms only add more confusion? Will these extra classifications be the straw that breaks the camels back? There are no short answers to these questions but my feeling is that "Classic" and "Selection" will be meaningless to wine buyers and consumers alike. There can be no coherent style and the placing of generic terms over non-generic products is only trying to legislate conformity. A customer tasting one bottle of a "Classic" Riesling might enjoy it, so purchasing another from a different estate and dislike it so forming mixed reactions about "classic" wines. In the worse case this might mean the consumer then feels he or she does not like "classic" wines. It again depends on their personal definition of the term and their expectations. Any initial help they might be giving the consumer will evaporate. The generic catch-all terms of "Classic" and "Selection" are like writing "fast" on a pair of running shoes.

A number of VDP members are using the term "Classic" on their entry-level wines. They are also using the VDP classification system. We are likely to see a pattern of this as producers sensibly use the regulation of sugar/acid balance to the benefit of their wine styles. Still, there is a lot of room for difference within this attempt at a style classification. Nägler is a case in point. His philosophy is well grounded, as he puts plenty of effort into his entry level wine, on which he is using the nonclamenture "Classic". It is the first offering of his estate people are likely to try. His 2003, Riesling Classic surprisingly had no malolactic fermentation despite there being some butter notes and plenty of *"panna cotta"* tones. Reductively made the tropical fruits, banana, and citric notes come through. The fermentation was stopped before complete dryness and the remaining residual sugar gives the wine some fatness without the appearance of being sweet. It is a delightful and skilfully made wine. Even so, this is not a "classic" Rheingau style. There is not the bracing acidity, huge structure, or petrol notes.

As it has been discussed, one man's "Classic" is another man's "International Style Riesling". Drawing Nägler out on this, his interpretation of what "Classic" should be means classic not for the Rheingau, not for Rüdesheim, but classic for his estate. These are the classic characteristics he can achieve in his wines. Despite the fact that this is not what I personally interpret as classic, he is making an excellent wine here which is released at a exceptionally good price and it is a wonderful international everyday drinking style. The situation indicates exactly the problem the German industry is going to have with using the term "Classic". If I ignore the term on the bottle then I just get a great wine for the price. If I want to find those flavours in another Rheingau producer's bottle labelled "Classic" then I am likely to encounter something else. This demonstrates that there will be a consumer interpretation and a winery interpretation. They are never going to mesh.

The only benefit these new categories will have is effectively behind the scenes. By making various tighter quality parameters there will be an increase in the quality of the wine. We can see from basic industry statistics that producers are warming to the term and the so-called style of "Classic". Producers are required to register a wine with the DWI for status as "Classic" so it is easy to see that the numbers have risen. As a winemaker, I must say that the rules regarding what fit the "Classic" suit are well structured, particularly in regards to the residual sugar levels that are permitted. This side of the operation has been well thought out and one suspects that they might have even bothered to have asked for some winemaker input. This would be the first for a marketing department anywhere in the world.

As is well known, the climate in Germany being at the margin for wine production means that different regions have considerable differences in the levels of acids that result in their wines. This is not to say that many German Rieslings ever lack a good fresh crisp acid structure and it would be rare to find a Riesling described as flabby. It is important to strike the right balance of acidity and sugar.

What is flogged off to us by the New World Riesling producers is often what is sweet enough to be considered half-dry by German wine laws. We do not notice this as it does not have "half-dry" written on the label and the wine tastes great. The acid/sugar balance is correct for the particular wine. The more acid the more sugar one requires to mask it. [101] An arbitrary number is just pen-pusher interference and has placed what would be otherwise very harmonious wines outside the consumer consideration of purchase due to the negative impression given by the label that the wine is not dry. This is a perverse reaction to the sweet and

---

[101] Winemakers are loath to release a *halbtrocken* wine unless this is a particular style that they sell. It might be in a particular year that a blend really needs just that extra gram of sugar in order to balance the wine, but it would not receive it due to the fact that the wine would suddenly cross the border from dry to off dry. No such problems in the New World, the wine just receives the right dose of sugar from winemaking point of view and leaves the winery with nothing declared in terms of sugar content. If the increasing levels of New World Riesling sales are to go by the consumer does not seem to be too fussed about the words trocken or *halbtrocken* missing from the label.

cheap disaster. Again it is an example of where legislative failures have tried to stem a haemorrhage with a sticking plaster rather than letting the wine styles and consumer sort things out.

The sensible consideration of the "Classic" regulations is that they have finally realised that what a consumer will taste as "dry" due to winemaking finding the right balance need not shoot itself in the foot by allowing some pen pusher to class it as half dry. The rules on sugar in "Classic" permit the wine to have 2 times the acid level up to a maximum of 15g/L. Now regional differences kick in. For instance, nearly 90% of the wines from the Pfalz would still be well within the class of *trocken* or dry. On the other hand, around 60% of the wines from the Mosel are over 9 gm/L of residual sugar. This means that if they were not in the "Classic" category they would have to be released as *halbtrocken*. Isn't it better to be making better wines rather than worrying about a cut off point. Say a wine needs 10 gm/L sugar, this still would be fine as a "Classic" rather than have to go out as a *halbtrocken* for the sake of one extra gram of residual sugar. This would likely mean is that the best balance for the wine, from a winemaking point of view, is that the wine would have been kept to under 9 gm/L of sugar so as to qualify for the *trocken* moniker rather than slip into the less saleable category of *halbtrocken*. Most estates will sell 9 bottles of dry to 1 half dry nowadays. "Classic" should provide an ideal shelter for the release of properly balanced wines which will still taste dry. This is the "international dry" taste that I would describe. It is the level of dry which should have been included in the 1971 laws. If this had been the case then many of the present problems would likely have been avoided.

Congratulations to the DWI for clever legal drafting here. The hope for "Classic" is that it is not abused. I do not mean by fraud here but with any winemaking by numbers with little subjective analysis, (with "Classic" there is none), there will be pressure from the large producers to jump on the bandwagon and try to "squeeze" as much of their product into a category that they will see differentiates and thus potentially gives them a marketing advantage. By dumping wines into these categories or slotting in the lowest priced wines they will potentially kill "Classic" as a concept. No matter what one feels about the sense of the title it would not be a positive thing to see it being abused.

The key to the success or otherwise of the "Classic" moniker will be in consumer and wine buyer acceptance. My feeling is that there is no real classic style. You can find a definition for a style which is classic. This would require extensive debate and at the end of the day the wines would be required to undergo sensory analysis in order to ensure that they met the flavours and aromas of what had been defined as classic. This is not the case. Further, my feeling is that by setting up an idea of "Classic" as a means of simplifying things detracts from a deep understanding of where much of the New World success with customers has come from. Much of the success has come directly from the fact that the simple use of varietal labelling. With "Classic" you are taking the focus away from Riesling as a grape variety. You have to spend a lot of money promoting and ramming the idea of "Classic" into the head of the wine buying public. This is not what is needed when you are talking about a variety. The focus should be on Riesling. People will return to or discover German wine via variety such as Riesling not by picking something up that is marketed as "Classic".

The reaction to "Classic" from major wine buyers in supermarkets is interesting. At the end of the day, this is the important first hurdle of acceptance as this is surely where the wines are targeted given the price and the desire to simplify the purchase decision is a stated aim of the push behind "Classic". UK buyer feeling, and these are only generalisations as it is impossible to ask them all, is that they can see some rationale behind "Classic", particularly with the acid/sugar balance basis. There is a feeling that Riesling, which should be the focal point, is being left behind and the money spent on promoting and providing the basic information as to what is "Classic" could be better spent on tarting up the image of Riesling.

Wines finding good acceptance in the market today, from a supermarket sales sense, are those based on heritage styles such as Chianti, regional differentiation, or French AOCs. The New World has little of this so has pushed with grape varieties and brands. "Classic" falls between these two pillars. It is a little bit with one foot on the dock and one foot on the boat. No matter what way you lean you are going to fall into the water. I cannot see the UK supermarket wine buyers listing these products purely for the fact that they are labelled "Classic". Such wine buyers will take the wine on the basis that given their customer base they have a place for a German wine. If it happens to be labelled "Classic" they are likely careless. If "Classic" is not a success or is seen as causing confusion we might well see the reverse reaction where supermarket wine buyers ask for the wine not to be labelled with "Classic" as it causes confusion for their customers and as a result sees them substituting to other wines.

"Selection", on the other hand is trying to take things up market a little bit. It is an attempt to be site specific. Looking at the winemaking controls on the category we can see a serious attempt to really produce top quality wines here. To my mind these wines are more likely what I would term as lending themselves to giving classic Riesling flavours. Surely the simpler of names should have been given to the entry-level point and the step up the more special name. This is, naturally, my opinion and others may well think that "Selection" sounds more important than "Classic". Have they got the names round the wrong way? The simpler wines now released as "Classic" could really be called "Selection" and the wines from the individual sites be termed "Classic".

The key here is that "Selection" wines must undergo sensory control and a period of maturation, basically a year before they can be released. I cannot really see this category taking off. I believe that most of the producers capable of making an application for the "Selection" category are likely going to be members of groups such as the VDP and their scheme is likely far more attractive for such producers. "Selection", is a category that would always be smaller than that of "Classic". Even so, my feeling is that the number of applications for "Selection" category status will run to low numbers and it will not be something that is successfully exported. This is simply due to the fact that the vineyard name is what drives the issue of the wine recognition and importance in this market sector. Adding "Selection" to the already cluttered label is not adding anything of benefit to the consumer.

The proof in the system is if it is initially embraced by producers and then if it translates into sales. It is too early to pass judgement upon. I would be willing to bet both "Classic" and "Selection" are not going to find favour in the export market. If they will be useful in the domestic German market is another question.

The VDP Premier Crew

The VDP have developed their own system in an attempt to sort out the mess that German wine has become. It is a hierarchical system and, in order to save you reading my conclusions, it is just about what the doctor ordered. It has been basically drawn together by a few loose cannons who were pushing for this sort of thing, albeit individually, (perhaps they had taken a lesson from the Italian estates), and it is not surprising that these people were from the leading wineries as judged by wine experts. There has been a lot of debate about the system among producers but I feel that the delay has been better than releasing something overly flawed. That is not to say that the system is yet perfect. The key aspect here is that the VDP are able to recognise their system is not yet perfect and remain willing to tinker until they get it right. Any German organisation behaving in a flexible manner deserves to be applauded just for that!

An overview of the Three Tier Pyramid or Classification Model is contained within Appendix Three. It provides a summary of terminology, where it applies, and the wine criteria involved for each level of classification. I feel it is worth having a quick look at this before diving into the rest of this chapter as it provides a useful outline as to what is being considered.

As previously mentioned the weight of wine journalists, often considerable even if they lack influence, has been squarely behind the development of a classification system. Tom Stevenson makes this clear in talking about the rejuvenation of the German reputation, "this would involve the classification of the country's top wine estates, but the owners are politically weak, while the large, commercial bottlers are strong. It is in the commercial interest of these large, powerful firms and cooperatives to keep export markets flooded with cheap, medium sweet wines made from almost every German white grape variety except Riesling."[102] Tom's statement is pertinent not merely for the declaration that a classification is needed but for the fact that such a classification must come from the top estates. He correctly cites that the Liebfraumilch Mafia have prevented in their own interests such a classification. There was no chance of such a classification becoming enshrined in law and as a result the only way for it to have taken place is in the hands of a private organisation filled and managed by the leading estates of Germany.

There have been many attempts at small regional groups setting their

---

[102] Page 259 Tom Stevenson, The New Sotheby's Wine Encyclopaedia.

wines apart and even estate in-house classifications systems. Examples are the Bernkasteler Ring in the Mosel and the various Barrique Forums. A number of elite German producers use an in-house classification system. This just adds to confusion. There are producers who use a system of "**'s" to indicate a level of must weight at harvest within a classification, another a series of different coloured capsules, and another who tries to pass off his own *cru* system by using the initials GC (von Guradze Christian) and PC (Philip Chrisitan) in an attempt to indicate Grande Cru and Premier Cru. The latter, Weingut Dr Bürklin Wolf, has done so much to demonstrate the best model for the future of the German elite estates and pushed the concept of pride in terroir exceptionally well. They have understood perfectly well the balance of label clarity whilst not foregoing tradition. Why they persist with this silliness of "GC & PC", I have no idea. As a certainly senior member of the VDP they would be better bringing their marketing under the *Grosses Gewächs* classification system, (which they use in conjunction with their GC/PC game), throwing their full weight behind the VDP effort of which they have at least six vineyards registered as *Grosses Gewächs*. Their "PC's" should be more focused at the second level of the classification pyramid, the *Klassifizierter Lage* wines.

The forerunner to the VDP classification system was the Charta movement. It is worth, I feel, giving some time to the concept of Charta. It was formed around 1983 in the Rheingau. The purpose of the association was to lift the image of the Rheingau Riesling and they were going to do this by promoting a style of wine which they saw as being traditional for the region. Further, they were going to regulate the winemaking so as that the requirements of wines falling into this category would have stricter parameters than that required by present legislation. To make a very long story short, the idea was to promote a wine style that under the existing legislation was effectively *halbtrocken* but at the same time the wine had to taste dry. This is the sensation that I have been referring to as "Internationally Dry". That is, given high natural acid levels in the Riesling a good serving of sugar could offset this whilst still tasting dry. This makes sense from a winemaking point of view and from a historical perspective. Without the ability in years gone by to heat cellars or tanks cold cellars would have meant that some wines were left with a level of sugar well away from dry. That is, the coldness of the cellars would have meant that some wines did not ferment all their sugars to completeness. The big guns of Rheingau wines were behind the creation of Charta including the late owner of Schloss Vollrads Graf Erwein von

Matuschka-Greiffenclau who also became well known as an ambassador for the importance of matching food with German wine.

As a marketing tool and sales device, Charta did not work. At the same time it provided a valuable legacy. First, we can see that the aims of creating a wine style based on a balance between sugar and acidity has basically transformed itself into what is trying to be achieved by the DWI with "Classic". Second, it meant a separate movement of quality and that quality push setting the parameters above what was required by law. Thirdly, it meant for a series of panels which had to taste member's wines before they could be granted the status of Charta in any given year. This has been adopted within the present VDP system. In addition, it was an attempt by a region to set aside wines and producers from within that region as offering something different and elite. As an aside, we can also see that the Charta idea of having a bottle with a logo embossed and the use of the three arched windows symbol[103] has been carried forth into the mantra of the VDP *Erstes Gewächs* classification for the Rheingau.

The late Georg Breuer was instrumental behind this system and was a highly interesting man as well as a great winemaker. He was a member of the VDP but left due to not seeing eye-to-eye with the new classification system. This basically came down to the fact that there were certain elements that he would have liked to have seen incorporated making the rules even stricter but the VDP would not do so. Basically, he thought that if you were going to legislate you had to make it strict so as that average wines could not sneak through. He felt there were too many loopholes in what was being proposed.

The lesson for the VDP is very important here. The history of German wine is littered with attempts at legislating for quality and forming mini-classifications. They must also watch closely what happened with Charta, in that its aims were fine but in reality it did not catch on with consumers. It is important that the classification system transform into market credibility and eventually sale but is not used to over hype the concept of terroir.

Effectively, the VDP system is a fusion of the estate classification as seen in Bordeaux and the vineyard classification as seen in Burgundy. The VDP has openly come out and stated that the classification of sites under their system would mean that nearly two thirds of existing *Einzellagen* vineyard appellations would not qualify. This is a dramatic statement and

---

[103] This 3-arched window symbol is taken from the balcony of the Graue Haus, arguably Germany's oldest inhabited house, located in the town of Winkel.

would mean that by the time the VDP scheme was fully functioning only around 780 vineyard site names would be able to be used, something that is certainly manageable. The pyramid nature would suggest a few hundred at the top and the rest sitting at the next step down. The VDP have no control over the wine industry in general; only their members. Thus, we will see the 2600 plus existing *Einzellagen* will continue to be used. Only those which are gazetted by the VDP in the classification system can be used by VDP members. If the VDP system receives solid backing from its members and consumer acceptance this will probably mean the consumer understands one simple thing and that is, a winery displaying the VDP symbol using a vineyard name is basically an indication of a quality estate, exceptional vineyard, and a very good resultant wine.

Reinhard Löwenstein states, *"Weinberge klassifiziert. Ist das nicht Feudalismus durch die Hintertür?"* <Vineyard Classification is that not bringing Feudalism through the backdoor>.[104] This in many ways sums up the attitude or failure in nerve from the German elite producers since the 1971 laws. The fear of elitism and the fear of walking onto the world stage announcing that their great wines are true the greatest white wines in the world is something no other wine country would have had the fear of doing. It is not Feudalism coming through the backdoor but finally capitalism sitting out front on the porch. Herr Löwenstein, one of the best producers on the Mosel and one with a complete grip on the idea of terroir. He describes the 1971 laws as basically the high point of the *"Süsse Welle"* or sweet wave. Löwenstein's article provides an excellent summary and finally a fight back from an elite producer against the mistakes of the past. He admits that the better producers are partly culpable for not having stood up to the politicians who were basically blinded or dazzled by the stainless steel of the major bottling operations. In addition, he ticks off the industry regulators for always pushing to make things cheaper and try to lay all the blame on bad marketing. There was no real concept or strategy from the top.

It is important to mention the intentions of the VDP. The idea the VDP is trying to communicate through their classification system is an advanced one for German wine. This has not received much discussion in the press, where the concentration has naturally been more on the actual rules and regulations of the classification system. Finally with this system there has been an expression of what should be logical to any person

---

[104] Reinhard Löwenstein, „*Von Oechsle zum Terroir*", Frankfurter Allgemeinen Zeitung, 7 October 2003.

deeply involved in German wine and that is that the sugar content should not dictate the quality classification level (QbA/QmP) of the wine. We have seen that this is the basis of the existing legislation and in no way takes into account the influence of terroir or recognises that quality level has more to do with just the resultant sugar level.

In the VDP scheme, only those wines reflecting their terroir are permitted to use the name of a vineyard site. They define a "magic triangle" of terroir.[105] Their triangle is composed of the vintage quality, skill of the grower, the overall quality and character of the vineyard. The vineyard character is further split down to being defined by soil, topography, climate, and microclimate. Further, only selected grape varieties are suited to a given terroir and these must also be approved.

I find the "magic triangle" a bit of a magic roundabout. All this talk of triangles and pyramids is starting to sound like a geometry lesson. The concept is the right one but the idea of terroir a little bit skewif. The concept the VDP should be pushing is more that the classification system is based on the knowledge of terroir absorbed over a considerable history of grape growing. This is something that is readily marketable and places reliance on fact. Cellars in the New World are always trying to find a marketing concept and for many years have relied upon technical wizardry. This is not exactly a romantic notion. Cellars owned by faceless corporate entities lack a marketing ingredient many Old World cellars take for granted. Think about visiting a large cellar in the New World and it is pretty stainless steel boring and there is not much to tell given the shortage of castles.[106]

The VDP consists of a national body grouping together regional associations. The national administration, in accordance with their members, has set the framework for the Classification system. This framework governs the overall administration and the basic foundation requirements. The regional bodies have the power to stipulate further conditions and even tighten quality criteria. This is a highly practical solution in giving the fine details of regulations to each of the regional bodies. With German wine it is possible to have a broad general

---

[105] Personal communication with VDP President, Prince Salm Salm.

[106] This is a generalisation; there are many boutique wineries with plenty of winemaking war stories to tell and the New World industry is filled with characters. One could visit a winery in Central Otago and ask one winemaker how he blew up both his Ute, *(ed. Australian pick-up truck)* and his dog at the same time during an attempt to eliminate rabbit burrows in his vineyards. Without castles, New World wineries have successfully geared themselves for wine tourism in other ways.

knowledge or be very wise in the specifics of a region. It is rare to find someone with a general knowledge which masters all the regional specifics. The best people to set the regional specific controls and the classification of estates are those who have grown up with the traditions of the region. In addition, such a group is far more likely to be able to have access to generations of understanding of the various sites. Further, in a group of quality orientated producers they are more likely to err on the side of caution and make quality standards and the achievement of classification harder than a national body merely listening to an application from a persuasive producer. The method of making open submissions for classification before the regional association also means it very unlikely that a producer will make a submission for inclusion unless they can be sure of it being accepted. Peer judgement, not wanting to push your own vineyard names forward, and not wanting to appear of having an overly inflated idea of the quality of your wines is likely to be a very effective method of self-restraint. Further, cast iron results over a lengthy period where the wines have been submitted to the VDP sensory examination will be used in order to determine what wines and thus sites are the best of the best and worthy of classification.

Rules are really only as effective as their enforcement. If the VDP wish to ensure the success of their system, or at least protection from criticism that it does not really classify only the best of the best, then they must be overly strict on what they permit to receive the premier appellation and subsequent steps down. To draw an aside with the Italian DOCG/DOC quality pyramid, it is one that permits entry to what in theory is the highest quality category (DOCG) based on the ability of an association to administer rules. Anything that can demonstrate an ability to strictly control a region and its winemaking can effectively be granted a DOCG status. As a result, it has meant in some cases less than what could be considered to realistically be the great wines of Italy enter into this category. The oft cited example is the Albana di Romanga DOCG; a well made wine but has nothing so special as to set it apart from a multitude of white wines and certainly could not be considered such an interesting or iconic style that it ranks alongside Barolo, Barbaresco, or Franciacorta DOCGs. The VDP must demonstrate not only the administration of their regulations is at the highest level but also that those vineyards brought into the classification are thoroughly deserving of such status. To err on the side of caution might initially be hard on some growers but will be for the long run benefit of the system.

Initially the vineyard site must receive nomination. Once it has been established that the vineyard has a long period of producing classic terroir specific wines that are considered to be at the pinnacle of wines produced in Germany then classification is permitted. In the highest category, this classification takes place as one of *Grosses Gewächs, Erstes Gewächs,* or *Erste Lage* depending upon the region. The VDP need to find a way to refer generally to these terms rather than the unromantic *1er Stufe*.

Common to all these descriptors are that there is a maximum yield of 50hl/ha, gazetted permitted grape varieties, strict VDP controls over vineyard management, required hand harvesting to a minimum of current *Spätlese* ripeness, a VDP sensory exam prior to receiving approval, and a mandatory period of aging prior to release of the wine. The VDP has understood that too much information on a front label has caused problems in non-German speaking countries. The entire movement is pushing towards the removal of terms such as *Auslese Trocken* and also to prevent the use of district names. This is the focus of the classification system and certainly an important step. It is important to ensure that the "window" to the wine is as uncluttered as possible. The VDP are requiring that members wines in the new classification system adhere to the following on a label; vintage, vineyard name, wine estate, variety, location and region. All other data, especially the legal stuff, is to be placed on a separate label.[107]

Grosses Gewächs or Great Growth refers to wines coming from the Ahr, Baden, Franken, Mittlerhein, Nahe, Pfalz, Rheinhessen, Saale-Untrit, and Württemburg. By extension, any wine reaching this level from Sachsen or the Hessische Bergstrasse would also likely enter under this category but as to date no such classification has taken place for sites in these regions. Given the fact that it covers most of the regions it is probably best seen as the overall idea and concept behind the classification system. As stated, each regional association has set in place rules pertaining to its situation avoiding an over generalised system. I make comments in the following passages in order to demonstrate these modifications not because they alter the overall aims but because they demonstrate the regional association's flexibility to determine what is in the best interests or represents their terroir. There are in all cases a minimum price for which the wines can sell set by the regional association. I choose not declare these, not out of fear of shocking the reader, (by world class wine standards they are very low), but due to the fact that they will rapidly date.

I should point out that *Grosses Gewächs* wines are dry but for those

---

[107] Refer to the Appendix One for a fuller discussion on labels.

designated as lusciously sweet, and these are identifiable with the designation of a *Prädikat* (*Auslese, Beerenauslese, Eiswein, and Trockenbeerenauslese*). Such wines as these have maintained Germany's status in the wine world as nothing can match these wines not even the great Sauternes. It is important that they retain their *Prädikat* as it makes a smooth transition from the consumers point of view to understanding that these wines have now been elevated to the status of First Growth, something which they have always effectively been.

In the Ahr, the permitted varieties are Riesling, Spätburgunder, and Frühburgunder. Riesling reaching a natural (non sugar enriched) must weight of 90 deg *Oechsle* and the reds 95 degrees. Wines must undergo a maturation period of at least 12 months in large oak vats and are tasted by the approvals commission both before and after bottling. They are permitted a maximum of 9g/L residual sugar for trocken wines and *edelsüsse* wines must be at least at the level of *Auslese*. There is a minimum price set for selling the wines and they may be released from the 1st of September the second year following harvest.

In Baden, the permitted varieties are Spätburgunder, Weissburgunder, Grauburgunder, Riesling, and at the time of writing further consideration is being given to Silvaner, Lemberger, Muskateller, Gewürztraminer, and Gutedel. Wines must reach at least Spätlese level of ripeness. They specify the bottle shape that may be used, Burgunder and for the Riesling a traditional *Schlegelflasche*. *Spätlese* wines are to be made in the *trocken* style and *edelsüss* wines must arrive at the *Auslese* level.

In the Nahe, the vineyards which enter the *Grosses Gewächs* classification are contained within a *Lagenkarte* or vineyard classification map that dates back to 1901. In this region, those sites classified can be used for the second tier *Klassifizierter Lage* wines and should they be good enough those sites used for *Grosses Gewächs*. Riesling is the only permitted variety. Here they define a certain bottle for use as the *Grosse Gewächsflasche* in either brown or antique green. The height of the bottle is too high for most supermarket shelves but I doubt that this sector is the object of the producers of such wines. A metal capsule is required as is a natural cork of 44mm. *Trocken* wines may have a maximum of 12g/L residual sugar with edelsüss wines having a minimum of 40g/L for Auslese and 60g/L for *Beerenauslese, Trockenbeerenauslese, and Eiswein*..

The VDP Pfalz, has classified vineyards based on those contained within the 1828 tax assessment records from the King of Bavaria. Later entry is permitted after demonstration of many years of top quality. Permitted varieties are Weissburgunder, Spätburgunder, and Riesling. 90

degrees *Oechsle* is required for the whites and 95 for the red. The bottle is a brown heavyweight *Schlegelflasche* of 350mm in height. *Trocken* wines are to have a maximum of 9g/L residual sugar.

The Rheinhessen classification is interesting for the fact that it has clearly set out the method by which a vineyard site can be elevated from a classified site (second tier of the quality pyramid) to that of being a *Grosses Gewächs* site. This sets out that a vineyard must have been at the lower level for a minimum of 5 years before it can even receive consideration for inclusion within the category of *Grosses Gewächs*. Naturally, there are some sites to get the ball rolling and these have been determined by the committee based upon historical documents and the resulting analysis of quality over a considerable period. Like the Pfalz, *edelsüsse* wine is permitted to use the vineyard site name but not able to mark the bottles with *Grosses Gewächs*. Residual sugar here is permitted to a maximum 1:1 ratio with the acid level which incorporates an important winemaking rule of thumb for the region. This should make the *Grosses Gewächs* wines from Rheinhessen balanced and show very well. Some very interesting wines should come out of here in the forthcoming years given the motivation of the young winemakers and the sensible framing of their classification regulations.

The Mittlerhein uses its initial *Grosses Gewächs* sites from those well regarded and found in a historical Prussian tax document. In the future sites may enter after having demonstrated many years of top quality. Only Riesling is permitted and the minimum level of ripeness is *Spätlese*. Those wines considered for the *Edelsüss* category commence from the level of *Auslese*. The wines should be trocken and what is appropriate for the terroir permits a maximum residual sugar equal to that of the acid level plus 5 gm.

Franken permits Silvaner, Riesling, Weissburgunder, and Spätburgunder with the white wines needing to achieve *Spätlese* level of ripeness. Here the *trocken* level is permitted to be the acid level plus 2 grams but at a maximum of 9g/L.

Württemburg is presently only permitting Riesling as a variety but expects to expand this in the next four years to include other traditional regional grape varieties. Interestingly, this region makes the permission to use a *Grosses Gewächs* claim or use of the vineyard name considered suitable for such classification dependent upon the sensory examination. This means that you might have a wine from site that is considered within the *Grosses Gewächs* classification but given the year or the particular wine you will be refused permission to use the *Grosses Gewächs* declaration when

143

in the decision of the examining commission the quality does not so merit. This is a very interesting system and means that no winery is able to effectively rest upon its past success. You are only as good as your last wine.

As we can see from the foregoing, each region using the *Grosses Gewächs* nonclamenture has taken a slightly different approach to what is best suited to their terroir. From a winemaking point of view this is a very interesting approach and demonstrates that the VDP well understand the making of blanket rules is not possible in a wine land as diverse as Germany and as subject to considerable variations in microclimate. Further, it respects the fact that the regions of Germany have different traditions and wishes to enshrine these appropriately without forcing a generalised standard from a national body. The age of centralised control has passed. Blanket rules require the setting of parameters that must by their nature encompass the lowest common denominator and this is not a suitable method with which to construct a system designed to celebrate the elite wines within an industry.

Erstes Gewächs, or *First Growth* refers to wines produced in trocken/dry styles and those wines which are lusciously sweet (*edelsüsse Prädikat* wines of *Auslese, Beerenauslese, Trockenbeerenauslese,* and *Eiswein*) from the Rheingau. The Rheingau *Erstes Gewächs* requires the use of an additional logo. This is the logo that was used in former times to identify the wines of the Charta movement.[108] The new classification system has in many ways absorbed the Charta movement even to the point of utilising this symbol.[109] This symbol is the Roman three arches, which as an aside can be found on the balcony of the Graue Haus. Riesling and Spätburgunder are the permitted varieties that reach a minimum level of *Spätlese* ripeness.

The Rheingau specifies that the front label must contain the year, variety, Rheingau designation, town, vineyard name, the term *Erstes*

---

[108] Charta as stated, were wines to be 100% Rheingau Riesling of QbA or QmP status. Residual sugar was permitted between 9 and 18 gm/L and the minimum acidity of 7.5gm/L. This means for pretty big wines, something the Rheingau can provide.

[109] There are some uniform packaging requirements and a sensory tasting requirement. Charta was a case of where a particular style of wine, a very traditional Rheingau Riesling, was pushed forward as an attempted standard. When one tastes Charta wines one is pretty sure of noticing a consistent style and flavour. This was a laudable aim and has worked. Even so, it has really gone unnoticed by consumers. It probably did not dare to go far enough, or perhaps the political climate within the Rheingau was not quite ready. It was certainly a stepping-stone in the right direction. Perhaps its focus on the Rheingau meant that it would always force its use and thus acceptance to be limited.

Gewächs, and the three *"romanische Bogen auf schwarzem Balken".*[110] They specify the back label is the primary label for the purpose of German/EU wine legislation. Wines that are within this First Growth are not released with the words *trocken* but *Edelsüsse* wines must carry the level of ripeness (from *Spätlese* to *Trockenbeerenauslese).* Riesling is permitted to 13g/L residual sugar but should taste dry. *Edelsüsse* wines vary in the level of residual sugar; *Spätlese* must commence from 40g/L, *Auslese* a minimum of 60g/L, and *BA/TbA/Eiswein* a whopping minimum of 100g/L. Spätburgunder is to taste dry and can have a maximum of 6g/L residual sugar.

Erste Lage, or First Site refers to wines from the Mosel-Saar-Ruwer with particular quality parameters for each *Prädikat* level. Experience has dictated in the Mosel, that this category should be open also to the *Spätlese* and *Kabinett* styles of wine. This will allow the dry full-bodied wines but also the elegant light *Kabinett,* elegant full *Spätlese,* and the full, nobly sweet *Auslese. Eiswein, Beerenauslese, Trockenbeerenauslese* come under the system. This is due to the special circumstances and tradition of the Mosel where balanced well-made wines are of a lower alcohol and likely that the residual sweetness comes from the stopping of the fermentation. Without this understanding of winemaking tradition it is unlikely that the Mosel-Saar-Ruwer could have adopted the VDP system. Again it demonstrates a well thought out approach of what is appropriate for one region is not for another. It is correct for the Mosel but not the other regions.

The Mosel can make dry wines but at the end of the day this is a region that can generally get grape must with a potential alcohol of around 10 to 11 degrees. More Southerly regions have not as much trouble to surpass these levels. As a result, the great sweet wines of the Mosel have an intensity of flavour not driven by overwhelming alcohol levels. The levels of acid and the dry extract[111] are often much higher than for top quality red wines, which provides an ideal component for ageing. This makes them ideal to cellar, collect, and auction. Rarity drives the price up and the best examples of such wines often sell for well above what the most expensive French wines. To have failed to bring such great examples of German winemaking within the umbrella of the cru classification would have been to ensure that the system was only a partial representation of the elite in German winemaking and excluding arguably the jewel in the crown.

---

[110] Roman Arches.

[111] Dry extract is the total dry matter, comprised of those substances which do not volatilise.

The regions have looked closely at what constitutes *trocken*. They have come up with formulas allowing a greater suitability to their terroir rather than imposing an across the board concept. We will see wines emerging that are basically "internationally dry". Finally, we will see great German wines that allow the winemaker to consider the acid/sugar balance without trying to force it under 9 g/L in order to qualify as *trocken*.

One of the most attracting factors of the VDP system is the concentration on terroir and the resultant wines. The foundation for the acceptance of a terroir as being suitable is based on primary historical information and further collaborated by peer assessment. This means that quality is determined by the interaction of terroir, (soil, topography, climate, micro-climate), and the winemaker interpretation. The latter can be the winemaker expression or it can be the expression of the "house" style. It is not merely my biased winemaking background that asserts the hand of the winemaker can direct the style of a winery and/or the way in which the terroir comes through in the resultant wine. Good winemakers spend their life trying to find in the right season the expression of what their vineyards can give and more particularly what they should demonstrate.

We can see that a famous name winery in the Pfalz, only recently been admitted to VDP and with no classified sites, has over a number of years made great wines. It remains an interesting question of if the class of the winemaker or the vineyards were responsible for this. The opinion of many in the region was that the vineyard locations were not the best but that the winemaker was making the difference. He was producing wines of such quality that his work inspired another generation of winemakers. Expert opinion supports that since this gentleman retired the wines have not reached the same level, despite recent excellent seasons. No prizes for guessing that I am speaking about Müller Catoir. It remains to be seen if the new guy needs some time to get to grips with the vineyards or if he is not of the same calibre. Wine journalists are often quick to judge and have little if any appreciation that it can take many years of tinkering until even a great winemaker finds the style of wine expressing correctly his interpretation of a terroir. Different conductors call a different tune.[112]

To further this winemaking theme, a great or potentially great terroir might exist but it is not classified or has been removed from classification

---

[112] It can be very frustrating as a winemaker to make some of the best wines in a region and understand that you are doing that with less than the best sites, often one drives past the better vineyards and one wonders what they could achieve with such wonderful material.

due to the fact that the current winemaker is not working it in the right way or is not producing a style that the terroir supports. There is plenty of room for argument here and this is the spice of winemaking. Winemakers must give much study to what is the right style for a particular terroir. The importance of the VDP scheme is that it allows declassification and the entry of sites. It is structured as a flexible operation above claims afflicting all other classifications systems in the world in that they are based upon the money, influence, or relentlessness of the estate owner. It is a false reaction to prevent a site entering the level of "greatness" classification when the wrong wine or style has been produced on that site. No one would argue that Chateau d'Yquem is not a pinnacle of winemaking achievement and deserving of elevated growth status. Even so, plant a variety singly unsuited to its location such as Syrah and you are going to end up with wines that are comparatively undrinkable.

Will there be a rush to release wines from all the potential classified First Growth sites? I think not. Producers are dealing with very fickle consumers who, understanding a site to be a First Growth vineyard, will expect to regularly see great wines emerging from that site. As a result, a winery will likely be very careful to release only those wines they know on a consistent basis will obtain suitable status. Thus, a winery is more likely to submit only those wines it is completely sure surpass the quality requirements on a regular basis. Where a winery has a First Growth classified site but is not sure of consistently hitting the quality levels then it is better to seek continued consistency within the second tier of quality and still be able to use the vineyard name. All-in-all, this means for an upwards push in what reaches the top level classification and tends to swell the ranks of *Klassifizierter Lage* wines. VDP members with classified sites are not required to produce First Growth wines if they do not think their production from a site measures up. There are going to be some wonderful wines in the *Klassifizierter Lage* section and this deserves a lot of scrutiny. As a winemaker the blending selection process is often one of things getting passed down the line; making the cut if you like. This is positive news for the *Guts* and *Orts* wines from VDP estates.

There has been some comment from the wine press regarding setting of wine yields per hectare as part of the criteria. At first glance the maximum permitted yields of 50hl/ha looks very sensible. We can understand that different regions have different planting densities especially due to the fact of their particular topography. It is easier to spread vines out in the undulating Pfalz. In the Mosel one has to plant closely spaced vines. The end result is that the individual vine in the densely planted regions must produce less juice in order to satisfy the quota. A vine forced into producing less in terms of volume is going to channel this effort into fruit intensity. An argument can be raised for tinkering with this in order to try to make it uniform across the regions but at the same time this is basically being raised by journalists who are demonstrating their ability to count rather than any actual knowledge they might have about winemaking.

A vine is able to support a prodigious amount of fruit. Naturally, there is a point where you are trading volume off against intensity of flavour and certainly sugar content. In the past there was no incentive to crop at low levels because you got paid on volume production. From a winemaking point of view a vineyard of 1ha with 10,000 plants limited to producing 50hl/hl is permitting each vine 500ml. A vineyard with half that planting density is permitting each vine to produce one litre of fruit. From a winemaking point of view I think it will be very hard to justify these sorts of criticism. The difference between 1 L and 500mls per vine in winemaking terms is immaterial. The difference between 1 L and 5 L is material and perhaps even 1 L to 2 L gap. Such calls neglect the fact that the vineyard planted with 10000 vines is restricting the soil that the vine has available and generally produces less fruit. In addition, the vines foliage and canopy growing space must also be limited if ripeness is to be achieved. These are techniques of vigour control and crop level management that have been practiced for centuries. A vineyard with 5000 plants per hectare is able to support more space between the vines. The vine is able to grow in greater space and thus form a larger canopy. This canopy is able to receive more sunlight and thus turn more sunlight into wine. At the end of the day, a vineyard difference between 500 and 1000ml per vine is splitting hairs from people who have not any winemaking. Quality producers under a scheme such as that proposed by the VDP are going to crop at the lowest level they can in order to achieve the quality they want. In addition, the wines have to go through a sensory analysis.

We can see the flexibility of the site classification rules from a number of the regional associations. It is key that the classified sites list must remain open. Some of the existing confusion is that the VDP have not been very clear as to what sites come under the *Grosses Gewächs/Erste Lage/Erstes Gewächs* list and what fall under the second tier classification. In time this should become clearer. What is important is that the list is open in both directions. That is, there is provision for removal from the list, (likely the ultimate sanction), and the addition of sites demonstrating their success. We can see some associations even confirm the permission to use their respective First Growth tag from vintage to vintage. Once you fall out with a bad year it will mean considerable work to get back to First Growth accreditation.

Gunter Künsler's of Hockenheim, has a number of vineyards that could come under classification but will not use the nonclamenture due to the fact that he found the level of Oechsle permitted too low, the non exclusion of concentrators, and the fact that chapitalisation can be used for a Grande Cru wine as being unacceptable. These I feel are all valid points and need to be considered by the VDP.

Not all the great producers of Germany are members of the VDP. Estates such as Molitor in the Mosel and Weingart in the Mittlerhein could certainly be members if they so chose. Further, there are a number of top wineries that have reservations about the classification system. Maximin Grünhäuser is one such estate. The owner, Dr Carl von Schubert is the complete gentleman. His estate in the Mosel is not part of the VDP but has close associations. His vineyards of Abtsberg, Herrenberg, and Bruderberg are his best. All these sites are certainly deserving of classification as *Erste Lage*. In discussion over the classification concept I knew that I was going to get an interesting perspective. Here is an owner with what are certainly seen as some of the best vineyards in the area and who is outside of the VDP. Thus, he has little benefit in only singing the praises of the system or being critical. He feels there is too much confusion with the system. There are some vineyards which are classified as First Growth whilst being owned by a number of different producers, not all of who are producing premier cru wines from that vineyard. He thinks that such producers then releasing their wines with the vineyard name on them but not as *Grosses Gewächs/Erste Lage/Erstes Gewächs* then takes some of the shine from the top producer using that site as his or her First Growth product. This is a very valid point and something that the VDP have to monitor. He agrees that *Spätlese* is the style to show Riesling at its best but knows all too well the dilemma of people then thinking these wines have to be sweet. At the same time, the best wines from his estate are those outside the *trocken* band, due to the need to balance acidity. These wines do not necessarily taste sweet due to the fine balance that has been achieved with the acid. His object is to let the fermentation stop before full dryness in order to retain natural sweetness in the wine.

His other comment about the classification system is that if he was to move over to this form of nonclamenture then he would loose the chance to distinguish many of his individual vineyard wines and would need to release nameless cuvees. He points out that one of his lower priced wines, the Abtsberg QbA Trocken, is terroir specific and demonstrates the characteristics of the Abtsberg vineyard. This vineyard, through selective harvesting, also provides a range of wines up to *Eiswein* level of ripeness. Should he use the classification of *Erste Lage* for Abtsberg then the lower level of ripeness wine would not be able to use the vineyard name. This is a valid point and to each his own. Dr von Schubert has a dedicated band of loyal customers and will have no trouble selling his wines no matter the name given their quality and extreme ability to age.[113]

Herr Selsbach of Weingut Selsbach-Oster in the Mosel has had remarkable success. By virtue of his exceptional wine quality and international recognition certainly he has the right to be heard on the VDP classification system. He is not a member of the VDP but he has vineyards that would come under classification should he so wish such as Zeltingen Sonnenuhr and Berkastel Badstube. He has a fear that despite being a good idea it is an attempt to fix something that is not already broken. He compares it to the classification system in the Alsace which through a series of complications largely cannot be described as having been successful.

He feels that the names of the great vineyards are already well known. I would agree, in the case of the German wine enthusiast, but the aim of the classification system is to bring to the attention of the wider wine public a method of quality declaration. The challenge for German wines is to lift or even create a positive image or brand. To achieve this will require more than recognition from the converted. Overall, Selsbach sees the EG/EL/GG idea as "not a bad one". This is qualified by his feeling that the practicalities are harder than the theory and with the EG/EL/GG names there appears to be no catch all description. They add to rather than reduce the confusion. There is enough confusion with the QbA/QmP "quality" ladder. This confusion is compounded by the fact that the individual VDP regional committees make many of their own rules on the platform of the national foundation rules. This is all factually correct and they are valid criticisms of the system.

---

[113] I have seen a respected journalist's recommendation of aging potential on his 2001 Riesling *Eiswein* and that is 2060. This wine has a full concentration of everything one wants to see in an *Eiswein* from the Mosel (surely the best place for this style). Apricots, honey melon, butterscotch, mango, pineapple, orange peel, and plenty of spices. Cream notes and plenty of acid to give this the holding time it needs to become even more complex.

Clearly the VDP need to rapidly address the cumbersome use of the terms EG/EL/GG. Is it First Growths, Premier Cru, or merely the modern marketing of "1ˢᵗ". The level of confusion that will be generated by adding the classification system to the existing model is a valid point. At the same time, in my opinion, one needs to look at the way the classification will be presented to the consumer, most of whom will not get beyond looking at "1,2,3, buy".[114] In my opinion, the fact that VDP regional associations can set or add stricter regulations is a positive aspect. We can see that a region such as the Rheinhessen, which has had a hard time being taken seriously, has beefed up their particular regulations. They have seemingly understood the stricter conditions will mean for fewer wines gaining 1ˢᵗ accreditation and those wines that do will be of such a standard to be the most positive publicity for the region.

Koehler-Ruprecht is another winery that could sell its production many times over. You are paying for rarity and quality at this estate. This is another estate that feels in using the First Growth name of a site means that they could not use it on other wines from those vineyards so hindering their particular marketing.

The VDP is extending the classification, to be open to producers other than those who are a member of the VDP. The VDP is a civil society and thus in theory their rules only apply to their members. At the same time the VDP understands the importance of having the *Grosses Gewächs/Erstes Gewächs/Erste Lage* and *Klassifizierter Lage* system accepted on an industry wide scale. It will not receive acceptance if it is merely a closed gentleman's club. The fear of many producers, and perhaps one of the reasons that the German industry was very much polarised in its representation in the past, was partly due to the impression gained that there existed a certain elite old boys club that did not want to see their important vineyard names downgraded or shared. This theory continually disproved itself given the fact that such sites generally attracted the highest prices when sold. Despite egalitarian grunting noises the sites with the best potential were always the most coveted. The VDP is willing to allow this classification to be used by non-VDP members if they meet the criteria. It is not impossible to imagine that this could happen.

---

[114] A simplistic concept that the consumer recognises the wine as belonging to a VDP member, is marked as EG/EL/GG, and has a vineyard name. No more is needed, in theory, to understand that the wine should be at the top level of industry production.

A Summary of the Two Systems

German wine is on the way back. For some it never left. Is this a hollow comment? In his 1991, book Ian Jamieson[115] made essentially the same statement and over a decade later the evidence of a German wine return has not been substantiated by export figures. If anything, the numbers suggest that the situation has worsened. Jamieson indicates that during the 1980's the image of German wine had become swamped with low quality commercial exports but that there were an increasing number of producers releasing dry superior quality wines. His contention in 1991 realistically represents the present situation. So what has changed in ten years to indicate that German wine is on its way back other than merely considerable talk as to the potential international recovery?

The change that has taken place has been a realisation at all levels of the German industry that the existing system was not capable of righting the capsized ship. This being so, producers have had to push for a change in system, something which does not come naturally to the German mind. No other country in the World has tolerated such inane wine regulations and blindly followed them. In the intervening period, German producers have concentrated not only on individual quality improvements but put in place the means with which to begin declaring their true quality wines to the public. These systems may well be those proposed by the VDP and DWI.

As we have seen, the reputation of German wines slipped drastically in the face of increased competition from New World producers and they appeared to have no unified voice as to how this problem could be solved. All Old World countries have suffered losses in the face of such a well-marketed and concentrated attack. This attack has been based on consistent quality and being very in tune with what consumers want both from a packaging and flavour point of view. We have to realise that the consumer base for wine has radically altered and perhaps the least well equipped people to deal with those new market demands are those who come from a wine background. Being passionate or experienced in wine are not necessary keys to successful marketing of a commercial product. Purists and the passionate are best placed to market their individual estate wines, and this is something that small German producers can do very well if they make themselves available in this regard.

---

115 "Wine-lovers will be glad to know that the future of German wine is not what it was" Page xiii, Ian Jamieson, German Wines, Faber and Faber, London, 1991.

In order to represent the industry as a whole there needs to be a different approach. The tactics in selling gym shoes are probably more suitable to selling commercial wines nowadays. Unfortunately, for German producers, their industry image was demonstrated with low quality poorly packaged commercial wines being sent onto the export market in great numbers. These commercial wines were neither consistent nor offering a "cute" alternative to the wines from the New World. When they were made consistently they had all character removed resulting in bland offerings that do not show well up against the fruit bombs from the Southern Hemisphere. The playing field changed and German commercial producers were the least equipped to fight that challenge.

Suffice to say, the reputation problems of German wine had reached such a level that all parties had to find a way to combat the inroads to their markets. So what are we left with? The German industry is now trying to face the world armed with a three-legged beast. Naturally, it makes for more confusion but this has become traditional when dealing with German wine. The stuff is just so good that the faithful are willing to spend the time trying to understand. If wider appeal is to be gained then this confusion will need rationalisation. Someone has to cut through all the confusion. The key place to start is with producer wine list and rationalise the array of products presented.

The existing variation of the 1971 laws remains as the basic structure and we can assume that this is unlikely to change. The consumer will start to look less at this law as a guarantee of quality, which it patently is not. Soufflés do not rise twice and the existing law will never be anything other than a handicap. The other two legs at an attempt to guarantee quality come from the VDP and DWI with their cru classification system and "Classic/Selection" respectively. "Classic/Selection" is the effort of the DWI and is part of the wine law, which brings me back to the analogy of the soufflé not rising twice. The VDP classification system is binding only on the members of their club. As we have seen the VDP are making the system available to non-members as well.

The DWI soufflé is an attempt to impose a set of names or new categories. The DWI idea of "Classic" and "Selection" is a system built from the ground up. It is looking at existing styles of wines and then trying to hive off two "special" categories as a means of making things easier for the consumer. In reality, "Classic" is making it easier for the producer to present balanced wines. On the other hand, the VDP have built a system from the top down. It is not surprising of why the two representative bodies decided to work from different directions. The mandate of the DWI has to be as egalitarian as possible, aside from the fact that it ends up representing more the wishes of the large bottlers, and thus has to cover the entire playing field. The VDP members are, in theory, included in the group due to their historical achievements of wine quality but only if they want to be members. As a result, their focus is on quality and with their programme they have been very strict in what passes. There are two schools of thought and there is nothing essentially wrong with that.

The DWI idea was grounded on the theory of lifting the lesser wine quality. Doing so would put Germany back on the world wine map. Trying to make better Liebfraumilch in other words. In truth, the aims of "Classic" and "Selection" go beyond trying to make better Liebfraumilch, as producers make individual wines but within the set parameters. The VDP sees it differently and feels, like France, the elite ones make people swoon and so that image trickles down to the rest.

We can see that there has been a considerable preoccupation with residual sugar levels. The VDP and its members understand clearly the problems German wines have suffered with being associated with sweet and cheap. As in the DWI's efforts with "Classic" and "Selection" there has been a firm codification of what is permitted. It is clear that for the first time, regulations have been drawn with consideration and thought given to actual winemaking issues rather than arbitrary numbers.

In essence the steps are correct, despite the questionable name of "Classic". This is the right direction in terms of trying to up the quality level and more importantly the perceived quality level of the supermarket sector wines. The name is completely subjective as to what is a "classic" wine. The term adds nothing but further confusion to the situation. The idea was that by trying to set a "classic" style with quality parameters and once the consumer had tried a wine tagged as such they would embrace this as being a quality indication for German wine. Following this through to a logical conclusion, the concept is one of trying to get a message to consumers of "Classic" wines being very good value for money and having certain quality parameters; resulting in an image makeover for German wine. There is hope consumers will then make the normal progression to the higher priced and in theory the more complex wines labelled as "Selection". Once people have tried something they like in the supermarket sector they are willing to trade up. At the same time, the producers of most of the wines labelled as "Classic" are going to find it hard to supply the volumes supermarket buyers want. This tends to suggest that if supermarket listings come then they will be for wines released by the large bottlers. Will this lead to a cycle of mass production wines being released as "Classic"? Only time will tell. In my opinion the moniker is only set to produce greater confusion. Perhaps it would have been better to avoid the terminology and just amend the *trocken* aspect of the existing legislation. This would have been less expensive and a public admission of what was clear privately.

A case in point is the 2002 Riesling Classic from Schlossgut Diel. The wine did not strike me as particularly being from the Nahe. The same went for the 2003 Classic that I tasted at a subsequent event. The wines are made completely for the international market or taste. There is no particular aspect of Nahe wines to them. Is this wrong? I think not. Quite the opposite. The wines are made to have universal appeal and do so exceptionally well. They are packed with fruit, rose petal notes, tropical characters, and are wonderfully balanced. Given the price and the quality level, I would argue you are hard to find such well-crafted white wines from other producing nations. Wines in these brackets need to be more general, in order to compete with the same sort of designed wines from the New World. You do not need to flaunt characters of the Nahe or even make a noise about them in this sector. Well-crafted, ready to drink, fruit driven wines will be attractive without needing to pin point them on a map as has been learnt from the example of Southeast Australia. The key should be balanced varietal Riesling. Classic allows this, given the modification to permitted sugar levels. Here is a smack in the face for German legislators. Damage could have prevented by so framing "dry" in 1971 as what passes for "Classic" now.

At present, to the best of my knowledge, in the United Kingdom market there is only one listing of "Classic" wine in a major multiple and no listings of the more expensive "Selection" wines. This is very disturbing for the DWI initiative which has taken a lot of time and money to develop as well as market.

The aims of "Classic" are a good thing. It stops the attempt to cram wines into the *trocken* bracket without a proper balance between acidity and sugar merely so as to avoid the negative "half dry" labelling requirement. The problem with "Classic" is the term has a plethora of meanings. Speaking with one producer recently and discussing his use of both the VDP *Erstes Gewächs* and the use of "Classic" for another it became apparent that interpretation of "Classic" was yet again different. His idea of "Classic" was not to demonstrate classic characteristics from the region but from both his vineyard and estate. In effect a classic house style. This is all well and good but if the consumer does not like that house style then where does this leave them with an impression of "Classic". I cannot imagine producers in Champagne releasing a fizz termed classic. What is classic Taittinger and what is classic Veuve Clicquot are two very different styles of Champagne. The end result is merely confusion. The public would still certainly see them as Champagne. At this point we should note in various regions such as Baden there has been for a long time the use of the term "Selection" and many producers in Germany have also made use of the term in releasing their own styles. As we have seen, the legislation permits this fragmented situation for some time to come but at the end of the day anyone who was formerly aware of what "Selection" might have meant does not now.

On the other hand, the VDP system of classification makes the first modern attempt by German producers to categorise quality based on terroir. It is complicated and difficult for the consumer without doubt. For it to be convincing, the VDP are going to have to be quick in educating consumers as to what the beast is and more importantly be ruthless in regulating what wines may pass. The system is certainly not without its flaws but if harnessed properly can provide a wonderful clarification for the consumer. Like all classification systems it is difficult to come to grips with but the challenge for the VDP will be to communicate the "nuts and bolts" of the system. The VDP have to administer the system ruthlessly in order to give it as much credence as possible and it not just become a marketing exercise. The other side of the coin is to find acceptance with consumers and avoid the fate of Charta.

The VDP system cuts out much of the excess information. It puts things into a quality cru system. There is First Growth level of *Grosses Gewächs/Erstes Gewächs/Erste Lage* wine, and if you have an interest in a region, there are not so many names to remember. Further, the wines are labelled distinctly as to set them apart as belonging to this club. At the next level, there are vineyards that do not make the top league but are still special enough to warrant the use of their site name. Again, not so difficult and the VDP can at the lowest level of education make it simple by stating if a wine is from a VDP member, (indicated on the bottle with the logo) and there are the words *Grosses Gewächs/Erstes Gewächs/Erste Lage* then this ranks in the premium level of wines. If the wine is from a VDP member and has a vineyard name without the use of the terms *Grosses Gewächs/Erstes Gewächs/Erste Lage* then it is from a classified site and sits in the bracket knocking on the door of the First Growths.

Take the approach of the consumer. He or she in time will have some understanding of the new system if it is well communicated. The VDP only need communicate the basics to the general consumer as I have set out above. The vast majority of wine buyers are not ever going to take in the mass amount of information behind the cru classification system. The purchase process needs to be made simple if markets are to be attacked. The VDP, if they promote their *verbund* and members well, are in a prime position to make consumers with only have a slight knowledge of German wine recognise those wines from the VDP members are largely the best Germany has to offer. This being the case, the consumer needs then only the basics of "1,2,3" in order to buy. (*eins, zwei, drei,* buy). It's a pretty simple dance to the checkout.

1.   the wine comes from a VDP member and thus is included in the best of German wines.

2.   the wine has *Grosses Gewächs/Erstes Gewächs/Erste Lage* on the label and thus comes from the First Growth level, and;

3.   the wine has a vineyard name but not the words *Grosses Gewächs/Erstes Gewächs/Erste Lage* but a vineyard name so it comes from the next tier in the pyramid. These wines provide excellent value for money.

The consumer will also wisely see a difference in price. The VDP by setting minimum price levels ensures there will be a differentiation between the levels. Wines from the top level cannot be sold for less than those down the quality pyramid. This is a particularly sensible tactic by the VDP. To those who might be worried that the prices are high, one can see that by world standards for premium wines that the prices are in fact low.[116]

Where does this create a difference from other German wines that are on the shelf? Sitting on the shelf next to them is a wine without VDP recognition and boundless amounts of information from *einzellagen, beriet,* and *gebiet.* We know that these factors are basically diluted and debased in the minds of wine consumers, largely being responsible for the present state of affairs with German wine. If the VDP are forceful and proactive they will try to re-inforce to consumers that on all wines other than those of their members the use of such a minefield of terms basically means nothing and that only their system provides a guarantee of both quality and of meaning something sensible. It is not egalitarian and probably not

---

[116] The Wine Spectator list of the top 100 wines for 2003 had in 8th place a German Riesling. This wine retails in the United States for $30. This was under half the price of any other wine in the top 100 listing!

very nice to do to brother producers but I cannot imagine for a moment Australian producers loosing sleep if they were faced with the same marketing decision. The VDP is there to represent its producers and having adopted the high moral ground on classification of terroir meaning quality they should not stand back from delivering the *coup de grace*. As a consumer what are you going to choose? The VDP have wisely created a *niche* which gives a guarantee. The other wine has none.

We have to be realistic and imagine that the vast majority of potential wine customers are probably not even interested in knowing this much about the classification system. The Italian classification system results in the highest priced wines often being from effectively the lowest wines in the pyramid. The consumer tells what is meant to be better quality by one determining factor and that is price. Still, German wines are a long way away from this luxury. Naturally, the VDP must spend time trying to educate about the entire system but should not fail to recognise the way with which most wine purchase decisions will be made. In order to reach those customers the VDP, in my opinion, needs to come up with point of sale marketing which demonstrates the quality pyramid in a nutshell. This is where the marketing boys can earn their money. Something along the lines of the "1,2,3" decision flow could be useful, perhaps it is communicated as "all you need to know about German wine".

The VDP classification is a very important step. This is the most major and well thought out piece attempt at codification in German wine history. There are still some rough edges but the key point is that the VDP have openly admitted this and have put in place a system that is designed with flexibility in mind. This works from the top down, in so much as the VDP has set uniform standards which go across the board and left matters of closer definition and codification to local regions. This is a major step and one which must be applauded. Regional associations or chapters of the VDP are able to specify matters such as yield, must weights, and select those sites which ought to be classified. It is a very healthy system. Not only for the fact that the people at the actual sharp end get to make a determination on what is happening in their region but it avoids the feeling of being directed from afar by pen-pushers who have never set foot in the winegrower's vineyard. All farmers are suspicious of regulatory authorities and the further the way you have controls the more it ends up looking like Brussels. The key is this interaction of local knowledge. This is a key feature as are the very un-Germanic statements by Prinz Salm Salm that things still need work and it is will be a model that takes place over time as things are developed. In addition, there is a way in and a way out. This means that a consistent non-performer can be "de-classified" and someone who has shown a long pattern of quality production can come in.

In brief, I believe that ultimate success of the VDP classification system will come in the fact that it will become a successful simple guarantee for consumers. The treasures of the First Growth wines will become special and sought after. With these the future reputation of German wine will rest. Anyone tasting German wines and wishes to compare them against the best from the rest of the world has a relatively small batch of wines to compare among the greats. This produces a trickle down effect, especially when wine advisors, sommeliers, buyers, and journalists are able to say good things about the best of the best but also mention that the quality of the next step down is also exceptional and provide great value for money.

Even so, there are a group of top German producers who are either not a member of the VDP or have not embraced the system. Their reasons vary but there is a unified theme that I have struck in talking with them. That theme is simply that if they are to use the classified site names then they are going to loose the ability to use anything other than classified site names on their wines. This means for many that they would have very little other than Guts wines or for simplicity estate wines. This would be the norm in the New World but for many traditional producers it means loosing something which has set apart their wines for a considerable period of time. If you are a small producer with an existing client base, it would be a drastic move to abandon the differentiation that you have built your selling base upon.

In addition, some producers feel that the system of classification means that in many cases only part of a vineyard is classified. Other producers who are not members of the VDP also may have holdings within that named site. Under the wine legislation, we must note that the VDP system is presently only applicable to its members, there can be a wine released as a First Growth wine by a VDP producer and labelled with the vineyard name and confusion created by another non-VDP member releasing a wine also with that site name despite the fact that it is not at the level of premier cru. This has the potential in some cases of debasing the value of the site name. Fortunately, the chances of this are few but it remains a disadvantage to the classification system and is only removed in the event that the scheme takes on universal effect.

Of the two new systems, the VDP classification has far more credibility and fewer holes than the system adopted by the DWI. This is not to say that the DWI system of "Classic" and "Selection" is without merit or application. In fact, many estates are using both "Classic/Selection" and the VDP model. Are producers having a bet each way? At the end of the day the proof will come in consumer acceptance of the wines. Producers are happy to use "Classic" in order to release entry-level wines finally with a correct acid/sugar balance. This sets such wines in a position to compete with the world of wine. German producers have been handicapped for too long with the under 9g/L residual sugar ball and chain and it is natural that they should want to utilise whatever the legislation allows them in order to better compete. At the other end of the spectrum, VDP producers, realise that to gain the lion's share of attention for great wines they must utilise the classification system.

Herr Löwenstein makes a very valid point in answer to the question of if elite terroir wines are the magic trick to rescue the German reputation. The key point of Löwenstein, and that I share, is that the concept of classification and terroir wine should not be used too heavily as a marketing tool. There has to be substance behind it and the challenge for the VDP will be to keep the First Growth system away from being merely a lot of talk.

Has all this tinkering made for a better system? At the moment it makes for yet another layer of information and confusion for the consumer. It could all go to mush and just make German wine more complicated. On balance I believe that the VDP classification will rise to the top due to the level of commitment behind it and for the fact that it is finally a return to a focus on the elite. "Classic" will also have its place, due to the fact that it finally frees producers from the strict *trocken* "prison". Not only is this opinion based on the belief that quality will out, but due to the fact that with the right push behind it the classification system can have a dual effect. That is, for the consumer with a high level of interest in German wine, they will make the effort to understand the classification. For the general consumer, if the marketing is kept simple by the VDP, then it has the potential to be a quality guarantee. This might not be quite what the VDP intend, but if it works then the VDP have achieved what they set out to do even if by a round about method. It is a step towards the hierarchical classification that is so desperately needed in order to bring the focus back to German wine and Riesling as its greatest varietal asset.

The Call to Arms: A Blueprint for Renaissance.

In the last 20 years Ernie Loosen hasn't got too many things wrong.[117] There is a first time for everything and I sincerely hope that he is proven to be incorrect about a "Riesling Renaissance"; that when it comes, it being lead by the New World. In my opinion, there can and will be a "Riesling Renaissance" and if played well it will come from Germany and its dedicated band of elite quality producers.

There is much work to do. It is a resurgence that will need to be lead ultimately by the producers. Their task is to continue to make stunning value for money wines, understand better marketing, and expect to have an overall strategy of representation clearly established by their representative bodies. A good encapsulation of the present situation facing small to mid sized elite wine producers is that it is hard to be a great winemaker, viticulturalist, and marketer all-in-one. Unfortunately, this is what is required. It suggests that there can only be a one strategy and that is to continue to make great wine, build the marketing around the tradition of the estate, and target the customer interested in knowing of the people behind the wine.

The clues to a renaissance are all there; an increase in sales, an increase in sales of more expensive wines, better winemaking, greater comprehension of marketing, and importantly a realisation that for things to get better a lot of effort needs to be made on developing what I would call the "brand German elite". Elite German producers should look to what has taken place in Barolo and Barbaresco. The wines from these regions were certainly always great, but the regions were sleepy and inward looking. With some changes in focus and the way they have been presented to the wine buying public they have gone beyond being a cult, reaching auction and allocation status.[118] Some cellars have modified their winemaking but in general they have relied upon traditional winemaking methods, just cleaning it up a little. They are not rushing to make wines that are for early drinking and releasing them in a Bordeaux shaped bottle.

It may seem strange to find this section is effectively the conclusion to my work, some distance from the end. The reason is a simple one.

---

[117] Ernie Loosen is one of Germany's elite producers and a leading figure in the industry. He has done much to set standards and outline the best pathway for the industry. This has not always made him popular with bodies such as the DWI.

[118] I use the term "auction and allocation" to indicate that these wines are now found in wine auctions around the world and many of the elite cellars are forced to sell their wines on an allocation basis much like the great names in France.

Consideration has been given to the source of Germany's wine industry woes in a world perspective and note made that the various regulatory bodies have understood this situation. Following from there, I have looked at both the DWI and VDP methods to bring about a change in this situation and return the image of German wines back to one of favour. This conclusion looks to the steps and direction German producers and their representative bodies should look to in capitalising upon their work. It is a drawing together of various points and thus serves as a conclusion. Part Four, which follows, is an analysis of the various terroirs classified under the new VDP system and is intended more as a reference section.

This text has largely centred on Riesling. Riesling defines the German wine industry in so many ways. Does this mean that all German wines benefit from a rebirth in the stature of Riesling? I think not. Müller Thurgau will never give great flavours and Silvaner, despite having its moments in Franken, will not be something to take on the World. Journalists have hammered this point for years but they will not solve the situation. A renaissance can have champions but it cannot be lead by great names in the wine writing field. It must be lead by producers and winemakers with a fundamental understanding that getting out and pushing your wines is the only true way to bring them to the attention of the wine buying public.

The strides made in wine quality have been more than evident to wine *cognoscenti* and German Riesling is on the way back. The keys to it will rest upon the fact that German producers have realised they can be justifiably proud about their wines. Sure, there is an element of elitism entering but given the fact that the Australian society prides itself on having an egalitarian attitude and remains highly elitist in terms of wine means that these two things can exist as harmonious if hypocritical bedfellows. By leading with your best foot forward people approach the lesser wines in a positive way.

There are some key points pointing as to why this renaissance is possible and they are probably more to do with an important shift in attitudes rather than as a result of a conscious industry plan.

First, young German winemakers are not abandoning the family estate for "city" jobs. Their parents have run estates during the period of the worst decline in German wine fortunes and gradually seen export markets erode. Vineyard land has its value, in the flatter parts, for building development and even if you wanted to sell the family business to someone interested in the backbreaking low profit work, they would unlikely be able to afford the price of the *"Winzerhof"* or building in which the winery is contained. Often they are of a historic nature, large, require expensive maintenance, and have a high value based on the real estate value rather than as a business.

Young members of traditional wine growing families, have probably like in no other time, been given the freedom to walk away from the work of their parents. Still many have opted for living what many office workers see as a dream. Many of the new generation have travelled to see what is happening in the New World and returned, realising, that with some effort and new thinking there is nothing stopping them shaping the future direction of their industry.

I feel the younger generation are look at the situation with a different perspective. Many of their parents came to the business out of family obligation, taking over when the good times were ending and the bad times beginning. As a result, they have only struggled and worked long hours including weekends, foregone holidays, and certainly no great financial reward. In making sure that they did not place the same burdens upon their children. They have been pleasantly surprised when their offspring voluntarily enter into the business.

This new generation enters with a different attitude, one that recognises quality only comes without compromise. If they plug away at it for long enough the world will notice this and start to pay a more realistic price. The young winemakers have the same goal and want to work together to set the direction of the industry. There is a greater general philosophy of pursuing top quality and an understanding that if they work together they can lift the image of the region, which in turn will benefit all. Part of the effort in this regard will to be to convince their peers that German wines are providing excellent value compared to imports. The convincing of their generation to be proud of German wines and the wine heritage will come with more international acclaim. First they require international acclaim to convince the domestic market that their wines are important.

Second, there is an increasing understanding that wine, especially top quality, is a hand sell product. This means getting out on the hustings; pouring wines at shows and at tastings. It means a lot of travel and effort but with high cost wines you need to get them closer to the end consumer in a variety of atmospheres. Wine event based tourism is becoming increasingly popular.

I attended a VDP step up tasting in London recently. Winery owner/winemaker/sales person/export manager attendance was optional meaning that there were plenty of wines to taste but few people standing behind them. This is not a way to get in contact with customers, journalists, importers, or restaurateurs. These wines are a hand sell product. Some days later I attended the Australia Day Tasting. There were in excess of 120 tables, often staffed by the winemaker, owner, or export manager. It costs a lot more to come over and explain the wines. Ryanair flys from Frankfurt Hahn, an airport bang slap in the middle of the best of Germanys wine regions, what I term the "Riesling Box".[119] Over early in the morning and out in the day means no hotel expense and the whole thing could be done for less than an investment of 100 Euro. What's going on?

After the Australia Day Tasting in London I prepared to set my appointments for Germany's big wine showcase ProWein. This is held every year in Düsseldorf and has steadily grown and now part of the annual wine show circus. The difference is astounding. Small producers, sometimes with 10 to 20 hectares had come to the London tasting in order to show their wines and try to find representation. It is a long way and despite the strength of the Australian dollar at present it is not a cheap exercise. On the other hand, when I called around various well-known German producers trying to set up meetings at ProWein I was left flabbergasted. At most, Düsseldorf is only a few hours drive compared to coming from the other side of the world. The 15 calls I made provide interesting results. All the wineries were rated "names" producing excellent wines after a long history of operation.

Of the fifteen, five were heading to ProWein with their own stand and one was going to be present on the stand of an importer. One never answers the telephone and another was able to get back to me by email that he would be there but without a stand. The rest are not in attendance. Only 2 of the effective 6 in attendance were able to provide via the first contact, (i.e. the receptionist) the hall and stand number where they would exhibit at the show. The others knew either something about it or had to put me in touch with someone else for the details. So much for the myth of German efficiency. I repeated the experiment with 15 similarly sized and status wineries from Italy. 12 of them were to be at ProWein and in 9 of the cases the receptionist was able to give me the stand location information at first attempt.

It is easy to take the moral high ground and say that this is one of the

---

[119] My idea of the Riesling Box is boarded by taking a line running from Neustadt a.d. Weinstrasse, Trier, Koblenz, and Wiesbaden. Inside this box fall the best Rieslings from the Pfalz, Mosel, Mittlerhein, Rheingau, Nahe, and Rhienhessen.

reasons the German wine industry has problems in selling and getting their message out to the world audience. Likely, it is not as simple as this. At the same time, it is only sloppy management that does not ensure the receptionist is part of the entire winery team and has such details to hand or is able to retrieve them without reference to the boss. If you have to lick the stamps then why do you employ someone to do it?

ProWein is an opportunity to sell. Yes, I can understand the response of some producers that do not go because it is expensive, or they do little business there. This is certainly the case also for many of the Italian producers that travel to ProWein, for them it can be more of a social occasion and one in which to network rather than a period of selling. I know from personal experience that it is hard to go to these shows and see very few people approach your stand. Many small to mid German producers seemed to have admitted defeat because this can be uncomfortable. Certainly the show is expensive but one can only use this as an excuse for non-attendance when the winery invests in attending other wine shows or events.

The comments of two of the producers I called were interesting. As family businesses of 20 hectares they thought they were too small to attend with their own stand but would like to attend in a group of other liked minded and sized producers from other regions. Nothing looks worse than a stand built to the lowest budget and without any customer footfall. Associates of mine in Italy have grouped together in such a way that they get together twice a year with a good-sized stand at two different shows. This makes for sharing of costs, better presentation, and more people moving about which also attracts interest. Such sharing of space can also lead to contacts being generated. The response from one of these German producers was that this sounded great but no one was making the initiative. I find this surprising as ProWein has a number of small groups that get together and present a joint stand. If you want to be in such a group, let's call it "small family producers" then call a few other such wineries and try to get together. You cannot expect it to be done for you.

Other wineries not in attendance stated that the show was too unspecific. This strikes me as strange. If you are a top German producer and want to make some noise then surely this is a place to do it. Ferrari always wants to win but especially at Monza. ProWein is the home circuit for German producers and they should be present. There will always be journalists and passing interest if you attack it full on. It is going to be difficult to attract journalists to one off visits to your winery. One winery was able to tell me that they sell all their wine and have no need for the show. This is great news for this producer and all around the world there are such examples. They are few and far between.

All of the wineries were exceptionally friendly and in some cases almost apologetic that they were not going to be in attendance. They need to find some way to band together in order to have some presence at the show.

Mass wine tastings can give a wonderful opportunity for both the big names and the small to attract journalists, clients, and give good public exposure. The VDP and DWI are highly proactive in setting these up. In the last few years the choice of venues and services, (such as clean glasses, spittoons, space at tables, prevention of smoking, and the like), have greatly improved. Even so, the timing of such tastings such give some wineries food for thought as to which are the key ones for them to participate. There is a seemingly endless stream of these "fairs" to attend and they are certainly not without their cost. A winery has to be realistic as to whom they can expect to see at such tastings and what state of evolution their wines are in before they stump up the funds for attending.

The Mainzer Weinbörse 2004, set up by the VDP, is a case in point. Held at the end of April most wineries were presenting a range of 2003 wines. These wines had generally been bottled in the last few weeks...if not days. Unfortunately, this means that most of their wines are suffering bottle shock (a phenomenon whereby the wine takes a wee bit of time before showing the fruit flavours it had just prior to bottling. This is due to high sulphur dioxide, final filtration, and hitting the bottle...hence the name). Professionals can get through this and make a mental adjustment but I wonder if for wine buyers, restaurant owners, and the general public if this is not a bit too much to expect. In fact, the wines show from 2002, demonstrated fantastic bottle development.

The DWI sponsors a tasting in the United Kingdom. Recently held at Lords' Cricket Ground, the show was well run and not different than those put on from Italy and other nations. In 2005, VDP members also had a separate presence. The event was well attended but mostly by students of wine schools and industry professionals tasting the opposition's wines. There were few actual buyers and members of the public were permitted to enter for a "happy hour" later in the day. Some criticism was levied and a feeling that the German Wine Institute in the United Kingdom needs to find a better way of presenting the wines to more eventual customers. Such criticism is a bit harsh given that those complaining were not able to make any suggestions as to how this should be done. If you do not think that it is working then you have to get in and make suggestions as to how you can do better.

There is a shift in the attitude of the German gastronomy sector, especially in the major metropolitan centres towards the listing of domestic wines. This is just what the Bernkastel Doktor ordered. Names that attract overseas attention are getting onto the right wine lists and giving greater credibility to the local wine scene.

There is a paranoid syndrome in Australia that visitors might not be finding the place good enough or not having a good time. It results in asking people if they are having a great time ten minutes after they have landed. It is a craving for approval from the rest of the world. To a degree I feel this also exists in relation to German wines. Gradually we are seeing that good world wide publicity for the elite German wines is turning into an awakening or understanding from German's that their wines really are very good. Our wines are trendy overseas? I better have a closer look. Germans are the first to admit that they will only think their products good if someone else from overseas tells them so. It is essential to ride this wave and capture this market in order to gain the attention of the next generation domestic drinker. The key is to avoid them thinking that only wines from Italy or the New World are chic. This is a generation not interested in egalitarianism. They are comfortable with elitism and do not want what every one can have. Exclusivity and hard to find things are good, it just must be also a mark that people know, otherwise it is not worth having. The age of people inside the Gucci, Max Mara, or Prada stores in Milan will give you this basic market research pretty quickly.

Publicity and strong links to lifestyle magazines, rather than just wine magazines, is key to advancing this cause. This brings attention from both a new audience and from a direction that allows diverse marketing attacks to be made rather than rely on specialist wine magazine; these are largely for the converted anyway. One has to think more closely to the marketing of premium beer.

The foregoing trends or shifts in market conditions can be primed or pushed by German producers. At the same time, it is impossible to be in the vineyard, winery, and taking care of marketing. Realistically, this is the work of representative bodies with limited funds. Producers must ensure that those funds are spent in the right direction by forceful representation inside both the VDP and DWI. Otherwise their contributions are being wasted.

No renaissance can take place without a patron. For so long the patron of the German wine industry had been the UK market and her journalists. No more. The English journalists will likely still write the most positive glowing articles about wonderful Riesling they find but their market is no longer geared to buying significant volumes of aristocratic German wines. Distribution channels, supermarket sales, the development of a public with a very "commercial" palate means that the best German wines will gain a foothold only in limited more specialised outlets, (which are becoming less profitable and thus further looking at their needs to turnover), and in restaurants. For the German producers to follow the UK market they are going to have to develop a means to attack these largely unfamiliar market channels and finding ways of getting their wines to far away restaurants.

It is hardly a surprise that the new patron of the renaissance for German Riesling will be the Americans and Japanese. They have the money, are less sensitive to price, and always keen to buy a slice of tradition. As a note to German producers, packaging must reflect that desire rather than a wholesale run to mimic the New World. In the case of the Japanese market, their food also fits well with Riesling and one wonders if as the future economic superpower of China can be convinced to take the odd bottle or two. Any rich patron of the arts will want the best. This is where the German elite producers stand the greatest chance.

We have seen that the main representative bodies have reacted to the situation facing German wine. The DWI have chosen to lead their attempts at rebuilding via the modification of the rules to permit two new "categories" of wine. These are "Classic" and "Selection". In summary, "Classic" provides a path for producers to finally release a wine that is "internationally dry". This is something that German producers have needed for many many years and is a way to at last let them release wines that appear dry which have balanced acid and sugar levels.[120] "Classic" will find widespread use, if not as a means of trying to market a wine but as a way to release an internationally dry style. Many producers will use the category and not make much noise if any about the "classic" aspect. "Selection" on the other hand, is a bastardisation of a single vineyard name. Very few producers will use it and fewer buyers will purchase based on the concept alone.

The VDP have, for the first time in the management of the German wine industry attempted to frame quality factors of guarantees based not on sugar levels but on terroir. They are to be applauded for taking on this

---

[120] I have seen a New Zealand Riesling recently listed in the UK, which has a residual sugar level of 12gm/L. It is being offered as a dry style.

task and getting solid support behind it. Full credit to the team at the VDP, lead by Prinz Salm Salm. Not only is there an understanding that terroir drives quality, but there is an understanding that one should not be afraid to say so. The VDP have understood that someone buying a litre bottle of Riesling really is unlikely to be fussed as to what vineyard it comes from whereas those buying at the highest level are likely to be more concerned. Their 3-Tier model provides a way of classifying vineyard quality. We have seen upon what factors this is based.

In addition, we have seen a number of the criticisms of the model by various leading players in the German industry. Further, we have seen that the first level of wines is complicated by not having any ready built name. Erste Lage, Erstes Gewächs, Grosses Gewächs, and Edelsüsser Spitzenwein are looking like four distinct categories. Despite the fact that they cover the same level of wines and merely delimit the region from which they originate, it is too much confusion for the wine buying public. It will be hard to get an accord from all the regions as to which, if any, should prevail. A universal "handle" is needed and quickly by the VDP. The additional challenge for the VDP is to communicate their classification system to the wine buying public and to demonstrate its merits.

The key to the VDP model is the way with which it can be communicated to the rest of the world. The particulars of it are difficult and not the sort of thing most wine buyers are going to spend any more time on other than to assess it is difficult. The VDP need to basically say, "over there are the rules, but what you need to simply know is….". The detail is there for those who are interested but the VDP must avoid this at all costs and merely hammer the thought through to consumers that "GG/EG/EL" is a guarantee that this is from the best of German wine. This is where one starts to question the wisdom of letting in both Weissburgunder and Silvaner. These grapes just provide white wine like many of the nondescript Italian white quaffers and questionably rank in terms of greatness, whereas no one can compete with the regal nature of Riesling, or its maximum expression, German Riesling. They are not international great varieties and have no real regal pedigree. It is hardly likely that the world is about to be wooed by an attack of the bocksbottle.

Despite these attempts at repair, there remain a number of problems that need addressing. Producers of wine in Germany still run excessively long lists of wines to the point of dullness. There appears to be a fear of making cuvees. Some producer's lists of wines run to fifty in any given year. This is generally composed of wines from various sites and then various levels of ripeness from them. Justification of this is only found on the fact that some of the wines have a particular market and without offering those wines clients go elsewhere. This is an understandable desperation to maintain whatever market a producer has no matter how small. One can imagine supplying a wine due to the fact that one has some remaining clients for it. This must be persuasive given the woes of the industry. At the same time, it is not forward looking and only serves to increase costs. In addition, it is impossible to market such an array of wines. Going to a particular wine tasting, how do you select from 50 wines those that you would present. Consolidation of the wine range needs to take place and in many cases the idea of keeping the juice from one particular vineyard separate from the other needs to be reassessed.

This consolidation needs to take place both at the level of assumed "quality" *prädikats* and with the *einzellagen*.[121] Producers are often taking from each vineyard fruit that goes into as many steps of the QmP ladder as they can. Others are harvesting at higher levels and downgrading so as to reach the more saleable *Kabinett* grade. Within all these prädikats there are often different expressions of styles. *Spätlese* is sometime sweat sometimes not. There is too much variation and this has made German wines difficult, unpredictable, and at worst confusing. The result of this we have seen. It is unrealistic to expect someone to come out and state, "all *Spätlese* styles are meant to be dry" (or better still internationally dry). Matters are well past the point of no return. Still, producers must understand the need to look at their entire winemaking portfolio and make some decisions. Certain vineyards should be the ones used for trying to get to the highest level of QmP ripeness each year and others providing a particular wine might be better as part of a blend. This, in turn, is likely to see less use of *einzellagen*, so reducing further the clutter and confusion.

Producing wines merely because they come from different sites is not a true justification for their release. This is narrow thinking, and from a winemaking point of view makes little sense. This is merely a liquid handling exercise, rather than a winemaker creating a blend from various assets in the cellar. It is a little bit like going to a restaurant and being given a bowl of flour and a bowl of eggs and having to make a cake in your stomach. A cuvee or blend can often be a better wine than the

---

[121] No one can be expected to remember many of these and basically the public understands them to be generally worthless as a descriptor of a particular site. At least in Italy when you see "Vigna" before a name you know that it is meant to come from one particular vineyard in the hands of the producer rather than a blanket zone.

individual parts. Cuvees can be made at both the entry-level wine and at the higher quality levels.

One winery that is doing this particularly well is Reichsrat von Buhl. They are evidence of a winery with a number of 1er sites and plenty of cru wines. In addition, they are releasing a number of cuvees, particularly at the *Spätlese* level with plenty of harmony and structure. These wines are ideal for the restaurant sector as they are multidimensional. Reichsrat von Buhl is very progressive and shows a comprehensive understanding of the need to release wines along such lines to target international markets.

German wineries need to understand a three-layer level of winemaking. The entire world of winemaking has understood this but the Germans have been handicapped by reliance on sugar as a means of supposedly determining quality. Perhaps the VDP 3-Tier model will help their members look more closely at wine categories. Many good estates are already doing this. Still, many have a basic entry level QbA wine and then move into the minefield of QmP ripeness levels. It is key to have an entry-level wine, a range of mid level wines, and your reserve. Should the winery be proactive enough these can also be distinguished by different marketing of each level.

Mosbacher, in the Pfalz, has the right idea. Their entry-level wines are made ready to drink with the maximisation of fruit characteristics. This has to be done with acid manipulation and reductive handling. There is good use of reductive winemaking going on in the entry and mid level with plenty of up front fruit drive in the wines. The mid level wines are looking to be terroir specific and demonstrate at the same time a "house" style. A "house" style in my opinion is where the winemaking methods used also accord with the overall philosophy of the estate and the owners. They say owners look like their dogs, but in the case of a good winery where the owners probably pay more attention to their wines than their children; one can see certain elements of character coming out in the wines. At Mosbacher the idea is also that the 1er wines (Freundstück and Ungeheuer) should look towards a niche. They will not be exactly what every one is after but at the same time the small volume means you only have to find a few like minded individuals in the world who adore that flavour profile in order to sell your product. This is the realisation of a three tier winemaking model. Your cash-cow volume wine is at the base, terroir specific wines sit in the middle, and your elite multi-faceted wine at the top.

In terms of releasing ready to drink entry level wines, the tag "Classic" should be ideal. At the same time, the VDP First Growth model is ideal

173

for the release of wines at the tip of the pyramid. It will come as no surprise that many of the VDP members are preparing to release their wines as such.

One error that needs to be avoided is too much focus on red wine production. Yes, you can make reds in Germany and good winemaking tricks turn out an acceptable drink. In some cases, such as Pinot Noir, excellent variations on this style can result. For the general red production we are seeing silly prices being asked for wines that are really not a match for equivalent priced offerings from elsewhere in Europe. In trying to get a consistent good red from most regions in Germany, it will mean the replanting on the best sites which, in my opinion, should steadfastly remain planted with Riesling.

Many German producers are correct in stating that there is no middle ground with their wines. That is, there are bargain basement wines and expensive wines. What they mean is that there is a wide gap between those wines at the entry level of the market and those at the top. Even if people try Liebfraumilch, there is no next step. Customers can only move onto the wines of the New World, which are rock solid at the mid price level. There needs to be a ladder. Large wineries or bottlers are trying to address this with their offerings such as "Bend in the River" by trying to improve their wines and effectively brand them. Will such "brands" bridge the gap between the image of Liebfraumilch and the level of First Growth? It remains to be seen.

In my opinion, the way to solve this problem is by developing better cuvees and using the fantastic winemaking talent that exists in Germany. I am not talking about the need to build cuvees at the QmP level as I have set out above. This is a different topic. Here we are looking at entry level bridging to mid level wines. German wineries need to think outside the square. The problem has been for mid to large German wineries to get listings with national distribution or major multiples. This has a lot to do with the fact that for German wines there is competition for maybe two or three shelf slots and one of these is likely taken by Ernie Loosen. Other countries compete for a larger array of shelf places.

All the same, one cannot give up without a fight. Resurgence in German wine popularity might see these slots expand slightly. The lowest price in a major multiple for German wines is likely one that they have arranged under their own label. Many good supermarkets and major multiples do have their own brand entry level German offerings. There will also likely be the ubiquitous Liebfrau. The challenge in this sector is to provide the bridge. I feel this can be done by looking not at small regions or particular sites. One has to study many of the wines from the New World that fit into this slot. Most of such wines are produced from grapes grown in an area called South East Australia. This is an area that takes in a massive amount of territory.

Why should German wineries limit themselves to blending from one region? No, I am not trying to reinvent Liebfraumilch in suggesting blending wines from various regions with out reason. We are talking about a different price level and if one looks closely there are a lot of very good wines that are made in large volumes in Germany. In addition, many mid sized producers make excellent wines for which they have no market. Interestingly, there is a project in the Rheingau to take some of this excess liquid from small top quality producers and release it as a branded offering.

Marks and Spencer have done exactly this. Gerd Step, who hails from the Pfalz, is the winemaker for M&S, has put together a wine released as "Mineralstein". It is a blend of wines from both the Mosel and Pfalz. This results in the wine being tagged a Deutscher Tafelwein, but who, when buying German wines in this category is really interested. Attractively packaged there is nothing to separate it in looks from most of the New World Rieslings that are trying to mimic German packaging. The only thing that separates it is that it is a wonderful cuvee and I believe provides exactly the bridge between the entry level and the reserve. Can medium to large wineries in Germany do the same? I believe so. Other cross regional wines will start to be developed as German producers see this as a way to build this bridge and make a wine showing off more than one stylistic aspect of German wine regions.

There is no quick fix, but at the same time one could only describe German producers as some of the most philosophical in the world. There is no blanket repair manual that can be given as each estate is different and founded upon a diverse set of values. This is what gives the wine industry its characters and charm. Even so, I feel there are some overall strategy directions that should be considered.

Essential is the need to understand each size wineries target market. Let us consider for argument sake that German wineries can be classified into effectively small, medium, and large. The small producer has to continue focusing much like they have effectively done. Their outlet is the passing public, private clients, their local (or even their own) restaurant, and at best domestic wine shops. They are limited by volume as to where they can look for markets. As a result, their costs are generally reduced by doing most of the work themselves. If they can make advances it will be likely in consolidating the range they offer and bringing their packaging into line with the requirements of the modern consumer. Saving costs, developing demanded reserve wines with a slight rarity factor, and working on entry level wines to give turnover will produce results.

The mid sized producer faces one of the hardest points in the current market. They do not have the critical volume mass to attack large distribution channels and must also serve the market targeted by the small producer. They must spend a lot time and investment targeting the specialist wine shop trade, restaurants, and at the same time potentially look to export. They are getting squeezed on both sides and have to play the game based largely on their individualism and quality. Most of the members of this group are effectively the elite producers in the German market. They have, in the past, often been very good at promoting themselves to their clients but not worked as a team in terms of trying to create a "brand German elite".

Until recently the elite were asleep and not talking up their wines with only a few exceptions. They were happy to provide information on their individual estate and their wines but there was not a unified concept of elite quality estates. The iconic producers largely had a different story and there appeared to be little industry vision as to the future. It was not difficult to understand from elite producers what was wrong in the industry but it was harder to find harmony on as what should be done. Effectively there was no segmentation of the German industry in the minds of the wine buying public. For instance, if you take the Italian industry during the same period, there became a group of elite producers (Sassicia, Gaja, and so on) who were recognised both by price and quality to be at the pinnacle of the industry. Then there were your everyday cheap co-operative produced wines. At the same time, there existed a middle bracket of producers that acted as a stepping-stone. Germany has for a long time needed to separate the elite and to demonstrate there are a lot of excellent mid sized mid level producers.

A mid sized producers need to look at cuvee building and also how they structure their entry-level wines. Often many of the wines so presented as entry level from these estates need to be considered as actually mid level. Due to the fact that the estate really has very little to offer as entry level they are forced to provide better wines in this category. They need to look at regional and cross regional blends in order to provide the volume for their estate wines, so shifting their own vineyard production up in to the mid level category. This should not sound strange. Consider how many wineries around the world work on this basis. In many cases they are not even crushing or fermenting the fruit but putting a blend together marketing it under their name. They do not need to crush, ferment, or hold the finished wine stocks. This dramatically reduces costs given the spare capacity in Germany.

Mid sized wineries in Germany seemingly make very little marketing use of their winemakers. This is likely because it is seen more as a job rather than somewhat artistic. The New World and even countries such as Italy use the winemaker as an effective marketing tool. This is something German wineries should make better use of.

We can also see the rise in producers releasing wines with particular names. This took off largely in California and spread to Australia. It is a means of differentiating your wine, be it a "Judge and Jury" Chardonnay, "Graveyard" Syrah, or a Grange (Hermitage). Like any other form of vineyard description they are generally based on historical geographic references. They are names that are effectively brands within the producer's range. The use of such names is basically to create an *einzellagen*. The fact that Germany has confusing use of *Gebeit, Bereich*, and *Einzellagen* means that in many cases these terms have become devalued as a marketing tool. The VDP direction is the way for their members to return some sensibility in terms of the names. That is, those wines at the top level will have the vineyard name as well as *EG/EL/GG* in order to delineate they are from the highest representative category. The next step down *(KL)* also permits the use of the vineyard name but for the *Guts* and *Ortswein* there can be no use of vineyard names. Such wines do not need the support of a vineyard name, nor do they need to be vineyard specific. Removing their use by VDP members means that their wines so released will be seen more easily as an estate cuvee.

We have looked at the requirements upon producers for labelling and how the artificial "quality" rules based on sugar is not a helpful system. German producers are handicapped in this regard. Some are learning they must keep all the unnecessary information on the "back" label. Further, the creation of "Classic" as a category will permit the release of internationally dry styles, so reducing one of the problems in needing to release trocken wines that are unbalanced. Many New World wines are half dry or halbtrocken but you will never see it on the label and few will detect it and only then if the wine is unbalanced. I witnessed a wine recently being considered for listing by a major UK supermarket chain. It was a New Zealand Riesling with 12gm/L of residual sugar but nowhere on the label was there any indication that it was halbtrocken.

It is important for all German producers, especially the mid sized wineries, to play a strong Riesling card. This is to ensure compact focus on what Germany is about. New Zealand Riesling is still a peripheral wine but their Sauvignon Blanc is not. Mid sized German producers need to show what fruity, crisp, and complex wines they have in order to ensure that this is the benchmark style of Riesling. No one in their right mind would argue that Pinot Grigio from Italy is anything like the personification of this style from the Alsace but the wine buying public has little understanding of Alsacian Pinot Gris and as a result, the Italians have taken not only the market but are dictating expectations as to what flavours should be found in the bottle. Italians are releasing Pinot Grigio of dubious origin in large commercial volumes. German producers must not let that happen to their Riesling.

Packaging is a key issue for all German producers. There needs to be some modernisation. I am not advocating the removal of traditional bottle shapes, colours, and labelling wholesale. In fact, rather the opposite, as I believe the traditional German package is one of the foundations of rebuilding. Certainly there needs to be some greater understanding of design and the removal of unnecessary information from the front label as this provides the first impression for customers. This is not difficult to do and I have considered this more fully in Appendix One. The potential new patrons of the German wine industry, (America and Japan) like the idea of tradition and as a result the label and bottle must reflect this. At present there is a trend by some German producers to ape New World packaging. Trying to hide your wines in things to look Italian or New World is not a long-term solution.

We see the use of non-traditional Anglo names, vile coloured picture labels, and the widespread use of the bordelaise bottle. In certain sectors, I am sure that this is not such a bad idea in order to pursue the entry level "Generation X" first time wine drinker. On the other hand, it is short sighted from mid sized producers to be going down that track. It is frightening that while many German producers are heading in this direction, the good producers of Riesling in the New World are trying to package their wines is Germanic style cladding. This is from the bottle shape, colour, and in many cases label design. The labels are not trying to fake family crests or German gothic script, but the set out and positioning, even if there is a sketch of their own vineyard, has a remarkable semblance to the German original. Pewsy Vale, Pipers Brook, and Petaluma are three names that if one looks at the packaging it is not at first blush Australian. The majority of Rieslings released in Australia now also use screw top closures. This is a direct example of the regions working together. Clare Valley producers got together and declared en masse they would move over to this type of closure. It has worked. The public do not think the wine is cheap, nor is it, and the quality backs up the price. The packaging has a German look and these wines are selling around the world. German mid level producers should study them closely.

In summary, the mid sized producer needs to promote their tradition and terroir. They need greater focus on the winemaker, cuvees, consideration of moving their current entry level wines to their mid bracket by putting together sourced wine blends, concentrate on their packaging, and be happy to see a movement focusing on the elite producers. It is not easy, but it can be done.

One has to be realistic. Overnight German wineries are not going to be able to convert to the production of only middle to upper level wines. There still needs to be some sort of outlet for the entry level. Even so, cleaning up the wines and emphasising the fruit structure should mean that they are ready to compete in these price brackets with the New World wines that are presently sector dominating. The key customer demands here are for fresh fruit and with a bit of zippy acid in order to give freshness. This is exactly what German wines at this level define. The historical problem has been poor winemaking in this sector. Faults were allowed to develop in the ferments. They received little attention due to the attitude of being able to clean wines up later on. Moving over to better winemaking means more factory like production but such wines must be produced on this basis. Australian wineries do not refer to parts of their winery as "tank farms" without having a resemblance to a paddock filled with stainless steel.

The large winery operation in Germany, or bulk commercial producers, need to shift their focus to better value for money wines. Largely they provide well priced wines and have understood that if they want to sell their wine they must respond to what the customer wants in order to compete on an international scale. Does this mean losing some of the tradition? Yes, to some degree. At the same time it is hard to really say there is any specific flavour or tradition behind wines in this market sector when they are blended from diverse vineyards. It can be said that in many ways these wines reflect very much the varietal, and that varietal is actually called German Riesling.

This is not such a bad thing as it can provide great value for money, incentive to trade up, acceptance, familiarity with German wine, and it importantly demonstrates exactly why terroir specific wines set themselves apart from the entry level. In order to produce consistency and volume, one requires a brand. We can see a number of major bottlers in Germany have been attempting to do this and with an international focus. At the same time, a number of volume producers who remain focused on the domestic market still try to release wines that are cheaply packaged and in one case retain, I kid you not, an embossed monkey climbing up the bottle.

The potential downside with big brands is that they tend to dumb down the whole wine scene. Can this be avoided? I think so. The idea must be to fight the New World at its own game. Using modern packaging, they are trying to copy cat the offerings on the shelf from New World producers at the same price. Will such wines just look like mutton dressed up as lamb or will they provide the bridge between the former cheap German offerings and making the majority of producers look presentable? In a real case of trying to hide where you are from we are seeing a lot of offerings in bordelaise bottles with names such as "Fire Mountain" and "Bend in the River". I feel these wines can meet with success. The producers have, from a commercial winemaking point of view, thought out the quality parameters. This was not something that happened in the past. Further, they are being targeted at a new generation of wine drinkers who has seen no great influx of New World offerings, as for them they have always existed. This is the market reality and effectively these "new" German brands are the market entrants. The challenge is to present a wine that can compete in terms of quality, flavour, and packaging.

The key for German producers as a whole is to ensure the entire industry is not tarred with the same quality image brush. In order to do so, there needs to be delineation between the big commercial operations and the more elite in the industry. Prior to the creation of the VDP Classification, there was no such tool. This time around the quality producers have found a way to differentiate themselves.

Consumers can easily see the difference in quality Australian wines and those that are more or less commercial products. This is done in the packaging, price, and style of promotion. German top class producers need to play the coloured cards and set themselves apart. The key will be to move attention and even production away from the Liebfraumilch and medium sweet offerings. Quality producers need to push their big asset; Riesling. Even big bottler's branded products are made from blends of varieties the key for the elite will be to make the Riesling grape the focal point.

White wine is under considerable sales pressure but this merely provides the right chance for German producers to fix quality, styles, and marketing in order to compete. Having looked recently at a swathe of New World Rieslings, the Germans have little to fear in terms of the gap in quality especially in terms of value for money. For the moment; pride comes before a fall. The New World will not stand still and looking at their interpretations of Riesling there are certain stylistic elements emerging. Wines with petrol notes are few and far between. The latest DWI statistics are starting to show a decline in purchases for the lower price category wines (under £2.50) and an increase in the over £6 bracket. This is all good news for quality producers. The trend also seems to see an increase in the mid level price point, largely on "branded" products. All-in-all this is most encouraging. It will take a long long time for Germany to rebuild its wine reputation and consumer trust.

The key is not to blush about what the big bottlers are doing. The key is to try to make them act responsibly and for the good of the industry. There will always be a market for bulk style wines. The tragedy in Germany was that the big guys continued to "flog a dead horse" with the production of such rubbish that was acceptable in the 1970s but only served then to give the entire industry a bad name. Most of the regions in Germany will always have the two-sided coin, such as top quality producers and the bulk bottlers. The latter must concentrate on finding their way with international styles. This means that well made, overtly fruity wines, giving good value for money, well packaged, and targeted to what is demanded by consumers then this should be able to be satisfied eminently well by the varieties and regions of Germany.

The smaller wineries have a different path to travel. This must be one of individualism. It is an individual story of family tradition, vineyard ownership, and particular wine philosophy. All these things can be communicated through ones winemaking and wine philosophy. Individual wines are an expression of the individual winemaker. This allows for more creative winemaking; from the use of indigenous yeasts to how the wines are matured (for example in old large oak casks).

Germany has a number of wine assets which have to date not been played well. If we look to Italy again as an example we see considerable focus on wine tourism. Wine events, cultural events, the development of a "Strada del Vino", agritourismos (or farm stay) linked to the winery, and "Cantine Aperto" where wine cellars in a region open on certain days of the year with a programme for inspection and tasting. Such concepts exist in Germany and have done for many years, (apart perhaps for the Cantine

Aperto). The marketing of tourism centred on wine has not been centralised, focused, advertised, or an overall direction attack developed. This is despite part of the Pfalz being described as the Deutsche Weinstrasse. Other wine events are gradually starting to emerge such as the Rheingau Gourmet Festival, which links various cultural events and the wine region. Other than that, the effort is largely made by the individual producer to develop their own cultural programme. This has been done well by cellars such as Dr Bürklin Wolf but few cellars in Germany have the size to run such an operation. Work needs to be done in finding an event for each region linking culture and wine.

Another area that needs industry focus is linking wine with food. "PacRim2 or Asiatic style cuisine is ideal with Riesling. Problem is that the DWI thinks that the way to promote German wine is with German food. This is not the way to promote anything other than a coronary attack. Asparagus might be the exception but for the rest they should be considering the shift in eating habits that have taken place across the world and look more closely to links with Asian and Mediterranean fusion foods.

There is a need to concentrate on the elite and attract the attention of powerful critics with flagship wines. The power of important critics shapes wine purchases. This is the way the market has moved. Anyone who has tasted great *Eiswein* will immediately recognise it is going to score huge points from such critics and in the simplistic translation of what Robert Parker gives 95+ for on Sunday, is certainly sold out Monday. Top German producers stand to only benefit from such reviews in a market that has the money to buy out top end wines. Further, there is a trickle down effect that produces an image benefit for other wines.

Quality and tradition need not be seen in a negative light. It is a time for aggressive tactics from representative bodies. Consider what Spurrier did in France many years ago with New World Chardonnay. Why not set up a similar taste off in London, Berlin, or for that matter in Sydney with the best of Germany? Fly out a group of journalists and put them to the test. If Jancis Robson writes that the top 15 out of 30 wines were all German then spend the money and stick it up the Australians by advertising in the wine press....and use an Ozzie expression such as "thanks for coming mate!" As an Australian I know this would drive them insane and the resultant fallout would bring considerable attention onto German wine in the world wine press.

To be well regarded internationally again the German producers are going to have to do what no one else can as well as them and that is surely Riesling. It is important that there is a mix of tradition and technology. There is no point in making tradition just for tradition sake. "World famous in Germany" can be moved on to real worldwide recognition.

Part Four

The Right Stuff

"Wine growers don't spend their winters pruning their vines with reddened hands or get up in the small hours to keep an eye on their fermentation for reasons of social prestige. The do it to express their passion for a place and a perfectionism felt by few of the workers who make the stuff that ends up on supermarket shelves."[122]

---

122 P.268 Patrick Mathews, <u>The Wild Bunch</u>. Faber

The Classifications and Their Teroirs

This chapter deals with the classification of German Estates. We have discussed the ratification of the VDP system. The aims of this chapter are to provide an *aide memoir* to the various cru. Matters at present are highly fluid, with modifications to the list of classified sites and the wines emerging from them. In writing about the sites I understand it is immediately out of date. Even so, the terroir basis remains constant.

It is hard to find a time at which to stop, or to want to, working on this section. In a lifetime things will not only change but so will winemaking philosophies at the various estates. Each vintage is different. Sites demonstrate different aspects which are more attractive in certain years. For example, sites with good water holding capacity will not suffer from water stress in hot years, so giving better-balanced and riper fruit.

During the 16th Century village names began to be used as a wine description. Later, the use of the year to provide vintage information came into vogue and this trend has not left us since. The Germans launched varietal labelling sometime in the 19th Century as they did with using the vineyard name in conjunction with the village to describe a wines providence. As a result, we have reached the present day system of describing a wine based on variety, vintage year, village location, and vineyard name.

Despite the focus of this book being largely on Riesling and why this variety is instrumental to the revival of the German wine image I have not limited the list or notes to only sites containing this variety. Riesling sites cover the major part of the classification as can be imagined due to its level of importance in the German industry but it makes sense to provide a better picture of the VDP classification as possible. Many producers such as Weingut Dr Bürklin Wolf and Weingut Heymann-Löwenstein have done extensive research on their terroir holdings. This chapter cannot expect to have the scope or intensity of such works.

Riesling, like no other white variety, gains incredible finesse with age. One must take this factor into account when looking at the First Growth wines in particular. Such wines will have a proclivity to age extremely well which makes it a shame to try to draw judgments on them in such an early phase of their development. Some can certainly be enjoyed now, but in general they will improve with age and start to demonstrate more of the differences in the terroir that creates them.

I must note membership of the VDP is meant to be for those wineries judged as belonging to be the elite of German wine production.

It is a fantasy to believe that the VDP has all the best of the German estates or that all those within the VDP are actually at that standard. Some of the industry elite chose for whatever reason not to be members of the VDP and some estates are probably very lucky to actually remain as members. We can see the recent welcoming of Weingut Müller Catoir to the ranks of the VDP Pfalz gives further credence to the VDP. Congratulations to both parties.

In many cases, I have assembled the notes on sites based on communications with the actual winemakers. Comments from the actual winemakers gives an insight into what aspects the particular terroir raises and what stylistic direction they wish to demonstrate. In some cases the winemaker is also the owner of the estate but I have tried to go direct to the source rather than having to read between the marketing lines. It would be impossible to thank all those who have given their time and wine to the completion of this section.

Further, I have been fortunate as a unknown budding author to have many producers pour their wines for me at tastings without their being any "official" basis to it. This has allowed me to taste wines as the public sees them and to make what I hope is a highly independent analysis. Any tastings of wines that are included in this section were made without the estate or winemakers knowledge that the wines were being tasted for inclusion within this book. Thank you to all those who have stood, discussed, and poured wines without any expectations.

I have tried to be as independent as possible in my assessment of any wines. All wine assessment is a subjective process. As a winemaker you certainly have your list of likes and dislikes. The advantage you have an understanding where some of the notes in wines have come from. Over pressing or poor post fermentation maturation can give an insight into the equipment a winery relies upon and the cellar practices. These matters are outside of style characteristics and poor performance in this regard deserves to be slated. Aspects that run more to the wines stylistic direction, such as heavy fermentation lees notes, or oak maturation are decisions of wine style and have been made due to the owner's philosophy, preference, or the historical production methods of the estate. I may or may not like them. At the same time, if the wines are well-made and express characteristics of their terroir then I must put my personal preferences away and comment on the value of the resultant wine.

Germany has a number of varied terroirs on a macro scale. In my opinion there are only a few grape varieties that can fully give expression to them. Riesling is one variety that can do this. It begs the question of if some of the Burgunder grape varieties, despite how nice they might be, actually belong at the level of First Growth in Germany. Their inclusion, despite the fact that they may be head and shoulders above the more mundane expressions of their production within Germany, does not make them anything of note on a world stage. It takes a bit of the gloss off the VDP classification.

The list of sites is as complete as possible at the time of publication. I doubt that there will be more than a handful of new entries and from some of the sites we may never see First Growth wines appear, given a decision of the owner regarding the wines.

Officially a detailed analysis of climate and terrain has only been made in the Rheingau. In other regions a handful of producers have undertaken studies with reference to their own sites in a sensible attempt to explain the differences in their wines. The lack of scientific backup is somewhat incredulous given the fact that so much about everything has always been studied in Germany. In addition, the wine regions are not so expansive that studies would be overly difficult. In the end result, a study of any wine region will most likely confirm local knowledge, hard earned in the school of life. A scientific analysis of a region's terroir means an additional weapon on the marketing front. It gives credibility to maintaining a discussion on "these sites are our best".

Of all the major regions, the Rheingau lends itself to an easy study given its geographical boundaries. The Rheingau study was undertaken by the region of Hessen, which indicates that there are funds available for this sort of thing. Many regions in Italy have undertaken terroir studies such as Franciacorta, the Valtellina, and Chianti. These studies were funded jointly by producers and the state. A scientific study can assist in suggesting what clones, varieties, and styles of wines could potentially be made on a site. Consultant winemakers and viticulturalists are often called upon to make such recommendations in order to find the best vines to plant on a specified site. They do so using analysis of soil, microclimate, and knowledge of what vines perform best under the conditions found.

At the same time, there are winemaking factors not taken into account by a straight scientific study. The elimination of sites based on scientific numbers took place with the late Georg Breuer in Rüdesheim. Due to the fact that one of his top sites did not come up best in the scientific analysis it meant that it was not considered by the Rheingau chapter of the VDP for inclusion as an *Erstes Gewächs*. I feel there would be little dispute that the site was anything other that First Growth. Still, the analysis ruled the day. One wonders if there might have been a bit of politics taking place.

All the regional boards, when selecting or ratifying the First Growth sites, used a combination of local knowledge, old tax payment systems (*steuerkarte*), and a system of inspection by their committee. The registration of the participating sites is as individual parcels or *parzellengenau*, which means a vineyard site can be segmented down into a particular delimited part to be used for only First Growth wines, whilst the remainder of the site would retain its *Klassifizierter Lage* status. In addition, ten vintages of wines had to be presented from the site and these all had to show outstanding quality in order to be regarded as great. In reality, most of those looking at the wines would have had experience of a greater number of vintages from those sites again demonstrating the value of local knowledge.

In the following regions the listings of the *Klassifizierter Lagen* correspond with the *Grosses Gewächs Lagen*; Mosel-Saar-Ruwer, Nahe, and Rheingau (with the limitation that for the *Erstes Gewächs Lagen* individual parcels have been defined.) What this means is that all the sites listed as *Klassifizierter Lagen* have the potential to produce First Growth wines. Thus, the First Growth category for those regions effectively "floats".

There are a number of *Klassifizierter Lage* (KL) and if you are a producer with such sites and feel that in a particular year the wines are of *Grosses Gewächs/Erstes Gewächs/Erste Lage* (GG/EG/EL) status then you submit them for approval. Naturally, the committee and the VDP are not really keen on seeing things make the cut and then fall back out. Neither are the wineries, as it is a risky game to say one year the wines are First Growth and the next not. Despite the fact that the wines are still likely of very good quality as *Klassifizierter Lage*, it is likely difficult to explain to customers that in one year the wines seem to have taken a backwards quality step. You are better to remain with consistency and as a result only select wines from sites that will consistently obtain GG/EG/EL status. When in doubt it is better to release the wine with KL status.

Tilbert Nägler, of Weingut Dr. Nägler, is a direct case in point. He has three premium vineyards which are all covered as First Growth. He is choosing to run with the Berg Rottland site for his annual stab at the *Erstes Gewächs* wine. This is due to the fact that the vineyard holds its water better than his Berg Schlossberg and Berg Roseneck vineyards. The Berg Rottland also has a greater level of quartz and slate giving, dare I say it, higher levels of "classic" mineral notes. The high the water holding capacity in the Berg Rottland means greater potential for ripeness and the wines that result being full bodied. Berg Roseneck wines are generally more fruity lending themselves better to expression as *Kabinett* or *Spätlese* releases. Looking at the wines, he has made the right choice. Despite having three EG sites he selects the Berg Rottland as his flagship wine and maintains the KL status, and thus uses the vineyard names, for Berg Roseneck and Berg Schlossberg.

The Classifications and Their Terroir

In the Mosel-Saar-Ruwer, Nahe, and the Rheingau the *Erste Lage, Grosses Gewächs,* and *Erstes Gewächs,* respectively, also apply as *Klassifizierter Lage* sites. We should note that for the purposes of the "Grande Cru" classification, some of those very sites have parcels within them that are delimited for use at the higher level and other parts which may come in for use at the second tier or *Klassifizierter Lage* level.

AHR

Sites with Gross Gewächs Approval

Heimersheim	**Landskrone**
Heimersheim	**Burggarten**
Neuenahr	**Sonnenberg**
Neuenahr	**Schieferley**
Ahrweil	**Rosenthal**
Ahrweil	**Silberberg**
Walporzheim	**Kräuterberg**
Walporzheim	**Gärkammer**
Walporzheim	**Domlay**
Marienthal	**Klostergarten**
Marienthal	**Trotzenberg**
Dernau	**Pfarrwingert**
Dernau	**Hardtberg**
Mayschoss	**Mönchberg**
Altenahr	**Eck**

The red wine valley of Germany dates back to Roman times. It is now Germany's premier red wine region. With over 80% of the vineyard holding planted with such, Pinot Noir is the king here. It is virtually impossible to use machinery in these very steep vineyards means that the wines come at a price. Only 520 hectares are planted and this number is continually at risk. Only 8% of vineyards are planted with Riesling.

The Germans will try to pretend that there is a Mediterranean climate here, but in reality there seems to me more than merely a bronzed bikini clad ragazza or two missing. Along with the Pfalz insisting on describing itself as the Deutsche Toscana this is one of the more enjoyable aspects of German tourism marketing by association.

At the same time, it has exceptional conditions for producing wonderful Pinot Noir wines. One should not invite comparisons with Burgundy; it is a different style as are the Pinot Noir from Oregon, Central Otago, or Tasmania. The steep slopes are from a vineyard and winemaking point of view hard work. Slate soils and walled/terraced vineyards trap heat creating a particular microclimate. The Rhein River provides both a heat sink, drainage of cold air (hence frost potential), and acts as a mirror reflecting the sun into the vineyards. Further, the region is sheltered from cold winds by the Eifel ranges.

Altenahr: Eck

Spätburgunder classified site. From 1249, very steep, terraced vineyards, Sandstone and weathered slate soils with a very high proportion of stones.

Maychoss: Mönchberg

A virtual cliff like vineyard. Woods at the top protect it from cold winds. Slate soils and vineyard walls act as heat savers. Weingut Deutzerhof considers this one of their best sites along with the Altenahr Eck.

Ahrweiler: Rosenthal

Sloped vineyards, high protective walls built up from the remains of a viaduct that the Germans are still waiting for the Romans to finish. 50 hectares with very mixed soils. Loam in central and upper parts, loess, and slate. A great site for J.J. Adeneuer with Spätburgunder.

MOSEL-SAAR-RUWER

Sites with Erste Lage Approval

Winningen	Uhlen "Laubach"
Winningen	Uhlen "Roth Lay"
Winningen	Uhlen "Blaufüßer Lay"
Winningen	Röttgen
Hatzenport	Kirchberg
Erden	Treppchen
Erden	Prälat
Ürzig	Würzgarten
Zeltingen	Sonnenuhr
Wehlen	Sonnenuhr
Graach	Himmelreich
Graach	Domprobst
Bernkastel	Lay
Bernkastel	Graben
Bernkastel	Badstube
Bernkastel	Doctor
Lieser	Niederberg Helden
Brauneberg	Juffer
Brauneberg	Juffer Sonnenuhr
Wintrich	Ohligsberg
Piesport	Goldtröpfchen
Piesport	Domherr
Dhron	Hofberg
Trittenheim	Apotheke
Trittenheim	Leiterchen
Trittenheim	Felsenkopf
Leiwen	Laurentiuslay
Eitelsbach	Karthäuserhofberg
Filzen	Pulchen
Wawern	Herrenberg
Kanzem	Altenberg
Oberemmel	Hütte
Wiltingen	Hölle
Wiltingen	Braune Kupp

Wiltingen	**Scharzhofberg**
Ayl	**Kupp**
Ockfen	**Bockstein**
Saarburg	**Rausch**
Serrig	**Schloss Saarfelser Schlossberg**
Serrig	**Schloss Saarstein**
Serrig	**Würtzberg**
Serrig	**Herrenberg**

With over 700 years of continuous winemaking culture here the Mosel-Saar-Ruwer is all about the winding of the river, creating pockets of potential vineyard sites. This is one of the largest Riesling areas in the world. It has a cool climate and requires a very long ripening period. Riesling, as we are aware, is not an early ripening variety in any event but this puts it always at some risk. In terms of getting a crop, one is better to plant earlier ripening varieties and this is the reason that various German research institutes spent many years developing vine crosses in order to provide plant material suited to providing earlier ripening crops. They neglected to consider that the Riesling grapes planted over such a long history of grape growing were there because of experience. This experience went against the modern technocrat wisdom and early ripening crosses were planted with much gusto. This has now come full circle. It is understood that great wines are generally produced from the most particular of sites; approaching marginal for the production of grapes.

The Mosel is a complete discussion of terroir. You need the right selection of site and grape in order to make something extra special. No matter how widespread plantings become around the world, there will always be just a few pockets of microclimate that produce that fantastic something when planted with the perfect vine combination. Barbaresco would not be the success it is if it was planted with Riesling and vice versa if the MSR was planted with Nebbiolo. In the rush to plant for ease of harvesting and early ripening crops the region would always struggle to produce something special and likely release bland wines.

The MSR, provides wines often with relatively low alcohol and high acidity, whilst having notably rich aromas and balanced natural sweetness. It is often described as the defining style of Riesling given the combination of balance with lower alcohol, crisp acid, hints of petroleum, and steely notes. It is interesting to note comments from New World winemakers at wine shows, where they will often describe their wine with reference to a European zone. Comments on their Gewürtztraminers such as, "its an Alsacian style" despite the fact that 90% of them have probably not ever tried more than one very basic wine from Alsace. Recently one Australian winemaker described to me his Riesling as being Germanic in its style but could not take this further when pushed on Germanic Rheingau, Germanic Pfalz, or Germanic Mosel. Again, I have to assert that if German producers do not react quickly to how they must present as a group their wines then they risk having the Australians kidnap what the wine consumer thinks is the style of Riesling.

Despite a flirt into the realms of dry wines, the producers of the Mosel now likely realise that the star products from their region will be the *edelsüsse* wines which also have the capacity to fetch high prices. One might think that *edelsüsse* wines have their origin in the Mosel but in reality they are an innovation of the Twentieth Century customer demand and technology in filtration.

Historically, Mosel wines have a chequered reputation and been seen as light and overly sweet. Over the years they have suffered their fair share of wine doctoring which was a common practice in the Nineteenth Century with various additions to the wine made to give it greater apparent strength but certainly did nothing for the overall quality or reputation.[123] Further, the wines were not seen to have any real aging potential due to their light body and low level of alcohol. Nowadays we understand the reverse to be the case and with changes in winemaking Mosel wines have some of the longest aging potential of all white wines. As a historical aside, the Australian industry managed to kick a dog when it was down by taking the Mosel name and effectively trying to make it a wine style. Spelt "Moselle", it was overly sugared bag-in-box rubbish largely made from Sultana grape. Generally got up in mock German packaging it was nothing short of an insult to the actual Mosel region.[124]

The region has around 11,000 hectares under vine of which around 50% is Riesling. Traditionally vines were trained around stakes in the ground resembling a small tree but many vineyards have converted to modern trellising systems. There are various trade offs to costs, light exposure, and labour for every type of trellis system and basically the traditional method will be the highest cost. This cost has to be weighed against perceived benefits in quality. I like the names of the indigenous

---

[123] Addition was often with Elderflower.
[124] I recall one bag-in-box with pictures of men in Lederhosen....perhaps this is more appropriate to Bavaria rather than the Mosel.

trellis systems; *"drahtramenziehung"* which means training the canes along horizontal wires, *"Trier Rad"* which is a system resulting in the vine looking like a wheel and the traditional binding of the vines to poles known as *"Pfalerziehung"*.

Devon blue slate is the best soil composition in the region giving a distinctive minerally steely note to the wines. In wet seasons the excellent drainage of the slate helps to get rid of excess sugar diluting water and vigorous vine growth. The slate is also a wonderful heat sink, providing radiated warmth and frost protection, something that can be of advantage in all seasons.

The Mosel is an excellent example of winemaking geography. Grapes of any quality can only reach maturity with the best sunlight reception making sites occluded by bends in the river and anything other than virtually vertical sites less than the best for catching the rays. Often the mid parts in the vineyard tend to produce better fruit given protection from cold winds at the top and from frosts at the bottom of the slope.

Steeper sites have the better drainage. This is immensely important given the propensity for rain around harvest time. It will come as no surprise that the cost of working the better steeper sites are much higher and border on the prohibitive given current returns for the wines. There becomes a cost-benefit analysis and much of the Mosel is retreating in hectares under vineyard cultivation. The lower demand for bulk wine has also meant the "closure" of uneconomic vineyards. Fortunately, it appears that the better sites have been retained, despite some losses. In some cases the estates having success have bought into the better sites at very good prices. The loss of the lesser quality vineyards can only be welcomed as it will consolidate the quality of what remains.

The reason the Mosel is cultivated with only around 50% Riesling is due to the fact that bulk producers planted on the flatter lands the mongrel variety Müller-Thurgau in order to satisfy the volume demands of sweet and cheap exports. As we are likely all aware, the misuse of Grosslage names post the 1971 Wine Law meant for the world being awash with examples of Piesporter Michelsberg.

From a winemaking point of view Mosel wines should have traditionally been slightly sweet. This would have been the case due to the fact that the late harvest in the region would have meant for cold cellars giving slow if not sluggish fermentations that struggled to finish. The wines, due to the high acid level, likely did not taste sweet.

The fear of the modern commercial winemaker is a "stuck" fermentation, or one that does not ferment through to dryness. This raises a plethora of wine and cellar handling problems. If a ferment does not go to completion it remains naturally sweet with a lower alcohol level than potentially could have been obtained. It probably sounds strange to non-winemakers that in many cases you would prefer the wines to go through to dryness and then adjust the sweetness with corrective sugar additions at a later stage giving the balance one seeks. With a ferment that chooses to stop, it means that the winemaker has no control over what level of sugar/acid balance.

At the same time, many winemakers will also try to stop a ferment when they feel that the residual sugar levels are right and the wine is in balance with the maximum fruit expression that can be masked with higher alcohol generation. The essence of Riesling is that the fruit aromas can become very lifted and pronounced at the right level of alcohol, acid, and sugar; so generating the most complex of wines. I would question if many New World winemakers actually have the feel or experience of when to stop a fermentation and if their training would even let them consider such a risk.

New World winemakers are far more likely to consider that the grapes coming in should be subject to acid adjustment (up or down) and ensuring the ferment goes to dryness. From there, they will work very skilfully on blends and putting the wines back in balance. The product that results from less interference will always be more interesting and complex.

The German Wine Law of 1971 went against all this hard earned winemaking knowledge. The Wine Law ensured that "dry" wines could have no more than 8gm/L of residual sugar. It mattered not that a wine might have fermented to 10% alcohol and been left with a natural residual sugar of 15gm/L which with a high acid might have not only tasted "dry" but been perfectly delicately balanced. No, the law made this fall into the virtually unsaleable category of *halbtrocken*. Many producers were faced with making wines that were not the ultimate expression of their terroir or their own winemaking potential due to the fact that at the end of the day they had to sell their wines. To do this it was virtual economic suicide to release anything other than what fitted within the dry category.

It is certainly possible to make dry wines in the Mosel but this is expensive due to the fact that the best sites have to be used and the grapes held out in the ripening window for the longest possible time. The winemaker runs the inevitable risk of the weather turning a years hard vineyard work into mush.

The classification by the VDP for the Mosel was based on a series of tax maps from 1868, 1804, and 1904. The consumer demand has been for fewer single vineyard names on labels as well as the removal of misleading *Grosslage* names. It looks like this is taking place with the work done by the VDP group in the Mosel.

The steep sites in the Mosel really make it difficult to tend the vineyards. Many sites use a mini railway in order to reach the tops of the slopes. The VDP use as their symbol a Traubenadler, an eagle with a grape cluster held in its talons, one wonders if this might be a more economic harvesting method when one sees the steepness of the sites.

To date there have been relatively few wines released from the Mosel under the new classification scheme but this is due to the fact that it has so recently been ratified. Given the string of recent great years we will see more wines emerge from the classified sites. Here I make note of those sites with wines released to date.

Winningen: "Laubach" Uhlen

This is a huge south and southwest-facing amphitheatre on the side of the river. The name has something to do with owls. Terroir is grey slate with large limestone segments, bringing very soft but full flavoured wines. Areas of the vineyard have blue slate with clay layers which give concentrated mineral flavours. There are really three distinct terroirs here so there will be some variation even within what is potentially shown from this *Erste Lage*.

There is the **Uhlen Roth Lay** with iron oxide characters in soil giving very aristocratic crisp wine, **Uhlen Laubach** with plenty of calcium in the soil giving full but spicy wines, and the **Uhlen Blaufüsser Lay** with the blue slate and clay soil giving the traditional mineral edge.

Winningen: Röttgen

With this site and that of the "Laubach Uhlen" stunning wines are produced by the groundbreaking winemaker Reinhard Löwenstein from Weingut Heymann-Löwenstein. The best site is that with the South to Southeast exposure, at about 100m above sea level. The soil is a mixture of quartz, clay, and slate which produces wines with great mineral content but a very soft rounded style. This is a classic Mosel terrace vineyard.

Bernkastel: Doctor

This is one of top vineyards in area and has just over three hectares of vineyards. It provides very mineral wines with pepper and flinty notes.

Despite this small size, it is probably one of the few vineyards that most wine buff around the world could name. In 1971, the vineyard area was expanded more than six fold, but this has been delimited for the purpose of VDP classification and is the legitimate part of the South facing Doktor.

We are likely to see other wines with *Erste Lage* classification from the Bernkastel area such as **Graben** which is southwest facing with very deep soils giving excellent water retention. Many of the big names have parcels on this site and they rate it as highly as the Doktor. Bernkastel **Lay** is a highly steep site of slate soils, a vineyard where Ernie Loosen often produces an amazing *Eiswein*.

Brauneberg: Jufer Sonnenuhr

To date nothing has been released as Erste Lage but the combination of botrytis notes and petrol tones that can often be found in the Brauneberger Jufer-Sonnenuhr wines, (currently released as Auslese), from Weingut Willi Haag demonstrate a combination of aromas that position this site and Haag's winemaking well into the outstanding class.

Wintrich: Ohligsberg

At start of 20th Century it was considered on a par with the Doktor given the prices the wines were fetching. Quartz soil, slate, and west facing slopes mean the grapes hang much longer on vines. When healthy the grapes can be harvested very late gaining the benefit of the autumn sun. The vineyard with a 70% slope had fallen into disrepair by the early 1990s but the vineyard was snapped up by Herr Haart, of Weingut Reinhold Haart. He has replanted and restored it to its former glory.

Piesport: Goldtröpfchen

The infamous village of Piesport has very little to do with this site. This was another great site that had its reputation raped and pillaged by the 1971 laws. This is a wonderful amphitheatre with good water retention in fine soils. It produces its best stuff in dry years with high levels of fruit at low levels of alcohol. If one was to describe a style as being the quintessential demonstration Mosel style, this would be the vineyard. It is an ideal site for the production of *edelsüsse* Rieslings giving some excellent botrytis affected wines.

Kanzem: Altenberg

Has a slope of 70% and weathered slate soils with red slate predominant. They need a very long time these wines to show their potential as they are very closed when young. This is a site capable of demonstrating the aging potential of Mosel wines, especially those from Weingut von Othegraven.

Both the Saar and the Ruwer have a higher risk of frost due to the fact that there is little if any climatic moderating effect from the Mosel River. They are both cooler sub-zones meaning generally higher acid and often the grapes can struggle to fully ripen. A long growing season means a greater risk of a poor harvest resulting from bad weather. Having experienced this "phenomenon" a number of times, it is a heart breaking feeling to see a years work washed away in a few days of bad weather. At the same time, such climatic marginality can give a stunning variation in vintages. Each season is an individual challenge and can provide wines of extreme quality. Wines from the Saar and Ruwer tend to give complex, persistent, and mineral flavoured wines. When they are good they are really good.

The Ruwer is predominantly grey slate as opposed to the Mosel with its blue slate. The area under vine is shrinking here due to the uneconomic costs of production and the fact that easier more financially rewarding work can be obtained not far away in large cities. One can only hope that this is a culling of the poor and mediocre sites leaving the best to continue the tradition of top wine production. A number of producers are gaining attention for their production of *edelsüsse* wines which is good news but we must keep in mind that despite the attractive prices fetched it is hard if not impossible to make a living from such wines. The effort will be in conversion of the consumer to the dry wines produced here and at a price sufficient to offset the high costs of production. It will be a difficult task now that competition exists on a worldwide scale.

MITTELRHEIN

Sites with Gross Gewächs Approval

Steeger	**St. Jost**
Bacharach	**Wolfshöhle**
Bacharach	**Posten**
Bacharach	**Hahn**
Engehöll	**Bernstein**
Oberwesel	**Oelsberg**

This region is predominately slate but soil formations offer vines deep rooting combined with a special microclimate giving fine aromas in delicate wines. This area also has steep vineyards that act as suntraps.

It is a region that will always struggle for recognition up against its big "brother" the Rheingau and big "sister" the Mosel. It is effectively sandwiched in between these better-known regions and with around 70% of its vineyards yielding Riesling its wines can generally be described as a mix between those you would find in the Rheingau and Mosel. Crisp wines with more acidity and less body that those in the Rheingau but with less acidity and more body than those in the Mosel. The sites that perform best conform to the "3 S" principle[125] of German wine growing; Sheltered, Steep, and South facing. The area under vine has fallen to around 500 hectares. This is due to the high costs of production and limited opportunities to sell. Without a string of big names, it does well with a few star producers and by concentrating on the regional restaurant trade.

Bacharach: Hahn

South to Southeast facing site with a very steep slope of 65% sits at one of the narrowest points on the Rhine. It is protected from cold North winds and its closeness to the Rhine gives a temperate effect. Sun is also reflected off the water surface into the vineyard. Stony weathered Devon slate soil structure. The Riesling planted higher up in the hands of Jost is some of the best and he is a producer capable of releasing very balanced and persistent wines.

---

[125] If this principle does not exist is does now!

Bacharach: Posten

Positioned at the place where the Rhein turns north. Cliffs of steep slate and quartz define this vineyard. The vineyard name comes from the watchtower that used to be here to control the river. The Rhein acts as a heat-reflecting mirror onto the slate terraces. The site has a 65% slope and Devon slate. Note that the heating of the slate in the daytime means a slow release during the night, moderating the microclimate around the vines. It generally has mineral flavoured wines.

Bacharach: Wolfshöle

This vineyard backs directly onto the Posten. It is south facing, with a 50 to 60% slope at a height of 100 to 200 metres. Soils change between clay slate and crystalline slate. Acid levels are high but the site can give very refined wines.

Engehöll: Bernstein

Lies in a side valley of the Rhein above the town of Oberwesel. Here the valley runs from East to West along the south side of the river. It is a type of amphitheatre. The high hills around protecting it from strong winds and the geological make up of soil is of brown/grey slate. The mineral rich soils warm easily due to the high percentage of stones. Again this provides a moderating effect at night and helps in creating a lengthy ripening window.

Oberwesel: Oelsberg

63% slope all south facing on a bend in the Rhine. Microclimate is also heavily influenced by the river giving a considerable balance. The Rhine flows towards the vineyard for a distance of 6km providing extreme light and heat reflection. The soils are slate, with some loess, and loam. Untypical rich soil for the region and the individuality of the wines is due to a layer of sandstone which is near the topsoil in this vineyard. Complex and interesting wines generally result.

NAHE

Sites with Gross Gewächs Approval

Münster-Sarmsheim	Rheinberg
Münster-Sarmsheim	Kapellenberg
Münster-Sarmsheim	Dautenpflänzer
Münster-Sarmsheim	Pittersberg
Dorsheim	Burgberg
Dorsheim	Goldloch
Dorsheim	Pittermännchen
Laubenheim	Karthäuser
Laubenheim	St. Remigiusberg
Laubenheim	Krone
Langenlonsheim	Löhrer Berg
Langenlonsheim	Rothenberg
Langenlonsheim	Königsschild
Wallhausen	Johannisberg
Wallhausen	Felseneck
Roxheim	Berg
Traisen	Bastei
Traisen	Rotenfels
Norheim	Kirschheck
Norheim	Dellchen
Altenbamberg	Rotenberg
Niederhausen	Felsensteyer
Niederhausen	Steinberg
Niederhausen	Kertz
Niederhausen	Hermannshöhle
Niederhausen	Hermannsberg
Oberhausen	Brücke
Oberhausen	Leistenberg
Schloßböckelheim	Kupfergrube
Schloßböckelheim	Felsenberg
Bockenau	Felseneck
Monzingen	Frühlingsplätzchen
Monzingen	Halenberg

The Nahe is a difficult region to describe largely due to the fact that it does not appear as a compact defined winegrowing region. It is focused on the Nahe River, which wanders all over the place sometimes running west-east and then other times towards the north. Of prime importance is the Upper Nahe, comprised mostly of Riesling on slate soils. This is of significance given that the region as a whole is planted only with 25% Riesling. We can see a very modern style results from the Upper Nahe, particularly from estates such as Dönnhoff that demonstrate a elegant balance between fruit, acid, mineral tones, body, and structure.

The region has some 4600 hectares under vine, with an interesting geological make up providing for some interesting wines. In the lower Nahe, in between Wallhausen and Bingerbrück there is Devonshire stone, Phylitte, green slate and quartzite. Here Rieslings have a greater level of fruit compared to mineral content.

Between Münster-Sarmsheim and Monzingen there is more red conglomerate and sandstone soils and in the upper layers of the vineyards red sandstone. This structure gives wines of greater fullness, body, and weight.

There exists weathered volcanic soils between Bad Münster and Schlossböckelheim in the central Riesling area of the Nahe and the wines have a correspondingly good level of acidity, fruit, and elegant structure.

It became known that the Nahe had its own form of vineyard classification based on tax payments over 100 years ago. Payment was based on pieces of silver. 15 to 120 silver pieces for the lowest category, 150 to 240 in the middle, and 360 to 600 for the top sites. This was documented in a 1901, <u>Nahe Weinbaukarte für den Regierungsbezirk Coblenz</u>.[126] The map was marked in dark red for those sites that had to pay the top level of silver and it follows suit that these were the sites fetching the highest prices for their wines. This map was somehow lost in a Germany that has thousands of perpetual students who write dissertations on the history of the ergonomic development of the steering wheel but seemingly mislay a manifestly important document which sheds light on an important industry from both a cultural and social point of view. Many of these small towns still today centre their yearly operations and social focus on wine. In any event, the map was located by the Nahe VDP and put into practice as a means of determining their top sites from a historical point of view leading into classification.

One of the lessons of this map re-released in 1997 was that the best

---

[126] Vineyard map of the Nahe for the region of Coblenz.

vineyards should only be permitted to be planted with Riesling and all other grape varieties including the Burgundian varieties should only be allowed to be marketed under their varietal names even if they were planted in one of the "grand cru" vineyards. One has to say this demonstrates the seriousness with which the re-classification of the region has been taken.

Münster-Sarmsheim: Dautenpflänzer
The vineyard is on the right bank of the Nahe and very steep slope facing to the Southeast. Due to the south-southeast slope and the last remains of the Münster forest, the Dautenpflänzer is protected from cold West winds. Grey Devon slate is the make up of the soil with loess and loam. This is a site recognised for producing ready to drink wines.

Münster-Sarmsheim: Pittersberg
Very close to the river and very well protected. Grey slate soils with a south facing aspect. The wines require considerable time to develop and show their best.

Dorsheim: Burgberg
On the North side of the Trollbach valley there are 4 hectares of vineyards sitting between 200 and 300 metres above sea level. A 45-55% sloped south-southeast facing vineyard bordered by cliffs forming an amphitheatre providing excellent microclimatic protection for the slate, quartz, gravely soil, and mixed with loam. This site gives Riesling of great aging potential. Cold nights at the bottom of the slope give a cold air hang and are ideal for the production of *Eiswein*. The wines from Diel show plenty of fullness and fruit. Given some aging the wines really start to demonstrate great Riesling characters.

Dorsheim: Goldloch
The golden hole is 11 hectares of top vineyards between 200 to 300 metres above sea level are partially terraced and south facing with a slope of 45 to 50%. Glacial deposits make up the soil here covered with a thin layer of silty loam. Very delicate apricot notes are found in these wines.

Dorsheim: Pittermännchen
The name derives from a silver coin or medal. This is on the north side of the Trollbach Valley with 8 hectares between 220 and 300 metres above sea level. This site borders the west side of the Goldloch vineyard, again

with a similar slope south facing. Soils are slate with gravel and quartzite. Diel is a major grower here and believes wines result with a racy acidity and thus likes to use them for their fruitier wines. I find the wines have a very good length and up front fruit.

Time gives greater development to many wines and those of the Pittermännchen are certainly a case in point. I made a tasting of wines from Schlossgut Diel in both Berlin and Mainz. Comparing my notes from tastings in Berlin during September 2003, and from Mainz in April 2004, allows one to check ones consistency and to see if there have been changes to the wines over the intervening period. Looking to my notes on the 2002 Dorsheim Pittermaännchen Riesling Spätlese, this wine struck me as having (in Berlin) some slight petrol notes and very subdued fruit with good minerally texture. Looking at the same wine down the track in Mainz the additional bottle age seems to have given strangely more pronounced fruit flavours and certainly greater length with more harmony from the petrol notes. Interestingly, the initial impression of the wine was of having low fruit notes. Just six months more and the wines were showing excellent fruit.

Wallhausen: Johannisberg

Extremely steep 60% sloped vineyard south facing. This is one of the oldest European vineyards going back to the 12th Century. 50-year-old vines on this vineyard with very deep rooting. Very complex wines result and they need considerable aging in order to show their potential and best attributes as well as their inherent complexity.

Monzingen: Frühlingsplätzchen

The name stems from the fact that the warmth of the site was such that the winter snows were first to melt here so it became known as "little Spring place". Soils on this south-southwest facing slope are weathered red slate mixed with quartz and basalt. These wines likely reflect the launch of Spring early as they are ready to drink sooner.

RHEINGAU

Sites with Erstes Gewächs Approval

Flörsheim	**Herrnberg**
Wicker	**Stein**
Wicker	**Mönchsgewann**
Hochheim	**Hölle**
Hochheim	**Stein**
Hochheim	**Königin Viktoriaberg**
Hochheim	**Hofmeister**
Hochheim	**Kirchenstück**
Hochheim	**Domdechaney**
Hochheim	**Stielweg**
Hochheim	**Reichestal**
Kostheim	**Weiß Erd**
Walluf	**Berg Bildstock**
Walluf	**Vitusberg**
Walluf	**Walkenberg**
Martinsthal	**Rödchen**
Martinsthal	**Wildsau**
Martinsthal	**Langenberg**
Rauenthal	**Rothenberg**
Rauenthal	**Gehrn**
Rauenthal	**Wülfen**
Rauenthal	**Baiken**
Eltville	**Rheinberg**
Eltville	**Sonnenberg**
Eltville	**Langenstück**
Eltville	**Taubenberg**
Eltville	**Kalbspflicht**
Kiedrich	**Sandgrub**
Kiedrich	**Wasseros**
Kiedrich	**Gräfenberg**
Erbach	**Hohenrain**
Erbach	**Steinmorgen**
Schloss Reichartshausen*	
Erbach	**Schlossberg**

Erbach	Marcobrunn
Erbach	Siegelsberg
Erbach	Michelmark
Hattenheim	Mannberg
Hattenheim	Wisselbrunnen
Hattenheim	Nussbrunnen
Hattenheim	Hassel
Hattenheim	Pfaffenberg
Hattenheim	Engelmannsberg
Hattenheim	Schützenhaus
Steinberg*	
Hallgarten	Jungfer
Hallgarten	Schönhell
Oestrich	Doosberg
Oestrich	Lenchen
Mittelheim	St. Nikolaus
Mittelheim	Edelmann
Schloss Vollrads*	
Winkel	Schlossberg
Winkel	Gutenberg
Winkel	Hasensprung
Winkel	Jesuitengarten
Johannisberg	Klaus
Schloß Johannisberg*	
Johannisberg	Hölle
Geisenheim	Kläuserweg
Geisenheim	Mönchspfad
Geisenheim	Rothenberg
Geisenheim	Mäuerchen
Geisenheim	Fuchsberg
Rüdesheim	Magdalenenkreuz
Rüdesheim	Klosterlay
Rüdesheim	Bischofsberg
Rüdesheim	Drachenstein
Rüdesheim	Berg Rottland
Rüdesheim	Berg Roseneck
Rüdesheim	Berg Schloßberg

Aßmannshausen	**Frankenthal**
Aßmannshausen	**Höllenberg**
Lorch	**Bodental-Steinberg**
Lorch	**Pfaffenwies**
Lorch	**Krone**
Lorch	**Kapellenberg**
Lorch	**Schlossberg**
Lorchhausen	**Seligmacher**

The Rhine river flows almost 1000km in a Northerly direction, the one exception being that at Wiesbaden the Taunus mountains block its path and for 30km and it runs West before again turning to the North at Rüdesheim. Protected on the North by the Taunus mountains and on the South by the Rhine, this so provided the ideal strip of land on which to base 1000 years of wine culture. This geographical and geological quirk provides space for 3200 hectares of south-southwest facing of slopes with around 1500 growers and planted with 80% Riesling. The zone is framed by the river and the forested hills at the top of their parallel slope. This compact zone is so protected from the cold winds and the Rhine provides a moderating climatic effect. There are massive differences in sites in terms of sunlight exposure, drainage, and soil fertility. Gravel, sand, loam, clay, loess, and marl soils all exist. In the higher vineyards around Kiedrich and Rauenthal there are soils of quartz and weathered slate. The sites closer to the river are generally seen as somewhat inferior, due to higher incidence of rot and the higher fertility of the soils pushing out vine vigour rather than pumping their energy into the fruit and accumulation of sugar. The Romans, Karl the Great, and the religious orders (wine producing nuns still remain) brought the region its vineyard fame and continued its tradition of top production. The quality steps of *Spätlese* to *Trockenbeerenauslese* stem historically from the Rheingau.

Wicker: Mönchsgewann
"Monks Victory" is a south facing 27% slope. This trophy site was in the hands of various religious teams from 970. Due to great water holding potential the site shows its best potential in very dry years.

Hochheim: Domdechaney
South facing slope at foot of the Hockheim church called St Peter and Paul. This was in the hands of the religious leaders of Mainz who used

the castle adjacent to the vineyards as their summer residence. There is evidence that in the 18th Century during hot vintages, water was brought from the mines to the vineyards. The soils are heavy limestone soils. This provides excellent water holding and vine the roots can tap it throughout the ripening season meaning the potential to late harvest. This begs the question of why water had to be brought from the mines but German history has a pattern of being made tidy.

Hochheim: Kirchenstück

This site is east of the Domdechaney and very different in terroir. It is a south facing slope and protected to the north by the estate buildings. The soil ranges from heavy limestone and loess to very light sand deposits over deep water retentive under soil.

Martinsthal: Langenberg

This is a South to Southeast facing sloped vineyard. To the west the soils are weathered slate but the more east one travels the higher the loess percentage. They are steep vineyards but with high water retention, especially in the middle of the slope.

Kiedrich: Gräfenberg

Southwest facing slope with up to 50% gradient. Soil structure is deep stony Phylliten. The site has excellent air circulation with a very long ripening period. Very elegant and fine Rieslings sometimes described as the Mosel wines of the Rheingau. Excellent wines result from Weil off this site.

Erbach: Hohenrain

This is situated behind Erbach and it is a south-facing slope with a gentle 10%. It gains all day sun and is bordered on the West side by a wall protecting it from winds. From 1543 the vineyard was know as Hohenrain, Soils are deep loess and loam with marl content. The wines generally present with plenty of acidity but in recent years the wines of Jakob Jung have become somewhat flabby in my opinion.

Erbach: Schlossberg

This is 6 hectares of vineyards adjacent to the Erbacher Marcobrunn. Only Riesling is planted on a south-facing slope. Good water holding loess soils help considerably in dry years. The name of the vineyard is a new one from 1972, following the infamous 1971 laws which permitted each winery to name one sloped vineyard of at least 4 hectares with the name of their choice. Schloss Reinhartshausen was one of these and the Erbacher Schlossberg resulted. Wines are generally more elegant than those of Marcobrunn but perhaps less complex.

Erbach: Marcobrunn

With a South facing slope the name originates from 1275 where it was the mark or border delineating Erbach and Hattenheim. This distinctive marker happened to be in the form of a fountain (*brunnen*). The soils are mica and have partial lateral water drainage. It is near the river but an exception in terms of quality due to the marl soils. Rich full bodied wines with at least four producers providing variations on a theme here. The site has become even more interesting since classification, due to the fact that there are four producers from which to compare their interpretation of the terroir. Producers are Baron zu Knyphausen, Schloss Reinhartshausen, Domäenweingut Schloss Schönborn, and von Oettingen. The wines from Reinhartshausen are likely the largest or fullest but von Oettingen leads the way with a combination of fruit and finesse. Schloss Schönborn sits somewhere in between.

Erbach: Siegelsberg

Directly above the Marcobrunn there is this wind protected 16% sloped vineyard. Perfect southerly exposure, this is an early flowering and early ripening site on clay with loess and loam deposits. If I was to select a favourite of the three Erbach sites, this would be it. Wines are generally similar to those of the Marcobrunn but tend to have just more chutzpah.

Hattenheim: Mannberg

In the possession of Freiherr Langwerth von Simmern since 1464 this site has a 500 year wine tradition on this south-facing slope of 18 to 27% with groundwater prevalent.

Hattenheim: Wisselbrunnen

The exposure is Southwest on this vineyard site. Light soils with some marl holding water well. A dry vintage performer again with some four producers exhibiting wines. Hans Barth, Hans Lang, Baron zu Knyphausen, and Josef Spreitzer all provide distinct wines with those from Spreitzer standing apart with greater complexity and fruit harmony.

Hattenheim: Nussbrunnen

Continuing the obsession with naming vineyards after fountains and suggesting that water must have been able to be drawn from relatively close beneath the surface indicating that vines would not have had trouble tapping water and in warmer years avoided water stress. South-southeast exposure at only a height of 87 metres above sea level but well protected from cold northern winds. Balthazar Rees producers an excellent fruit structured, mineral, creamy, full wine from this site with marmalade and apricot tones.

Hattenheim: Hassel

100 metres above sea level with a south-facing slope. The site was named in the 14th Century after hazelnut trees.

Hattenheim: Pfaffenberg

Just over 6 hectares in the hands of Schloss Schönborn.

Hattenheim: Steinberger

This vineyard is in the possession of Kloster Eberbach. With an amazing 34 hectares it is the largest single vineyard in the Rheingau. It is completely enclosed by a 3.8km wall to prevent grape thieves. This now more likely creates a microclimate of protection. Deep slate soils.

Hallgarten: Schönhell

30% slope south facing protected from cold winds by the Taunus. The name comes from the 14th Century; meaning beautiful slope. Deep loess with loam layers, excellent water holding capacity.

Oestrich: Doosberg

South facing slope with a single bank of slate but exposed to wind. This might not sound ideal but given the other microclimatic effects of the site the airflow provides good canopy drying and so avoids the development of rot. Humus soil with clay loess, loam, and gravel deposits. Peter Kuhn from Weingut Peter Jacob Kuhn creates some stunning wines from this site. A family run estate demonstrating the versatility a wine producer needs to have today.

As an aside, he is moving over to using crown seals for his wines. One should not be alarmed. These seals are made from stainless steel and have an inert insert making the seal between the wine and the glass. Thus, there is no risk of cork taint with his wines. They are capsulated so as to effectively hide the crown seal. From a winemaking point of view this is going to provide a wonderful means of closure. These seals are not like those you see on beer bottles but rather more robust and are used to seal bottles of champagne and sparkling wine whilst they undergo their secondary fermentation and often lengthy ageing.

Oestrich: Lenchen
Very deep soil with a gravely loess, some loam, and heavy tertiary deposits of marl. This southwest-facing slope can be found in the 1867 Royal Prussian classification at the highest level. In 1920, a Trockenbeerenauslese was harvested with 303 degrees Oechsle. The vineyard is subdivided by locals into Eiserberg, Eiserweg, Hölle, Pfaffenpfad, and Rosengarten. It was the Eiserberg portion that was mentioned in the 1867 documentation.

Winkel: Jesuitengarten
The Jesuitengarten runs along the the Rhine at the river's edge. 26 hectares between Winkel and Geisenheim. These are South-southwest facing vineyards with a microclimate giving an early flowering and thus early ripening of the grapes. Soils are part of the bank of the Rhine and thus sandy loam with some gravel and layered silt. Easily warmed soils make it one of warmest vineyards in the Rheingau.

Winkel: Hasensprung
Southeast facing slope with very deep loess soils and some gravel. The name comes from the time when a hare or a rabbit was a sign of fertility and appears to have been used as some sort of confidence boosting Viagra for the grapes.

Winkel: Schloss Vollrads
Schloss Vollrads goes back to 1211, with a documentation of wines sales. South-southwest sloped at 140 metres above sea level and protected from northerly winds by the woods above the Schloss. Soils are loess, loam, and quartzite. The Rhine reflects light up to the vineyards.

Johannisberg: Klaus
A 1248 named vineyard, south facing slope of only 2 hectares. Deep limestone soils with patches of gravel. Very well protected.

Johannisberg: Hölle

First mentioned in 1180 it is a south to southwest facing slope of 150 m above sea level with a situation over Johannisberg. Quartzite with loess and loam soils.

Rüdesheim: Berg Rottland

This has a 33% south facing slope to the west of Rüdesheim. The vineyard goes back to 1051, when the Bishop of Mainz presented it to the people of the town. The soil is changeable and goes from stony to partly slate, quartzite, and gravel lightly covered with loess. I have covered why Tilbert Nägler of Weingut Dr. Nägler has chosen this site as his *Erstes Gewächs* vineyard due to the better water holding capacity. Balthasar Rees produces a fantastic long life wine from this site, which is full of mineral, tropical, and over time petrol notes. Herr Rees feels that petrol notes are an integral part of Riesling. We can contrast the wines of this site with his *Erstes Gewächs* production from the Hattenheim Nussbrunnen, which have a greater cream notes to them.

Rüdesheim: Berg Roseneck

This is divided into East and West parts. The west is the steepest, having deep gravel and much stone. The east is almost running to a flat plateau, with deep loess and loam. Over the complete site is there is a slope of 33% facing to the south. Producers here are Allendorf and Fendel but both of them have consistently slipped through my tasting net so I am unable to make any comments about the wines.

Rüdesheim: Berg Schlossberg

The 70% slope is the steepest vineyard in the Rheingau it is composed of slate and Taunus quartzite. The Hessische Staatsweingüter Kloster Eberbach wines from this site have been discussed in the winemaking part of this text regarding the development of petrol notes. Comparing the 2001 to the 2002, there is a complete change. The 2001, is full with petrol and the 2002 has less structure and no noticeable petrol tones. We will have to wait to see if these notes come out in the future. If not, the wines will have changed. As I have discussed before, the move to irrigating their part of this site might well remove the petrol notes. Some clients are likely to be attracted to this change in style, but others will miss the predominance of the petrol nose. Changes in winemaking philosophy can and do change the resultant wines which is why it is often hard to describe the wines that result from the terroir. The Balthasar Rees wine from 2002 has a far greater intensity and will develop a delicate petrol nose and in my subjective opinion is now superior to that produced by Kloster Eberbach.

Lorch: Kapellenberg

Although this vineyard is in the Rheingau it is in the direction of the Mittlerhein. It is in the monopoly ownership of Weingut Graf von Kanitz and amounts to 3.5 hectares. First mentioned in 1480 the deep soil has loess with some weathered slate. This vineyard produces a bridge between the Rheingau and Mosel styles of Riesling. There is good balance and harmony as well as plenty of potential for aging. The wines in the last year have demonstrated a great suitability to the international market, toning down some of the heavier Rheingau characteristics.

RHEINHESSEN

Sites with Grosses Gewächs Approval

Bingen	**Scharlachberg**
Bodenheim	**Burgweg**
Nackenheim	**Rothenberg**
Siefersheim	**Höllberg**
Siefersheim	**Heerkretz**
Nierstein	**Brudersberg**
Nierstein	**Pettental**
Nierstein	**Hipping**
Nierstein	**Oelberg**
Nierstein	**Orbel**
Oppenheim	**Kreuz**
Oppenheim	**Sackträger**
Dienheim	**Tafelstein**
Westhofen	**Aulerde**
Westhofen	**Kirchspiel**
Westhofen	**Morstein**
Dalsheim	**Bürgel**
Dalsheim	**Hubacker**

Could this region be termed Germany's Chianti? It is responsible for so much of Germany's bulk wine it has a hard road to reach universal acceptance. Given that it produces around 25% of all German wine, one cannot expect much. It is a large triangle bordered by Bingen, Mainz, and Worms. The area is protected by the Donnersberg hills to the west and its closeness to the Rhein. This is one of the driest regions in Germany with an average rainfall of 500mm. It is characterised by rolling hills which unsurprisingly lend themselves to mechanical harvesting. Vineyard management has been characterised by over cropping on highly fertile soils in the past. This was standard practice during the days where quantity was the driving factor. The region has been forced to closely re-examine its position due to the fact that the fall in demand for such wines has reached crisis point and the prices fetched for such bulk dross is now basically uneconomic. The regions quality producers are the prime example of the theme of this book. That is, if you have good sites, good winemaking, and work together to increase the profile of your region through tasteful marketing then you will see the results. This is exactly what is happening in the Rheinhessen. Those with good sites have invested heavily in making better wine, working closely together on winemaking and especially marketing. This marketing can be contrasted with the efforts from Baden.

There are a number of young winemakers who, faced with their lot in life, who have gone overseas in order to see what all the fuss is about. Coming home full with ideas they have understood their terroir of rolling hills and fertile soil does not differ substantially from what many New World regions have. In fact, their more marginal climate should give them a flavour advantage. They have been quick to grasp both the style of Riesling that they should be trying to produce from their terroir and how to market it.

Constant in the theme of Germany's wine regions, is the influence of the Rhein that indicates the best sites. For ease of discussion, the Rheinhessen can be divided into three sub-regions of Bingen, Nierstein, and Wonnegau. Wonnegau is the engine room of high yielding vines providing the flood of uninteresting bulk wines and deserves scant attention. History has shown that the area around the Rheinfront (Nierstein to Nackenheim) is the dress window to the region.

The name Nierstein will be familiar to most people whom have looked at German wine due to the fact that this excellent site was one of those who suffered from gang rape at the hands of the 1971 Wine Laws. How the Deutsche Wine Institute could not have campaigned against the abuse of such a name is beyond belief. When the Grosslage of Niersteiner Domtal was "created" under the 1971 law, it naturally included the site of Nierstein. Revoltingly, this wonderful site now only contributes around 3% of the territory inside the delimitations of Nierstein-Domtal! If you sold someone a product labelled Real Orange Juice with only 3% real orange juice inside you would not only be swiftly out of business but in need of a good lawyer. The actual Nierstein vineyards are also known as the Rote Hang in describing the "red slope" comprised of clay, iron, and slate. The extreme iron content in the soil gives a mineral note to the wines that have considerable aging potential.

Attempts at making quality improvements are not limited to the Rheinfront. A number of growers have looked closely at their vineyards and made changes at to what they grow. There is an increasing tendency to the Pinots (White and Red) but disturbingly high levels of Dornfelder and Portugieser appearing.

The Rheinhessen has made many diverse attempts at remarketing their image. Full points for trying and one can see there is solid support behind the VDP effort in classification. One can imagine that it is not so easy to reverse a regional focus on bulk wine and move to quality production. This goes for anywhere in the world which is trying to reverse its image and levels of quality. Once can see that this is taking place in the South of Italy where producers are also trying to escape from the vicious cycle of bulk wine production.

Bingen: Scharlachberg
During 19th Century it was considered as one of the best sites in Germany. South to Southeast exposure with weathered slate stone containing high levels of iron oxide lead to soils with an irregular rusty colouring. Strong winds coming from the Hunnsrück maintain good airflow and reduced rot potential. Excellent pineapple and passionfruit notes can be found in these wines.

Bodenhcim: Burgweg
First mentioned in 1364, the view is to the Taunus to the North and the Odenwald in the East. Loess and sandy loam produce light wines and are better suited to the Burgunders (Spätburgunder/Pinot Noir, Weiss Burgunder) rather than Riesling.

Nackenheim: Rothenberg (Roter Hang)
The vineyards lying between Nackenheim and Nierstein were historically described as the Red Slope or Rotter Hang. They are South to Southeast facing slopes, which tend towards due South the closer one gets to Nierstein proper. The Rote Hang is like an island within this territory with a specific terroir strip of red slate, mineral rich iron soils, and clay. Together with the microclimate this is producing some of the best wines in the region.

The vineyard of Rothenberg is at the Northern end of the Roten Hang making up some 20 hectares of vineyards having an extreme slope of between 50 and 80%. It is very much influenced by the effects of the Rhein and holds heat extremely well. Combined with the rays reflected from the Rhine it results, during very dry years, in water stress giving extremely concentrated fruit. Elegant wines with mineral notes and often combined with some aromas of spice and nutmeg can be seen.

Nierstein: Pettenthal (Roter Hang)

This lies on the same South-facing slope as the Rothenberg. Very deep soil profile with red slate. It also gains the reflection of the suns rays from the Rhein. Wines are always very well developed and have a great substance. It is different style from the Rothenberg despite their proximities. The wines have exotic fruit when young and are very fresh after lengthy aging due to the acid structure. Drier years give wines of greater structure. There are a number of producers using this site, chiefly, Weingut St. Antony, Weingut Kühling-Gillot, Freiherr Heyl zu Herrnsheim. St. Antony also has Grosses Gewächs vineyards at Hipping and Oelberg.

The production philosophy of St. Antony has been described elsewhere in the text. They talk a lot about letting things just make themselves but given the wines I believe there is little left to chance at this estate. The winemaking is well thought out and interestingly I struggle to find a great gap between the entry-level wines and those destined for Grosses Gewächs classification. There is really tight consistent winemaking at this state from year to year. Their Pettenthal is extremely full and complex.

Interestingly the organic pioneering estate of Freiherr Heyl zu Herrnsheim has wines from this site. The 2001 has considerable notes of petrol. In addition, there is a butterscotch note on the nose and the winemaker insists that there has been no malolactic fermentation, (which can tend to give butter flavours) and insists that it is a characteristic of the terroir.

Gunderloch also has a vineyard on this classified site but it will not be released as a *Grosses Gewächs*. They remain in the VDP but will not use, for the moment, the *Grosses Gewächs* classification due to the fact that they did not support the inclusion of Spätburgunder in the classification for the Rheinhessen due to its lack of tradition in the region. Their wine has a slight asparagus note, spicy flavours, and pronounced aromas of honeysuckle. This suggests the butterscotch/honeysuckle note must be an aspect of the terroir.

Nierstein: Hipping (Roter Hang)

This is a very exposed part of the Roter Hang where the Southeast-facing slope meets the South-facing slope. It needs very much the warming effect of the suns rays reflected from the Rhine. The vineyard is known for its very small yields and produces lighter wines with fine mineral notes. The wines tend to be more complex rather than demonstrating up front fruit.

Nierstein: Oelberg (Roter Hang)

This Southern section of the Roten Hang has old deep-rooted vines in very stony soil also red slate. Very different wines from the full-bodied wines of the Northern part of the Roter Hang result. The wines are fine, elegant, and almost styled by their fresh acidity with excellent apricot and bitter chocolate notes.

Oppenheim: Kreuz

Southeast facing slope with prevailing mild winds give good aeration to the vineyards. It is a huge loess bank dotted with limestone containing fossilised seashells and evidence of fig leaves providing an interesting climatic perspective. It is a Spätburgunder site for classification purposes.

Oppenheim: Sackträger

Mentioned as early as 1541, it is name translates as "bag hauler", leading one to believe it was connected with shipping on the Rhine. (Oppenheim Docker in English or Oppenheim Wharfie in Australian). The people of Oppenheim specialised in this particular type of labour. There are some 29 hectares of sloped vineyards and it has formed a bay opened to the East to Southeast. In summer it stores the heat very well, giving a longer ripening season. The soil holds water well. The wines have a high mineral content and often extremely high dry extract levels. The wines do not tend to show their full character when young but after around two years they seem to open up and show very lifted fruit tones. There is considerable potential on this site to release wines that reach the Beerenauslese or Trockenbeerenauslese level of ripeness.

Weingut Kühling-Gillot, in addition, to their *Grosses Gewächs* sites at Nierstein Pettenthal (Roter Hang) and Oppenheimer Kreuz, have a parcel in Sackträger. The 2002 Sackträger *Grosses Gewächs* Riesling is a balanced, full, crisp, and prominent fruit driven wine, (this is a complete reversal of what I found with the 2001 which was exceedingly thin.). I hope that they stick with the style of the 2002.

Dienheim: Tafelstein

South Southeast facing slope of which the west side is given to Grosses

Gewächs as it is better protected from winds. Due to excellent water supply likely due to the spring in the vineyard it gives very fruitful wines. It has deep-grounded loess soil with chalk and marlstone underneath covered by a humus deposit. Complexity is the key here in that the wines are not hugely full but have exotic fruit, mineral notes, and are particularly persistent.

Westhofen: Aulerde
South Southeast facing slope, stretching up from the Rhine to a high plateau, protected from the east and southeast winds. A small part of the Aulerde, the *Grosses Gewächs* section, shows a mix of soils with clay and loess loam with small limestone outcrops to an under soil of yellow clay sandstone ranging to gravely sand. This is in contrast to the majority of this vineyard. Fifty-year-old vines from Weingut Wittmann give highly concentrated fruit with much complexity.

Westhofen: Kirchspiel
Kirschspiel is open to the Rhine like an amphitheatre where the vineyards lie in the centre part of the slope facing east-southeast. They are protected from cold winds as a result. Soils are clay and limestone, with the deeper soils being dominated by limestone. Wines tend to display plenty of citrus, apricots, and some mineral complexity.

Westhofen: Morstein
Limestone cliffs are the feature of this vineyard. The soils are of clay and limestone layers. It has great water retention and in warm years this allows exceptional ripening with tropical fruit, honeysuckle, grapefruit, and pineapple notes.

Siefersheim: Höllberg
A South-southeast orientated site with the best vineyards sitting at the upper to mid point of the slope which is delineated by an old stone wall. Sandy soils sit over a clay base giving very ripe fruit after a long growing season. Very typical mineral notes and solid acid platform on a varietal fruit base generally result. These full wines have considerable ageing potential.

Siefersheim: Heerkretz
This is a south facing 30% slope with good shelter from the cold east and west winds. Soils are composed of red quartz over sand having high

calcium content. Wines are very powerful with a prominent firestone or flint note.

Dalsheim: Bürgel

This is a vineyard known for its white and red Burgundy varieties. A South facing slope, the soils are locally known as Terra Fusca. High limestone content pushes the acidity, and water stress tends to occur in hot years. This can tend to reduce vigour and allow for the ripening of varieties other than Riesling. I only mention it due to contrast this with the Dalsheim Hubacker site, which generates *Grosses Gewächs* Riesling.

Dalsheim: Hubacker

Mainly clay and limestone soils, this lies some 1km north of Dalsheim and is made up of a 6 metre high slice of limestone rocks. A 4 hectare vineyard with a 25-30% sloped Southeast facing aspect produces interesting Rieslings of with high levels of passionfruit and apricot flavours.

Bingen: Scharlachberg

This is a wind-exposed site, noticeably affected by winds coming off the Hunsrück. As a result the wines tend to have lower levels of fruit. The wines are interesting due to the high level of iron oxide in the soil.

FRANKEN

Sites with Gross Gewächs Approval

Bürgstadt	**Centgrafenberg**
Homburg	**Kallmuth**
Thüngersheim	**Johannisberg**
Würzburg	**Stein**
Würzburg	**Innere Leiste**
Randersacker	**Pfülben**
Randersacker	**Sonnenstuhl**
Sommerhausen	**Steinbach**
Frickenhausen	**Kapellenberg**
Escherndorf	**Lump**
Volkach	**Karthäuser**
Volkach	**Ratsherr**
Rödelsee	**Küchenmeister**
Iphofen	**Julius-Echter-Berg**
Iphofen	**Kronberg**
Castell	**Schlossberg**

Along the Main River, this region has a particular geology. This is a region demonstrating that weathered sandstone gives good results to the Silvaner variety. Prone to frosts and having a harsh winter climate, Franken tends to produce few Rieslings given its need for a long ripening season. There are some good Rieslings produced, tending to have an earthy note but the specialty will always rest with Silvaner. The potential for consumption of this wine outside of Germany is low unless consumer tastes change dramatically.

Bürgstadt: Centgrafenberg
Spätburgunder classified site.

Homburg: Kallmuth
This site is orientated west southwest, and slopes up to 74% rising from around 140 to 210 metres above sea level. It is a very dry site, being basically in a rain shadow receiving around 300mm per annum. The position permits a long daily window of sunlight interception. Weathered sandstone with a limestone outcrop, in very dry years it is prone to water

stress. The wines of Fürst Löwenstein demonstrate almost Chanel No.9 aromas. Robert Haller, the winemaker at this estate, has continually improved with wines year-after-year and provides a convincing demonstration of terroir potential. The wines from this site and those of the Löwenstein estate in the Rheingau show the importance of a winemaker who can correctly interpret the terroir. Löwenstein has become one of the key estates in Franken due to wise investment in the cellar and backing a winemaker with a clear vision of the terroir.[127]

Würzburg: Innere Leiste
This is a steep slope on the left side of the Main River. It demonstrates the microclimate effects on a terroir being protected from cold Northerly winds. Soils are deep clay limestone with layer of humus.

Würzburg: Stein
Open vineyard facing South of considerable beauty. This is another unfortunate site that has given its name to a "style" of wine. In the past, such was the fame of the Steinwein. Unfortunately, classification has not really cleaned up the situation and confusion is likely to continue given that a number of estates have holdings here. Moreover, these estates are making *Grosses Gewächs* wines from Silvaner, Weissburgunder, and Riesling from this site. The site is a good one, but given the lack of specificity in what wine style will emerge with the *Grosses Gewächs* classification tag makes for too much confusion and dilutes the effect of naming a site as a premium growth. This should not be what the classification is trying to achieve. Can there really be a site that virtually no matter what you plant on it results in *Grosses Gewächs* wines? I think not.

Randerscker: Pfüben
Bounded on both sides by valleys having a 70% slope. This is a South Southwest facing site, this vineyard profits greatly from the reflection of the sun off the Main River. Very good water holding capacity means little water stress and both Weingut Juliusspital and Schmitts' Kinder produce full, ripe, fruity, and mineral Rieslings.

---

[127] The wines of Furst Löwenstein from the Rheingau were for many years "utilised" by Schloss Vollrads. Since regaining control of his vineyards in that region the wines have demonstrated their superior nature once again. It has been a long process for Haller to get things to this level and he should be feeling very satisfied.

Sommerhausen: Steinbach

This is a South Southwest facing 80% slope well protected from winds and with excellent sun exposure. Good drainage on limestone based soils mean it is ideal Riesling country. The wines of Schloss Sommerhausen, in my opinion, continue to improve and the Riesling Grosses Gewächs from this site shows racy acidity and balance with good fruit and mineral notes. It is a wine that must be knocking on the door of 90+ points, and likely needs just a little bit more complexity that might be found in old oak maturation on fine lees for a longer period of time.

Frickenhausen: Kapellenberg

Silvaner classified site.

Escherndorf: Lump

This would have to be included on its name alone. Legend has it that it was named after the lazy son of a vineyard hand but there is little if any evidence to sustain this. Those who wax lyrical about its features talk about the kettle effect of being protected in winter from North and East winds and trapping in the summer heat. It has clay and limestone soils. Due to the sheltered effect this is a better site for late ripening Riesling. Weingut Horst Sauer is one of the greats. An international award winner many times and deservedly due to delivery of some excellent wines at competitive market prices. As well they make some of the best wines of Franken from Riesling on this *Grosses Gewächs* site. His wines are the place to start when looking for absolutely typical pure no nonsense varietal Riesling notes.

Volkach: Karthäuser

Weißburgunder classified site

Volkach: Ratsherr

Silvaner classified site

Iphofen: Julius Echter Berg

This is a steep South facing slope, 280 to 380 m above sea level. A forested belt above the vineyards protects it from cold Northerly and Eastern winds. Grey brown copper sandstone soil reflects heat and gives wines of high dry extract and minerally spice. The wines have great longevity.

Iphofen: Kronsberg
Weißburgunder classified site.

Castell: Schlossberg
This vineyard sits at 340 metres above sea level. It has a South Southwest facing aspect with a slope of 48%. It is protected from cold winds by a belt of woods. The clay with copper content soils produces wines that are very mineral and tend to be spicy. The vineyard is held by the interesting producer Fürstlick Castell'sches Domäneenamt.

SAALE-UNSTRUT

Sites with Grosses Gewächs Approval

Freyburg	**Edelacker**
Karsdorf	**Hohe Gräte**

Keeping with the German wine marketers attempts to project a Mediterranean or Italian equivalent to their regions; such as the Pfalz being termed the "Deutsche Toscana", Saale-Unstrut must surely be seen as the Deutsche *Mezzogiorno*.

This is one of the most Northerly wine growing regions of Europe and only has around 650 hectares. It tends to produce some minerally Rieslings. This region is likely included out of deference to the unified Germany as the wines I have tasted do not merit inclusion in the status of "Grande Cru". With the rapid onset of global warming this region might improve.

Freyburg: Edelacker
Terraced vineyards with a South facing slope of 45%. Continental microclimate.

HESSISCHE BERGSTRASSE

This small region has no current classified site in the *Grosses Gewächs* scheme. The number of VDP members here are also few but in theory there is nothing stopping sites being classified. The Hessische Bergstrasse has sites such as the Bensheimer Kalkgasse, Heppenheimer Centgericht, and Heppenheimer Steinkopf, which could contribute part of their holdings to a *Grosses Gewächs* classification. I am at a loss to explain why during all the set up of the classification system that they did not make the effort to put forward for classification part of these sites.

The region relies on local consumption and little if any wine is exported, in fact Frankfurt airport is probably the most international exposure any of their wines get. This is a pity as from all the regions of Germany it produces; in my opinion a Riesling that is likely the truest varietal examples. They tend to be pure expressions of Riesling as a grape without too much acid or robust structure. They are very ready to drink styles and this is reflected in their immediate commercial appeal.

PFALZ

Sites with Grosses Gewächs Approval

Dirmstein	"Himmelsrech" Mandelpfad
Laumersheim	"Steinbuckel" Mandelberg
Großkarlbach	"Im großen Garten" Burgweg
Ungstein	Weilberg
Ungstein	Herrenberg
Bad Dürkheim	Michelsberg
Wachenheim	Gerümpel
Forst	Pechstein
Forst	Jesuitengarten
Forst	Kirchenstück
Forst	Freundstück
Forst	Ungeheuer
Deidesheim	Kalkofen
Deidesheim	Grainhübel
Deidesheim	Kieselberg
Deidesheim	Hohenmorgen
Deidesheim	Langenmorgen
Deidesheim	Paradiesgarten
Ruppertsberg	Reiterpfad
Ruppertsberg	Spiess
Ruppertsberg	Gaisböhl
Königsbach	Idig
Gimmeldingen	Mandelgarten
Kirrweiler	Mandelberg
Duttweiler	Kalkberg
Godramstein	"Schlangenpfiff"
Siebeldingen	Im Sonnenschein
Birkweiler	Kastanienbusch
Birkweiler	Mandelberg
Leinsweiler	Sonnenberg
Schweigen Kammerberg	Sonnenberg

This is one of Germany's truly international wine regions, releasing wines in styles most suited to international markets. It is avant garde region not only from a winemaking point of view but due to the fact producers here appear to understand well changes in marketing needed to bring international attention, focus, tourism, and sales. One of its many terroir secrets is found in the protection by the Haardt Mountains from both wind and rain. This same protection is afforded to Alsace, which borders the Pfalz. The region has a wonderful tourism aspect, as the Deutsche Weinstrasse runs its length of some 80km. As a region it has a diverse range of soil types so there is no typical characteristic generalising this region.

Even so, the core area for top Rieslings is the Mittelhaardt from Kallstadt to Deidesheim. The zone of Kallstadt to Bad Dürkheim is based on limestone soils whereas the area around Wachenheim is weathered sandstone based. This is not a hard and fast rule, witness Forst. Forst has everything from limestone, layered clay, basalt, and loam. The volcanic basalt sets it apart and makes it arguably the best zone of the Pfalz and a commune to rival the top 10 vineyard areas in the world.

Forst holds the Kirchenstück vineyard, which is the domain of the Pfalz winery dream team, (on historical track record). The famous "3 B's" all have holdings in this site and produce variations on a theme. This will be looked at in some detail due to the fact that there is effectively one terroir for one *Grosses Gewächs* but with three different winemaking focuses. The "3 B's" are Weingut Dr. Bürklin-Wolf, Dr. von Bassermann-Jordan, and Reichsrat von Buhl. Some like to extend this to four, with the inclusion of Biffar but this estate has had a succession of winemakers over the last years, meaning a shift in styles. With the talented winemakers leaving one can generally read between the lines and imagine that the overall estate management lacks neither strategy nor a willingness to adapt to a changed playing field. It remains to be seen if the present incumbent will be able to influence this situation, allowing the vineyards to better show their potential on which the management seems to be willing to rest upon past laurels as a defence from having to modernise or invest.

Dr Bürklin Wolf has a traditionally focused winemaker interested in low vineyard yields giving superbly concentrated fruit which should largely be left to make its own wine. Fritz Knorr seems to be left to get on with just making great wines and steadfastly avoiding or perhaps just plain ignoring capricious involvement from the owner Christian von Guradze who to his credit has understood clearly both the needs of customers, the concept of protecting Bürklin Wolf's great fortune in terroir and the concept of reducing the confusion in getting this message across in marketing. If they concentrate more on the *Grosses Gewächs* concept rather than their own elaborate in house attempt at sneaking the idea of Premier Cru and Grand Cru past the customer then they will look somewhat more grown up.

Stephen Weber at Reichsrat von Buhl has the difficult task of keeping, no doubt bottom line focused, investors happy but this seems to have lead to a change in jockeys for whatever reasons. It remains to be seen if the new winemaker can approach the style, class, and quality that Frank Johns was bringing to the wines. Johns is an undeclared meister of the *edelsüsse* wines from the Pfalz, knowing exactly when fruit expression, acid, and sugar balance were perfectly tuned. If the last vintage is anything to go by the new winemaker is having trouble filling the shoes of Johns, releasing good workman like wines but nothing matching the star quality his predecessor put out. If anything, this reinforces the concept that a good winemaker can release good wines from great terroir but a great winemaker can do something else with the same fruit.

Ulrich Mell and Gunter Hauch's styles of work compliment each other at Bassermann-Jordan and at present they are the form team of the "3 B's" making the least noise, and for my money, the best overall collection.

Travelling further south, one hits the Sudpfalz, which realistically commences after Neustadt. There are fewer chances for great Rieslings given the soils which are highly fertile. This is the Südliche Weinstrasse, where there has tended to be the production of bulk wines. This is now moving to more focus on Pinot varietals of Pinot Noir and Pinot Blanc (Weissburgunder). The changes in the market for bulk wine have meant that a number of quality producers have emerged giving their more recognised neighbours of the Mittlehaardt a run for their money.

Dirmstein: "Himmelsrech" Mandelpfad

This vineyard is only 120 metres above sea level having a gentle slope and being south facing. Protected by a neighbouring valley from westerly winds it has porous limestone soils and relatively high sunshine hours resulting in exotic fruit and fine acid structure. In saying this, Knipser's wines from this site often show a marked acidity giving the wines plenty of longevity and being some of the best made in Germany.

Laumersheim: "Steinbuckel" Mandelberg

This site is South Southeast facing and protected from Northern and

Westerly winds. Thick loess layer over limestone rock and the wines are greatly influenced by the limestone soils and reach their full potential only after many years.

Grosskarlbach: "Im Grossen Garten" Burgweg

The Grossen Garten is the central piece of this vineyard with a Southerly facing aspect. The soil is very changeable ranging from gravel, clay, to weathered limestone.

Ungstein: Weilberg

The core of this vineyard is known locally as *Roterde* or Red Earth. The soil is intensively red coloured coming from a huge ferric dose and gives extreme mineral characters to the wines. This *Grosses Gewächs* classified section runs to around 1 hectare giving wines with plenty of acid, apricot, peach, and full bodied resulting in excellent ageing potential.

Bad Dürkheim: Michelsberg

This is a South-facing site of around 4.8 hectares. Terraced vineyards are well protected from frost and have good wind shelter. The vineyards are terraced using the red sandstone of the region which makes them particularly attractive. The wines have plenty of body, mineral tones, citrus fruit notes, and typical apricot flavours.

Wachenheim: Gerümpel

Biffar asserts this as a *Grosses Gewächs* site, whereas other owners see it as not quite making the cut. Reichsrat von Buhl and Bürklin-Wolf keep their wines at the *Klassifizierter Lage* (or second tier level), and both their offerings are superior to what Biffer is releasing at the ostensibly higher classified level. The wines are still wonderful and the site has an East Southeast facing slope. The name likely derives from a former owner Gerympel. Soil is sandstone sandy loam with some limestone layers. The vineyard rows are extremely widely spaced and a replanting of the vineyard on closer spacing might limit the vine vigour somewhat and make for wines von Buhl and Bürklin-Wolf feel are deserving of the *Grosses Gewächs* classification.

Forst: Pechstein

This site has a Southeast slope bordered by a forest. Black stone soils result from volcanic basalt and there are craters from volcanic eruptions situated behind the vineyard. There are also red weathered sandstone, sand, and loam aspects to the soil giving highly structured wines with great ageing potential. The wines develop intense petrol characters over time whereas when young they tend to give liquorice, peach, and flinty notes. These wines have a huge ageing potential and excellent length.

The Pechstein vineyard has around 12 hectares. It scored 56 out of 65 in the 1828 Royal Bavarian Land Classification and the high level of volcanic basalt in the soil gives considerable flinty notes to the wines. The flavours from this vineyard read like a list of condiments with notes of white and black pepper, spices, and Earl Grey tea. Wines from Pechstein need a minimum of 5 years before they can begin to show their terroir characteristics.

This is one of my favourite Pfalz sites, not only because the wines are superb but also due to the fact that along with the Kirchenstück site it is one where the "3 B's" face off against each other. Their wines all exhibit terroir specific characters; there is certainly a common theme of structure and power but overall I would say that Ulrich Mell's effort comes out with greater complexity and greater notes of flint combined with fullness of fruit. The Bürklin-Wolf version shows a milky note in the palate and has a greater petrol note propensity verging on being able to set up a refinery. The wine from Reichsrat von Buhl has greater fruit expression than their neighbours but lacks their body and fullness. As an aside, Bürklin-Wolf have for many years made a selective harvest from part of their Pechstein parcel and fermented it separately in a colder part of their cellar. The result is not released as a Grosses Gewächs wine but as Pechstein Fass 71 and is simply another dimension to the wines from Pechstein, resembling more closely the fruit notes and full mouthfeel of the Bassermann offering. Superb wines all round.

Forst: Jesuitengarten

This is the second most important vineyard or second highest valued vineyard in the Pfalz according to the 1828 Royal Bavarian Classification, scoring 60 out of 65 points. It consists of 6 hectares and sits on a hill, with facets in all directions but has predominantly an East facing slope with excellent sunlight exposure. The soil is based on volcanic stone and warms quickly retaining heat. There are some clay and sand layers giving a considerable fine mineral edge to the wines with notes of apricot, peach, and plums.

Forst: Kirchenstück

The Kirchenstück vineyard is around 4 hectares and is the only site rated with 65 out of 65 points in the 1828 Royal Bavarian Land Classification. It is surrounded by a sandstone wall that releases stored heat during the night and helps to create a funnel of wind. This tends to dry the vineyards and minimise problems with rot. Unsurprisingly the name stems from the fact that this vineyard was a parcel attached to the church. The soil is really what makes it special. Compact layered clay, weathered sandstone, sand, loam, limestone, and with a basalt composition an amazing complexity to the wines. The site is southeast facing and the topsoil is of volcanic basalt, helping with heat retention. Wines have very tropical fruit notes and combinations such as mango, orange peel, nougat, citrus, flint, and almond are not uncommon. The wines can tend to be a bit eccentric when younger but in time displays the multilayers of complexity that they contain. Given their huge ageing potential they start to unfold layers of their terroir over time.

This vineyard rightly is the best of the Pfalz; if such a claim can be supported given the healthy competition. Again, the finishing and structure on the wine from Bassermann-Jordan sets it slightly apart from that of Reichsrat von Buhl but I have the feeling there is a much lower yield at Bassermann giving the fruit greater concentration. At the end of the day, the crown jewel of wines from this site belongs to Bürklin-Wolf, gaining one of the highest scores I have ever given for a dry Riesling.

Forst: Freundstück

This is the smallest parcel in Forst with only 3.5 hectares. The soil is red and weathered sandstone with some limestone layers. Very mineral notes and concentrated aromas of peach result in the wines.

Forst: Ungeheuer

This is a large vineyard site of some 29 hectares having a gentle slope facing to the Southeast. This site scored 60 out of 65 points in the 1828 Royal Bavarian Classification. The composition is one of volcanic basalt topsoil, weathered sandstone, clay, and limestone. The soils provide a considerable heat sink. Like all Forst vineyards the wines are very powerful with a huge aging potential and this site gives more mineral tones than the others. If any Pfalz wine could be described as masculine, then this is the one. This is well evidenced in the styles being released from Bürklin-Wolf. I should also note that Georg Mosbacher produces a top class wine from this site with a full structure and evidence of early petrol note development. The vineyard's wines are typified by having notes of peaches, pineapple, and melon. Mineral notes are evident, with a particular white pepper note.

Deidesheim: Kalkofen
This is a 5-hectare gently south facing site with the best vineyard in a warm zone in the middle of the slope. Kalkofen or "limestone oven" suggests the soils to be predominantly limestone, which in fact is correct, with a clay base. The combination of the limestone and clay gives a very mineral driven wine by Pfalz standards with prominent flint notes.

Deidesheim: Grainhübel
Soil is sandy loam and clay giving good mineral notes to its wines.

Deidesheim: Hohenmorgen
This was classified as the best vineyard in Diedesheim by the 1828 Bavarian Classification. It has only 2 hectares divided between three wineries. It is Southeast facing on the very edge of Deidesheim. There are a mixture of soils with basalt, weathered sandstone, loam, sand, and some limestone stratification. Complex wines with good structure, spice, and fruit result. Bassermann, Bürklin-Wolf, and Christmann are owners here. The form team is Christmann but there is not much to separate all the wines which are exceptionally interesting and well made. Perhaps Christmann develops greater primary fruit and the combination with some spicy notes makes the slight difference.

Deidesheim: Kieselberg
Having around 15 hectares, the site is a suntrap. The soil structure is changeable throughout vineyard. The gravely base to this vineyard provides both retention of heat and good drainage.

Deidesheim: Langenmorgen
A southeast facing slope with sandy loam, red and yellow sandstone layers provide very good water holding capacity and show wines of considerable elegance in dry years.

Deidesheim: Paradiesgarten
Only the central part of the vineyard is covered by the *Grosses Gewächs* classification. It is again a bit of a borderline case like Wachenheim

Gerümpl. It should either be grande cru or not; or the vineyard further delimited in order to correctly define and limit the terroir.

Ruppertsberg: Gaisböhl

The Gaisböhl vineyard has been described as one of the best in the World. Weingut Dr Bürklin Wolf is the sole owner of this 8 ha vineyard with 5 hectares currently used as Grosses Gewächs having vines of around 30 years of age. The other 3ha will become used for Grosses Gewächs after the replanted vines reach suitable maturity. They list their wines from the vineyard under their own private classification of "GC". This site was classified amongst the best vineyards in the Bavarian Classification and is the top point scorer for the village of Ruppertsberg. This vineyard has a South facing slope that is somewhat plateau like soaking up sun into its red and yellow sandstone soils. Underlying sand and clay retain sufficient water to feed the roots and water stress does not seem to be a problem in most years. The wines from this vineyard give in general aromas of pear, peach, grapefruit, mangos, and apples. Full wines with an excellent fruit and acid balance result.

Ruppertsberg: Spiess

This is a 5-hectare Southwest-west facing site with sandstone and loam soils.

Ruppertsberg: Reiterpfad

This is a Southeast facing site, bordered by the woods at the summit of the hill. It is a walled vineyard which both reflects and acts as a heat battery releasing moderating warmth after hours. The soil is sandy clay with limestone deposits. Wines are extremely complex. Again it reads like a who's who of the Pfalz in terms of ownership. There is nothing to separate the class wines of Acham-Magin, Bergdolt, Reichsrat von Buhl, or Christmann here. Bergdolt likely lacks some of the finesse of the others but all the wines are extremely full, big structured, and possess considerable fruit intensity.

Königsbach: Idig

This is a Southerly facing slope with a slight westerly tilt. Protected from cold winds the soil is dominated by limestone. This is prime Riesling country. At the same time, the fact that the soils do not act as a heat sink to the degree of the vineyards on volcanic soils means that there is a big swing between day and night temperatures, making this ideal for the colour fixing in Pinot Noir whereas it provides mineral notes in Riesling.

Gimmeldingen: Mandelgarten
Weathered sandstone soils and a very deep water table provide highly fruit driven wines with particular notes of pineapple.

Kirrweiler: Mandelberg
Weißburgunder Grosses Gewächs site.

Godramstein: "Schlangenpfiff" Münzberg
The limestone soils make the Burgunder varieties the better performers. Weissburgunder classified site.

Siebeldingen: Im Sonnenschein
One of the few Southerly facing slopes in the Southern Pfalz. It has varied soils with a high level of marine sediment. Sandstone and gravely clay soils provide the basis for top Rieslings here whereas the limestone marine sediments provide better material for the Burgunder clones.

Birkweiler: Kastanienbusch
The vineyard name comes from the prevalence of chestnut trees in the vineyards pushed forward as evidence of a warm climate. The forests around protect it from cold winds and the vineyard is enclosed within a natural protective "kettle". It has a South to Southeast aspect and the soil structure is very complex with different parts more suited to *Grosses Gewächs* Spätburgunder and others to *Grosses Gewächs* Riesling.

Birkweiler: Mandelberg
An excellent suntrap based on its South to Southeast aspect. The soil has marine sediments with white limestone pockets. Again, the limestone making it more suited to the production of Burgunder clones.

Leinsweiler: Sonnenberg
This Southerly facing slope has a 30% gradient. Limestone deposits and marine sediment give the Rieslings here a light mineral tone.

Schweigen: "Kammerberg" Sonnenberg
Classified for Spätburgunder.

WüRTTEMBERG

Sites with Grosses Gewächs Approval

Gundelsheim	**Himmelreich**
Neckarsulm	**Scheuerberg**
Verrenberg	**Verrenberg**
Weinsberg	**Schemelsberg**
Weinsberg	**Ranzenberg**
Heilbronn	**Wartberg**
Heilbronn	**Stiftsberg**
Schwaigern	**Ruthe**
Stetten	**Pulvermächer**
Stetten	**Brotwasser**
Neipperg	**Schlossberg**
Hohenbeilstein	**Schloßwengert**
Bönnigheim	**Sonnenberg**
Maulbronn	**Eilfingerberg**
Mundelsheim	**Käsberg**
Besigheim	**Wurmberg**
Kleinbottwar	**Oberer Berg**
Kleinbottwar	**Süßmund**
Fellbach	**Lämmler**
Untertürkheim	**Gips**
Untertürkheim	**Mönchberg**
Untertürkheim	**Herzogenberg**
Schnait	**Altenberg**
Schnait	**Burghalde**
Winterbach	**Hungerberg**
Schozach	**Roter Berg**

Centred on the Neckar River and Stuttgart with deep grounded and mineral rich soils. Like Baden this region has its production dominated by co-operative cellars and mechanical harvesting of vineyards. Unlike Baden, Riesling is more widely spread here but its style lacks balance or strength. Better winemaking is seeing a more mineral style of Riesling produced but there is a long way to go until it rivals those of the Rheingau, Mosel, Pfalz, or even Rheinhessen.

Estates such as Grafen Neipperg are leading the way in terms of both Riesling winemaking and the overall wine style production philosophy. There is a logical structure to their winemaking and marketing that needs to be commended. Their idea is to make three levels of wines. Their entry level wines, which should be easy and ready to drink upon release meaning lower acid levels and good fruit flavours, are achievable given the relative warmth of the Württemberg region.

The mid level wines exhibit their terroir and attempt to be a primary display of the house wine style. The Grosses Gewächs wines are small volume and niche market orientated. That is, when you only potentially have a few thousand bottles of a wine you can tend to work it in an eccentric way developing a flagship wine showing off the estate terroir, philosophy, and winemaking talent knowing that it is not your fighting line. As a result you can expect to attract a few hundred like minded customers. This estate also agrees with my stance that the wines in a *Spätlese* level of ripeness are best able to demonstrate the "house" style of wines.

Fellbach: Lämmler
Good fruit aromas are present in the wines largely due to the low levels of rot and drying airs that pass through the vineyard.

Hohenbeilstein: Schlosswengert
This site has copper deposits in the soils and vines of over 50 years of age for Schlossgut Hohenbeilstein. There is potential for very concentrated fruit material but the wines at present seem to lack punch or complexity.

Stetten: Brotwasser
No one is volunteering much information about what makes the terroir special here which begs the red card question.

Stetten: Pulvermächer
Partially terraced vineyards and well protected from winds. South facing.

Schnait: Altenberg
Not named after an old castle but because the old winemakers used to look after it and many of them died there. I am not sure that this fact has anything to do with the soil characteristics but it is well protected from wind. The site has sandstone soils with copper deposits and a Southwest exposure with a slope of 30 to 40%.

Bönnigheim: Sonnenberg

This is a south facing slope of around 50%. In permitting the classification of the site, they are banking much on the future of the Lemberger variety here. There is a patch of Riesling which can tend to be minerally and have a good aging potential but they are far from the greatest of wines.

Schwaigern: Ruthe

This is an early flowering south facing terraced vineyard with a 45% slope. The soils are magnesium and calcium based with fair water holding capacity. The wines from Neipperg demonstrate good oily, petrol notes with exotic melon flavours. Well structured and terroir specific with flinty, gun smoke, mineral, and fruit notes.

Verrenberg: Verrenberg

South facing slope.

Maulbronn: Eilfingerberg

This site has easily warmed sandstone soils giving elegant and racing Rieslings which in good years demonstrate considerable finesse from Weingut des Hauses Württemberg.

BADEN

Baden: Sites with Gross Gewächs Approval

Sulzfeld	**Burg Ravensburger Löchle**
Sulzfeld	**Burg Ravensburger Husarenkappe**
Sulzfeld	**Burg Ravensburger Dicker Franz**
Neuweier	**Schlossberg**
Neuweier	**Mauerberg "Mauer-Wein"**
Neuweier	**Mauerberg Goldenes Loch**
Neuweier	**Heiligenstein**
Durbacher	**Plauelrain**
Zell-Weierbach	**Abtsberg**
Zell-Weierbach	**Neugesetz**
Berghaupten	**Schützenberg**
Hecklingen	**Schlossberg**
Malterdingen	**Bienenberg**
Sasbach	**Limburg**
Jechtingen	**Eichert**
Burkheim	**Schlossgarten**
Burkheim	**Feuerberg**
Oberrottweil	**Eichberg**
Oberrottweil	**Kirchberg**
Oberrottweil	**Käsleberg**
Oberrottweil	**Henkenberg**
Achkarren	**Schlossberg**
Ihringen	**Fohrenberg**
Ihringen	**Winklerberg**
Glottertal	**Eichberg**
Freiburg	**Schlossberg**
Auggen	**Schäf**
Schliengen	**Sonnenstück**
Istein	**Kirchberg**
Mauchen	**Sonnenstück**
Michelfeld	**Himmelberg**
Tiefenbach	**Schellenbrunnen**
Tiefenbach	**Spiegelberg**

In such a wide-ranging area it is hard if not impossible to generalise. It is a region of geographical boundaries rather than geological. It is too diverse in order to have either a uniform characteristic or even a consistent marketing focus. The vast majority of production is in the hands of co-operative cellars that in turn often on sell wines to third parties for bottling. As one can imagine, this is hardly likely a step towards estate certified quality. In addition, Riesling is not the main focus here. From a Riesling point of view, there are only a few pockets of interest such as the region running from Heidelberg to Karlsruhe, (known as the Badische Bergstrasse) with clay soils giving full-bodied wines and the Ortenau region near Baden-Baden. If the German wine identity is in a confused state then Baden is even worse. There is little overall direction or marketing strategy that goes beyond a yellow stuffed smiley-faced sun with arms and legs called the Sun Man if I recall correctly.

Sulzfeld: Burg Ravensburg Husarenkappe

This is a 6.5-hectare Southwest facing site with a thin layer of topsoil over very stony soil.

Neuweier: Mauerberg

This is a terraced vineyard of largely granite deposits. This is further split into the "Mauer Wein" and the "Das Goldene Loch" sites. The soils are the same but very different wines are produced. The Goldene Loch is a warmer vineyard due to more reflected sunlight and a 60% slope. The Mauer wines are very mineral whereas those of the Goldene Loch have more structure and fullness.

Durbach: Plauelrain

A 70% slope with Southeast to Southwest exposure. A wooded area through the vineyard protects it from harsh winds. Sandy soils with weathered granite provide strikingly intense wines with crisp acidity. Andreas Laible produces some excellent full structured wines here.

Zell-Weierbach: Neugesetz

This is a Southwest facing slope in a side valley of the Rhine. It is very well protected and has a warm microclimate. Weathered granite soils allow Freiherr von und zu Franckenstein subtle terroir specific wines.

Burkeim: Feuerberg

This site sits at between 230 and 240 metres above sea level in the West

Kaiserstuhl. Southerly facing and protected from cold northerly wind they are prime vineyard land. The soils are volcanic with sandy loam and act as a heat sink.

Ihringen: Winklerberg

Dr. Heager is top name in the area but has left the VDP. This site is not far from Basel and only a few kilometres from the Rhine. Vineyard is terraced and protected by stone walls.

Oberrotweil: Eichberg

Grauburgunder classified site with a dark rich soil.

Oberrotweil: Kirchberg

Burgunder variety classified.

Time to get the German wine label decoder rings out.

The Third Reich-esq Eagle is the symbol of the Staatsweingut or Staatsdomain and should not be confused with the VDP logo of an eagle holding a grape bunch in its talons. The VDP logo is known as the "*Traubenadler*" and is generally seen on the capsules of member's wine bottles.

---

[128] Wine label from author's cellar.

This estate used to be under the control of the State in much the same way as the Hessische Staatsweingut Kloster Erberbach and their affiliate Staatsdomain on the Hessische Bergstrasse are today. The Eagle was common to all of them as a symbol. The Eagle is still in use, despite a slight modernisation where the wings have been given a slight upward curve rather than this rather "art deco" look. Taking the words apart we can see;

Nahe, is one of the 13 specified *Anbaugebiete* and this indicates the region from where the wine originates and where the grapes were grown.

1973er, is obviously the vintage year. The "-er" is only correct German grammar. 85% of the wine must come from the year indicated.

Niederhäuser Hermannsberg. This refers to the *Grosslage* of Niederhäuser and the vineyard site of Hermannsberg. Today this is a *Grosses Gewächs* site in the Nahe.

Riesling obviously indicates the grape variety.

Auslese indicates the QmP level of ripeness achieved, and this wine happened to be an **Eiswein**. Up until 1982, *Eisweins* were able to carry the level of ripeness at which that Eiswein was harvested. Wines would need to have conditions suitable for *Eiswein* production and the level of ripeness they had reached at that time such as *"auslese"* was recorded on the label. This made for an array of *Eisweins* potentially at each QmP level depending on the sugar ripeness that was achieved. Thankfully, now they must be a minimum of *Beerenauslese* level and carry only the predicate *Eiswein*.

I opened this wine in late 2002 it was packed with complex fruit, honey tones, and a delightful "wiff of the forecourt". The wine was fresh, full, and retained a delicate hint of acidity. The label is a classic example of over complexity and un-user friendly script. Many German wine labels continue into this day to labour tradition and refuse to streamline matters somewhat. I am not an advocate for abandoning tradition completely as will have been detected in the text but there are degrees with which wines can be made more saleable by looking somewhat less hostile.

Qualitätswein mit Prädikat. The wine is one in the highest quality bracket of German wines under current laws.

Amtliche Prüfngsnummer. The AP number is to be printed on all QbA and QmP wines. As this needs to be different for each bottling, it keeps printers in business and makes for a good amount of added costs not to mention paper waste. A fuller discussion of the AP number follows below.

Verwaltung der Staalichen Weinbaudomänen, (Under the management of the State Vineyard) at *Niederhaussen* (at) *Schlossböchelheim.* This is the name and address of the wine producer. In the 1970's the estate produced some stunning wines and the Hermannsberg *Eiswein* has often been some of the most magnificent of its offerings. The property was privatised in 1998, and has struggled to find the old form. It is hard to credit that on this label you have to really struggle to find the name of the winery.

Erzeugerabfülling, in 1973, this would have meant estate bottled. The misuse of the term by large bottling firms meant that it became more of a term for bottled by this producer and gave no guarantees whatsoever. Changes took place to require now the term *Gutsabfüllung* means bottled at the estate of production. With the very heavy German respect for qualifications the term can only be used if the estate winemaker has a degree in Oenology. If you have learnt the trade hands on and probably know ten times as much as any recent university graduate you are lumped with the old *erzeugerabfüllung* until such time as you become Herr Professor Doktor.

Nowadays, the label must have *Produce/Product of Germany* to ensure that the wines are of German origin, the volume, and the alcoholic strength.

More modern labels that still retain a traditional look are starting to appear. The concept of "less is more" is starting to be understood and the need to keep as much of the unnecessary information off the "front" label. Labelling laws require the main label to have all the legal information on it.[129] One label must have volume, alcohol, region, producer name, AP number, winery address, QmP/QbA, level of dryness, and so on. As a bottle is round it is hard to really say what the

---

[129] This uses the typically inane legal terminology of "in the primary visual plane".

main label is and many wineries are now using the "back" label as a place to put all the required information leaving an uncluttered presentation of what they want to present as their first impression to the consumer on the "front".

We can see from the following label that the only information on the front label is the vintage and the Gross Gewachs vineyard site name. The back label contains all the legally required information. As a result the back label is the primary label despite it being secondary. Wineries such as Dr Bürklin-Wolf have for a number of years understood the need to provide uncomplicated and "clean" labels, often with toning down the gothic script. This does not mean the abandoning of tradition as one can see from the highly elegant style used by Bürklin-Wolf.

---

130 Weingut Dr Bürklin Wolf labels used with permission of the winery.

We can see the "back" label contains the full legally required information. The vintage year, alcohol, volume, recycling information, winery name, winery address, QbA designation, estate bottling indication, region, variety, AP number, and level of dryness are required. It is not permitted just to use the vineyard name of Gaisböhl, one is also required to use the town name of Ruppertsberg where it is located. One should not this is not done on the "front" label. Using the ending "–er" merely means that it belongs to Ruppertsberg or more specifically that it is from there. The VDP Trabenadler is used as a requirement of membership within the VDP and is not legally required nor is the bar code.

The *Amtliche Prüfnummer / Amtliche Prüfungsnummer*, AP number is required on all QbA and QmP wines. All European wines are required to a have a lot number. This is so that all bottlings can be traced back in case of problems with quality. The lot number must be any series of letters or numbers which the producer selects and can effectively identify that bottling run. The German AP number is far more stringent than the general "lot" number as the wine has had to receive approval for bottling and so gain the number from a regulatory examination board.

This board looks to the providence of the wine. That is, they control the winery paperwork detailing the vineyard and blending of the wine. This is designed to ensure that it comes from where the producer says it does and that all aspects of the wines particular category are correctly met. There is also a sensory examination where the wine can be eliminated for not being typical.

The number is a readable code and can be broken down as follows, using the wine from Schloss Böchelheim as an example.

A.P Nr.	1	750	053	20	74
	Number of the examination board	Each community has a particular number and this indicates where it was bottled	This is the registered number of the bottler within that community	This is the application number of the bottler in the year (indicated by the next two numerals	This is the year in which the application for the AP number is made

The last four numerals are the key. We know that this wine comes from the vintage 1973. We can see from the APN code that the producer went to bottle this wine in 1974 from the last digits "74". This was the producer's 20th application for an AP number in 1974. For Eiswein or many of the QmP wines this is probably of little significance due to the fact that the small volumes involved likely mean only one bottling of the wine is needed or even sensible. Where the numbers can give an indication to the consumer is often in the case of QbA wines.

Take for example a general estate Riesling. This could make up a sizable proportion of a producers production. As a result, he or she might make separate bottlings throughout the year. This may have to do with tank space, bottled wine storage space, or a cost factor. Each batch of wine, despite how similar is going to be slightly different. As a result, each time we see a bottle of say the 2001 XY Estate Riesling on the shelf it need not be the same as the last we purchased. This is not something unique to German wines or wineries it is a worldwide factor, try imagining Gallo bottling their ocean of Chardonnay in one run.

The Germans let us see what is going on if we are interested. Each time the producer goes to bottle he or she must apply for a new AP number. (Here we can see the increase costs in label printing). So there might be four bottlings of an Estate Riesling. In the interim period the producer might have bottled other wines and thus made other applications for an AP number. As a result, we might have a 2001 Estate Riesling from the producer with the following last for digits 05 02, 12 02, 26 02, and 01 03. The ultimate batch having been the first bottling application in the new year of 2003. Thus a consumer could make life hell for your average wine shop worker by seeking out the particular lot they liked, or looking for the "freshest" bottling rather than just buying on the vintage. Now you know.

Appendix Two
German Wine Regions

The following table lists the split of Germany into various zones of *Tafelwein*, the *Landwein* regions within those, and the overall region to which they belong. As discussed in the text, considerable wasted effort takes place with the *Landwein* and *Tafelwein* categories given that only two percent of industry production is classified as such, serving only to further clutter wine labels with unnecessary information.

Deutscher Tafelwein Regions	DT Sub Regions	Landwein Regions	Anbaugebieten
Rhein-Mosel	Rhein	Ahrtaler Landwein	Ahr
		Starkenburger Landwein	Hess. Bergstrasse
		Rheinburgen Landwein	Mittlerhein
		Nahegauer Landwein	Nahe
		Altrheingauer Landwein	Rheingau
		Rheinischer Landwein	Rheinhessen
		Pfälzer Landwein	Pfalz
	Mosel	Landwein der Mosel	
	Saar	Saarländischer Landwein	Mosel-Saar-Ruwer
		Landwein der Ruwer	
Bayern	Main	Fränkischer Landwein	Franken
	Donau	Regensburger Landwein	Franken
	Lindau	Bayerischer Bodensee Landwein	Württemberg
Neckar		Schwäbischer	Württemberg

		Landwein	
Oberrhein	Römertor	Südbadischer Landwein	Baden
	Burgengau	Unterbadischer Landwein	
		Taubertäler Landwein	
		Mitteldeutscher Landwein	Saale-Unstrutt
		Sächsischer Landwein	Sachsen

I see no point in merely listing all the *Anbaugebiet, Bereich, Grosslage,* and *Einzellagen.* To do so is the place of a text purporting to be an encyclopaedia of German wine despite that the knowledge is without real practical value. For those interested in seeing this done well, they can refer to the Deutsche Wein Institute **WeinAtlas** which contains lots of well done interactive maps. In order to demonstrate the enormity of this task here I will provide a summary table which looks like a complicated lottery numbers system and for consumers it may as well be.

Anbaugebiet	*Bereich*	*Grosslage*	*Einzellage*
Ahr	1	1	43
Baden	9	15	315
Franken	3	22	211
Hess. Bergstrasse	2	3	24
Mittelrhein	2	11	111
Mosel-Saar-Ruwer	6	20	507
Nahe	1	7	312
Pfalz	2	25	330
Rheingau	1	11	120
Rheinhessen	3	24	442
Saale-Unstrut	2	4	20
Sachsen	2	4	16
Württemberg	6	20	207
TOTAL	39	167	2658

German Wine Regions
(Reproduced with permission).

Appendix Three
The 3-Tier VDP Classification Model

- **Grosses Gewächs**, or Great Growth refers to dry/trocken wines from Ahr, Baden, Franken, Nahe, Mittelrhein, Rheinhessen, Pfalz, and Saale-Unstrut.
- **Erste Gewächs**, or First Growth refers to trocken wines or lusciously sweet wines (edelsüsse Prädikate wines of Auslese, Beerenauslese, Trockenbeerenauslese, and Eiswein) from the Rheingau.
- **Erste Lage**, or First Site refers to wines from the Mosel-Saar-Ruwer with particular quality parameters for each Prädikat level.

Grosses Gewächs
Erstes Gewächs
Erste Lage

Edelsüsser Spitzenweine

- Maximum Yield = 50hl/ha
- VDP Gazetted vineyard sites
- Grape Variety VDP determined
- Vineyards controlled by VDP
- Hand Harvesting
- Minimum must weight of Spätlese
- Wines undergo VDP sensory approval
- Wines have a minimum period of aging prior to release

Klassifizierter Lagenwein
(wines from classified vineyard sites)

- Vineyards, for classification and their wines must display discernable terroir specific traits.
- Grape varieties permitted are determined by the VDP regional association.
- Hand harvesting with a maximum yield of 65hl/ha.
- As in QmP wines no sugar enrichment is permitted.

Regional VDP associations set those vineyards or parts thereof that are deemed suitable for classification at the second tier of cru appellation. VDP members will only be permitted to use vineyard names on labels when they have been so classified. No other vineyard or site names to be used by members.

Guts and Ortswein
(wines from the estate permitted with name of region and/or village/ort)

Wines must comply with minimum standards of VDP wines as set out below.

- Hand harvesting of grapes for Auslese and riper quality levels.
- Vineyard and winery procedures controlled by VDP.
- Wines undergo VDP sensory examination.
- Estates are subject to a VDP inspection audit with specified criteria to be reached.

- 80% of an estate's vineyards planted with traditional grape varieties typical of their region as recommended by the VDP.
- Maximum yield of 75hl/ha.
- Minimum must weights are set at a higher level than as prescribed by law and determined by the VDP regional associations.

Appendix Four
Selected Terms

Abfüllung; bottling

Amtliche Prüfung; state required quality analysis and tasting resulting in granting of an **AP** number which in effect is permission to bottle. Refer to **Appendix One** for a fuller discussion.

Apfelsäure; German term for malic acid. In very general terms wine acid is largely made up of Tartaric Acid and Malic Acid. Malic acid undergoes a transformation to Lactic Acid via a biological fermentation known as malolactic fermentation, or in German BSA (Biologische Säureabbau). It can give a buttery note and is more suited to wines such as Chardonnay.

Auslese; selective harvesting.

Bereich; a smaller part of a Gebiet q.v. which is a major vineyard region.

Beerenauslese; a wonderfully rich wine a step in sweetness above Auslese generally from *Botrytis Cinerea* affected grapes. Will always require a higher level of ripeness than Auslese.

Biologische Säureabbau; (BSA) see Apfelsäure q.v.

Bocksbeutel; traditional bottle of Franken designed to make wine transport and shelving an absolute nightmare. Similar shape of bottle made iconic by Mateus Rose.

Botrytis Cinera (noble rot)/ **Edelfäule**; the spores which weather permitting turns rot into liquid gold.

Chalk; an alkaline soil with excellent drainage and the ability to permit good free root penetration. Plenty of mineral notes result in wines on chalk soils.

Clay; a soil with a very high water holding capacity and poor drainage. Tends to give more acid wines.

Einzellage; single vineyard site.

-er; thankfully disappearing from use, historically written after the vintage i.e. 1999**er** meaning coming from that year, grammatically er correct and all eh?.

Erzeugerabfüllung; in theory this should mean estate bottled wine but really it is producer bottled. See Gutsabfüllung q.v.

Fass; general term for tank but more specifically a wooden barrel of various sizes used for vinification and/or storage.

Feinherb; a meaningless term for halbtrocken/half dry. It is merely a complicated way of avoiding using those words which spell immediate commercial doom and at the same time making for more confusion for the consumer.

Flint; like **slate** (q.v) it stores and reflects heat. A flinty or gun smoke note in wine can be noticed.

Flurbereinigung; a system of vineyard ownership rationalisation. Basically it is a way where compulsory acquisition is more or less a compulsory swap/consolidation of land holdings. It is an attempt to make vineyard work simpler by giving a grower consolidated holdings rather than pocket-handkerchief holdings spread widely. Its goals have been successful and it has meant that there are wonderful roads, turning places, and erosion prevention in German vineyards. This is probably one example of state intervention in the short history of man which has been a success

Gebiet; significantly sized vineyard region.

Gerbstoff; German term for tannin.

Gewächs; growth.

Grosslage; a lumped together vineyard designation containing any number of Einzellagen or single vineyards.

Gutsabfüllung; effectively estate bottled.

Halbtrocken; half or off-dry.

Hochgewächs; beefing up of the 1971 Laws by requiring a minimum of 65 degrees Oecshle and a score of 3.5 out of 5 at the AP Number tasting. Completely, totally, and utterly irrelevant.

Internationally Dry; a term used by winemakers, journalists, and the public alike to indicate a wine that tastes dry despite the fact that the Residual Sugar (q.v.) level might not come under the legally set level for Trocken (q.v) but given the actual balance between sugar and acid has the taste of being dry.

Jahrgang; the vintage year.

Juice; the product of pressed/squeezed Must (q.v) which has been clarified either by settling, centrifugation, filtration, or floatation. The process is simply that the grapes arrive at the cellar, whereupon they are crushed and so becomes termed grape must. Once it has been pressed it is termed juice which goes for fermentation to become wine.

Kabinett; entry to the QmP q.v. wines.

Kellermeister; master of the cellar, can be someone who controls the cellar or even the winemaker.

Lese; the actual harvest

Lieblich; sweet wine.

Limestone; this soil type tends to give high acid wines due to its alkaline nature.

Loam; mixed clay, sand, and silt soil that is very fertile and not tending to give great wines. Better suited to the production of high volume wines.

Loess; a soil with exceptional water holding capacity and good warming properties.

Marl; a calcareous clay soil which gives wines of higher acid due to the fact that it tends to delay ripening.

Muschelkalk; this is a descriptor of soil which can cover sandstone, marl, or shingle.

Must; the mass of grapes and juice after crushing and/or desteming.

Oechsle; measurement system of sugar in grapes based on specific gravity.

QbA; Qualitätswein bestimmter Anbaugebiete or quality wine from a designated wine region.

QmP; Qualitätswein mit Prädikat; or quality wine predicated by ripeness. The level of ripeness is expressed in degrees Oechsle and a minimum level required for each QmP varies depending or the region and the grape variety

Quartz; a high pH soil so lessening wine acidity. It has excellent heat retention characteristics and as a result gives a beneficial boost to ripening.

Restzucher (RZ) / Residual Sugar (RS); what is left in or added to the wine at bottling.

Sand; a very free draining soil and this can help in sites prone to higher rainfall. The opposite can be true, in very dry years quickly resulting in water stress.

Schist; this type of soil holds heat exceptionally well.

Schwefel; sulphur dioxide.

Slate; exceptionally fast to heat up, reflects heat into fruiting zone, and maintains warmth, so modifying the microclimate in a vineyard.

Spätlese; late harvest material.

Süssreserve; grape juice unfermented which is later added to finished wine in order to give a level of residual sugar so balancing the acid levels or making the wine reach levels of halbtrocken for market reasons.

Trocken; dry, legally in Germany under 9 gm/L or Residual Sugar q.v.

Verband; an association or group such as VDP (Verband Deutscher Prädikatsweingüter.

Vorlese; harvest pre the main harvest (*lese*) in order to remove unwanted and/or rotten bunches.

Weingut; a wine estate.

Weinkelleri; winery.

Winzer; literally a wine grower.

Winzergenossenschaft/Weingärtnergenossenschaft;   co-operative winery.

Selected Bibliography

Eno, Brian (1996), <u>A Year with Swollen Appendices: Brian Eno's Diary</u>, (Faber & Faber), London.

Matthews, Patrick (1997), <u>The Wild Bunch, Great Wines from Small Producers</u>, (Faber & Faber), London.

Deutsche Wein Institute, Deutscher Weinatlas, CD ROM, Directmedia Publishing GmbH, Berlin 2002.

Unwin, Tim (1996 paperback edition), <u>Wine and the Vine</u>, (Routledge), London.

Harpers Wine Magazine, German Supplement 2003.

Johnson, Hugh (1994), <u>The World Atlas of Wine 4th Edition</u>, (Mitchell Beazley), London.

Johnson, Hugh (1999), <u>Story of Wine</u>, (Mitchell Beazley), London.

Stevenson, Tom (1999), <u>The New Southeby's Wine Encyclopaedia</u>, (Dorling Kindersley), London.

Kröll, Dr. Ralf and Löwenstein, Reinhard, (2003), „Erste Lage Uhlen", (Weinguts Heymann-Löwenstein Verlag), Winningen an der Mosel.

VDP, Grosses Gewächs Berlin 2002, launch catalogue.
VDP, Grosses Gewächs Berlin & Kloster Eberbach2003, launch catalogue.

Ainsworth, Jim (1991), <u>White Wine Guide</u>, (Mitchell Beazley), London

DWI & Association of German Oenologists, Dr. Ulrich Fischer, Aroma Wheels, no date, Mainz.

Noble, A.C, (1987), et al, Modification of a Standardized System of Wine Aroma Terminology, American Journal of Enology and Viticulture, Vol. 38, No. 2, 1987.

Von Bassermann-Jordan, Friedrich, (1923), <u>Geschichte Des Weinbaus I & II Bands,</u> (Frankfurter Verlags-Anstalt AG) (1991), Frankfurt-am-Main.

Verein zur Forderung der Riesling-Kultur, (1086), „Der Riesling und seine Weine", Trier

Deckers, Daniel, „Zur Lage des deutschen Weins Spitzenlagen und Spitzenweine", 2003, (Klett-Cotta), Stuttgart.

Diel, Armin and Payne, Joel (2001), <u>Gault Millau Weinguide Deutschland 2002</u>, (Heyne), Munich.

Ray, Cyril (1977), <u>The Wines of Germany</u>, (Allen Lane), London.

Robinson, Jancis (1997), <u>Confessions of a Wine Lover</u>, (Penguin), London.

Löwenstein, Reinhard (2003), "Von öchsle zum Terroir", Frankfurter Allgemeine Zeitung, 7 October 2003.

Pigott, Stuart (2003) <u>Schöne neue Weinwelt</u>, (Argon), Berlin

About the Author

Flying Winemaker O. J. Bird, vintage 1968, studied Law and Economics before practising as a Barrister in his native Tasmania. He returned to University in order to study winemaking and viticulture, graduating with Distinction in 1993. He has worked around the world as a winemaker in Australia, New Zealand, South Africa, Germany, Hungary, Italy, Georgia in the former Soviet Union, and having on occasion undertaken four separate vintages in a calendar year.

He is an invited judge at a number of international wine competitions around the World and considered expert on both German and Italian wines.

He is presently Group Winemaker, (overseeing Italy, Australia, California, and Germany) for WaverleyTBS Ltd UK, the wine division of Scottish & Newcastle Brewers, one of the United Kingdom's largest wine importers. Married to contralto Kirsten Schwarz they live with daughter Freya near Heidelberg in Germany.

Printed in the United States
50951LVS00001B/14

9 781845 490799